Curriculum Change in The Primary School since 1945

Dissemination of the Progressive Ideal

Studies in Curriculum History Series

General Editor: Professor Ivor F. Goodson
University of Western Ontario, Canada

1. Social Histories of the Secondary Curriculum: Subjects for Study
   Edited by Ivor F. Goodson, University of Sussex
2. Technological Revolution? A Politics of School Science and Technology in England and Wales since 1945
   G. McCulloch, E. Jenkins and D. Layton, University of Leeds
3. Renegotiating Secondary School Mathematics: A Study of Curriculum Change and Stability
   Barry Cooper, University of Sussex
4. Building the American Community: Social Control and Curriculum
   Barry Franklin, Kennesaw College, Georgia
5. The 'New Maths' Curriculum Controversy: An International Story
   Bob Moon
6. School Subjects and Curriculum Change
   Ivor F. Goodson, University of Western Ontario
7. The Formation of the School Subjects: The Struggle for Creating an American Institution
   Edited by Thomas S. Popkewitz, University of Madison — Wisconsin
8. Physics Teaching in Schools 1960–85: Of People, Policy and Power
   Brian E. Woolnough, University of Oxford
9. The Making of Curriculum
   Ivor F. Goodson, University of Western Ontario
10. Curriculum Change in the Primary School since 1945: Dissemination of the Progressive Ideal
    Peter Cunningham,

Studies in Curriculum History: 10

Curriculum Change in The Primary School since 1945

Dissemination of the Progressive Ideal

Peter Cunningham

The Falmer Press
(A member of the Taylor & Francis Group)
London · New York · Philadelphia

UK The Falmer Press, Falmer House, Barcombe, Lewes, East Sussex, BN8 5DL

USA The Falmer Press, Taylor & Francis Inc., 242 Cherry Street, Philadelphia, PA 19106-1906

First published 1988

Library of Congress Cataloging in Publication Data

Cunningham, Peter.
Curriculum change in the primary school since 1945.
(Studies in curriculum history; 9)
Bibliography: p.
Includes index.
1. Curriculum change—Great Britain—History—20th century. 2. Education, Primary—Great Britain—History—20th century. 3. Progressive education—Great Britain—History—20th century I. Title. II. Series.
LB1523.C85 1988 372.19′0941 88-3637
ISBN 1-85000-194-4
ISBN 1-85000-195-2 (pbk.)

Jacket design by Caroline Archer

Typeset in 10/12 Century School Book by Imago Publishing Ltd, Thame, Oxon

Printed in Great Britain by Taylor & Francis (Printers) Ltd, Basingstoke

Contents

For Jim and Marjorie

Abbreviations

ACE	Advisory Centre for Education
BB	Building Bulletin
CACE	Central Advisory Council for Education
CCPR	Central Council for Physical Recreation
CEO	Chief Education Officer
DES	Department of Education and Science
EFVA	Educational Foundation for Visual Aids
EPA	Educational Priority Area
HMI	Her Majesty's Inspector(ate)
ILEA	Inner London Education Authority
INSET	In-service Education and Training
LCC	London County Council
LEA	Local Education Authority
NAPE	National Association for Primary Education
NFER	National Foundation for Educational Research
NFF	National Froebel Foundation
NUT	National Union of Teachers
PP	Parliamentary Papers
PTA	Parent-Teachers' Association
RIBA	Royal Institute of British Architects
SLA	School Library Association
TUC	Trades Union Congress
UDE	University Department of Education
WREC	West Riding Education Committee

Preface

On first visiting Oxfordshire primary schools in the later 1970s I was deeply impressed, as Vincent Rogers (1970) and so many others had been. Most admirable was a social respect for the children conscientiously realized in terms of daily routine. The provision of a respectable and comfortable working environment, and the absence of whistles and bells, are just two examples. Another impressive feature, so markedly different from my own primary schooling, was the degree of responsibility for their own learning taken by children, and the high quality of work displayed.

Exploring further and listening to teachers, certain paradoxes and contradictions began to emerge. Between some of the better known and much visited schools, there were marked consistencies in curriculum emphasis and in styles of presentation, yet other schools within the county appeared relatively untouched by these characteristics, apparently not sharing in what was celebrated as the 'Oxfordshire tradition'. Some teachers shared a strong sense of identity as 'Oxfordshire teachers' and many from outside the county identified an 'Oxfordshire style'. Others within the county felt that some of the principles were too dogmatic, and that their independence as teachers was constrained by the teaching methods advocated.

The paradoxes will be familiar to many. If curriculum was carefully linked to children's individual interests, why were certain themes and motifs so recurrent? A gap remained evident between the popular cultural interests of many children outside school and the curriculum content in school. Another paradox was embedded in the importance accorded to display: why was the *product* of curriculum given such emphasis when the underlying educational philosophy seemed to assert the importance of *process*? Displays were important in communicating the ethos of the school; tasteful and stimulating as they often were, styles of display were uniform and certain rules seemed to apply. The quality of work was so consistently high, was it representative of the whole range of ability?

Particular curriculum emphases were evident, and a prevailing style of presentation was so marked, that questions of organization and administration were implied. How were the more 'progressive' ideas and practices disseminated? Why was their application irregular? How did a sense of county identity emerge? Of course the phenomenon was not exclusive to Oxfordshire and so I was led to explore a wide range of sources. And in a broader context still, how far were the features observed the product of a specific pedagogical approach, and how far the reflection of a particular cultural context?

Many individuals helped me by answering questions and suggesting lines of further enquiry. It seems almost churlish to acknowledge this help in a simple alphabetical list, yet those named below will know how readily they have offered help and advice. Many of them will dissent from various of my interpretations and conclusions, but that the phenomenon of 'progressive primary education' is worthy of historical exploration is a tribute to the energy, commitment and conviction that was put into improving schools for younger children in the decades since 1945. To examine the ways in which reform was effected, and to attempt to place curriculum improvement and innovation in the context of changing economic, political and cultural circumstances, is not to undermine its achievements but the better to understand its processes.

I wish to thank Jo Armistead, Graham Badman, George and Judith Baines, Carey Bennet, Leslie Bennett, Philip Best, Deanne Boydell, Graham Burchell, Tim Brighouse, Ralph Brooke, Len Cowee, John Coe, John Davidson, Sue Davies, Harold Dent, Keith Dent, Jim Fairbairn, David Gadsby, Julie Hatton, Ted Holloway, George Inger, Christopher Jarman, Paul Keates, Wendla Kernig, Bill Laar, Joachim Liebschner, Stuart Maclure, Edith Moorhouse, Ann Price, Arthur Razzell, Philip Robinson, Ed Salt, Harold Silver, Brian Simon, Robert Smith, Robin Tanner, Joan Truby, Ruth Wertheimer, Anne Yeomans and Sylvia Young. I also gratefully acknowledge the help of the following libraries and institutions: Bodleian Library, BBC Written Archive, NUT Library, National Froebel Foundation, Early Childhood Archive, Froebel Institute, Oxfordshire County Council Record Office, Oxfordshire Local Education Authority, *Times Educational Supplement*, Westminster College, Westminster College Library.

Reference

Rogers, V. (1970) *Teaching in the British Primary School*, London, Macmillan.

General Editor's Preface

The volumes in the *Studies in Curriculum History* series have, to date, been concerned with the secondary school curriculum and in particular, with the school subjects taught at that level. Future volumes will not only look towards non-secondary sectors, as is the case with Cunningham's work, but will also seek to look beyond the espoused curriculum to the lived experience of the classroom. For instance, the latter focus will be employed in Barbara Finkelstein's forthcoming book, *Governing the Young*.

In moving away from secondary subjects towards primary school progressivism Cunningham explores a tendency in schooling which, although multi-faceted, is often fundamentally antipathetic to the central project of secondary subject teaching. However, the current climate in Britain is plainly hostile to such challenges. As Cunningham states:

> What may be seen in the documents is a clash between the pedagogical tradition of child-centered learning and political pressures for accountability fuelled by concern about education and economic performance.

Given the driving force of the latter concern in the present government regime the direction of change becomes clear. What is interesting however, given the central concern of this series of research monographs, is how the political pressures for accountability and economic priorities finds expression in the reassertion of subject-centered criteria.

Thus the Department of Education and Science document, *Education 8 to 12* stresses the need to 'extend teachers' subject knowledge' in the primary school. Understanding is now once again allied with subject knowledge. But previous volumes have posed question marks about this alliance; showing that far from becoming divine, it is often malign. Rowlands has eloquently pointed to the ambivalence in the DES document:

> Education 8 to 12 may well be interpreted by teachers and others as recommending yet another move in the trend towards a more schematized approach to learning in which the focus is placed even more firmly on the subject matter rather than the child. The evidence it produces however, points to the need to move in quite the opposite direction.[1]

We are back then with subject-centeredness and the loser is child-centeredness. One is sadly reminded of the old schoolmaster's joke: 'Damn these children: They've been getting in the way of education for years.'

Ivor Goodson
Professor of Education
University of Western Ontario

[1]Stephen Rowlands (1987) 'Where is primary education going? *Journal of Curriculum Studies*, 19, 1, p. 90.

Introduction

Primary Progressivism

On 1 April 1945, under a war-time coalition government, Part II of the 1944 Education Act came into force. It introduced free secondary education for all, and defined primary education quite simply, as that 'suitable to the requirements of junior pupils', a junior pupil being 'a child who has not attained the age of 12 years'. In May Berlin fell to the Russian forces and Germany capitulated; in July a General Election returned the first ever Labour majority to the House of Commons. The development of primary education since that time, especially in its relation to political, social and economic change, has been little studied. Primary schooling does not take place in a vacuum; the impact continues to be felt in the primary classroom not only of shifts in pedagogical theory, but also of domestic politics, such as the contest for curriculum control, and of international affairs, such as the state of world trade. Whilst on the one hand the importance of developing young children's skills as independent learners is encouraged, on the other there has been a growing tendency to centralize curriculum control and to introduce mechanisms for teacher accountability. In 1985 was published the most recent in a series of HMI surveys of primary and middle schools, the first of which appeared in 1978; Rowland (1987) has identified an underlying contradiction in these documents, which at the same time record an observed lack of independent learning by children, whilst calling for an increasingly mechanical approach to curriculum development with detailed schemes of work and assessment.[1] What may be seen in the documents is a clash between the pedagogical tradition of child-centred learning, and political pressures for accountability, fuelled by concern about education and economic performance.

Current debate on primary practice has encouraged a narrow interpretation of progressivism. Classroom enquiry by HMI and by educational researchers has isolated particular features of progressive teaching such as 'collaborative group work' or 'discovery learning', only to find that these are much more rarely or inadequately implemented than had been presumed. In the broader sense with which this book is concerned, progressivism embraces many aspects of classroom practice from attempts at curriculum integration to detailed approaches to display of children's work. Exposure by such projects as ORACLE, of the 'reality' behind the 'myth' cannot, however, blind the historian to the perception that most primary classrooms of today are different from those of forty years ago. Some of the changes have been due to the dissemination of ideals within the profession (however those ideals may have been misinterpreted or badly practised); others have resulted from the changing social and cultural climate. Furthermore, the research reported below is concerned with the phenomenon of professional discourse (how teachers described their practice, or how they were encouraged to work) which, however inadequately applied, is widely documented. Professional discourse concerns the 'espoused' rather than the 'enacted' curriculum. In the example of a 'progressive county' such as Oxfordshire, a 'county ethos' was promulgated, though less than two dozen schools were considered to be good practitioners. This research has not set out in the manner of Bennett and others to categorize and measure styles of classroom practice or qualities of learning experience, though the public and professional debates engendered by Bennett's findings are very much a concern of the last chapter. The lived curriculum of the classroom has been badly neglected by historians, and though its importance is acknowledged, it is not the purpose here to make good that neglect.

Various taxonomies of primary education have been proposed to order our understanding of developments. Blyth (1965) identified three traditions in their social and cultural contexts, the 'elementary', most closely identified with nineteenth century concepts of working class education, the 'preparatory', from the traditional organization and curriculum of the independent sector, and the 'developmental', which evolved in the twentieth century, concerning itself with the stages of child development.[2] Golby (1982) classified three traditions: the 'elementary', bent on communication of essential knowledge to passive pupils, the 'progressive', celebrating self-expression, autonomy in learning and personal growth, and the 'technological', a return to the utilitarian orientation of 'elementary',but now concerned with the pursuit of technology and science demanded by a new technological age.[3] Alexander (1984) also adopted a tripartite model, but in taking account of the more recent development of middle schools, he referred to the secondary (subject) tradition, represented in the arrival of ex-secondary teachers in these schools, by contrast with the 'elementary' tradition still pervading some junior schools and departments, and the 'developmental', seen as particularly strong in infant and first schools.[4]

Richards' (1984) classification of four 'contrasting views' of primary education, justifiably ignoring the 'elementary' view as by now presumably defunct, embraced 'liberal romanticism', 'educational conservatism', 'liberal pragmatism' and 'social democracy'.[5] Richards, however, neglected to place these in their historical interrelationship which is required to understand them fully. For him, the 'liberal romantics', the main focus of the chapters below, were represented by writers such as Molly Brearley, Christian Schiller, Leonard Marsh and Sybil Marshall, and, of course,by the Plowden Report; however, the Plowden Report could also be said to have embraced aspects of the 'social democratic' view — school as a means of realizing social justice. There is something of a natural continuity between these two, though the latter also represented a challenge to 'liberal romanticism' arising from the changing social circumstances in which the primary curriculum was delivered in the later 1960s. 'Educational conservatism' represented by the Black Paper movement, was explicitly a reaction against these two educational trends, though it had deeper political and cultural roots. Conservatism gained increasing dominance in national politics in the later 1970s, and the 'liberal pragmatism' of the DES and HMI may be seen as an attempt to hold the line between prevailing professional opinion on the one hand and political pressures on the other.

A recent school of criticism, rather than a school of practice, and not included by the taxonomies so far described, was that of Sharp and Green (1975). They saw the basic liberal assumptions of progressivism, which had preoccupied educators for so long and which had appeared to offer a challenge to the dominant hegemony, as ultimately supporting the maintenance of the status quo in the social and economic structure. A parallel critique was embedded in the work of the Centre for Contemporary Cultural Studies (1981). Though concentrating more on developments in secondary than in primary education, they criticized the educational settlement of the 1960s, which included the Plowden Report, for its reliance on 'educational experts' as opposed to political intellectuals; they identified ambivalence both in the social democratic ideas of this settlement, and in their partial application.[6] From a less extreme political position, Denis Lawton (1981) offered a salutary reminder that schooling takes place under state compulsion which considerably restricts the freedom of children for ten years of their lives, a constraint which the 'liberal romantics' have preferred to ignore.[7]

Armstrong (1980) and Rowland (1984) may be seen as the heirs of progressivism insofar as they have held true to the principles of autonomy and choice for pupils. Their significant departure is in laying more emphasis on the teacher's intervention, and on a more rigorous attention to the structure of knowledge in the process of children's intellectual formation.[8] There is emerging an approach to the primary curriculum which represents more of a synthesis and less of a contradiction than HMI statements on the curriculum. Recent work by Blyth has taken the old shibboleths of the progressives, notions of 'development', 'activity' and 'experience' and has subjected them to close analysis. By contrast with the 'liberal romantic' trend of progressivism, Blyth has allowed that the nature of knowledge and the social context of schooling require consideration alongside our understanding of the child's development.[9]

Progressivism has been a customary label embracing the 'developmental', 'liberal romantic' and to some extent the 'social democratic' views of primary education. The term 'progressivism' would appear to have in-built obsolescence. In the normal course of history, there is a limit to the length of time a set of ideas or practices can remain truly progressive. Yet in the educational world the term has enjoyed long life, so what is the key to its longevity? Maurice Ash implied the problem in his account of a Dartington Hall colloquy in 1965, *Who Are the Progressives Now?*. Tension was evident in the proceedings, between the representatives of the old independent school progressivism going back to Abbotsholme and Bedales of the late nineteenth century, and the more recent progressivism of some local authority schools. Said Christian Schiller, concerning the latter:

> The ideas which interest me now are rather more 'progressive' than were those of forty years ago; and my concern has been, and is, to contribute to their fulfilment in state schools.[10]

In this Introduction, the purpose is not to begin defining progressivism, which is a task for the chapters which follow, but to illustrate the problematic nature of the concept. W.A.C. Stewart, in his account of 'the educational innovators', studied exclusively the experimental independent schools of the period 1881–1967.[11] He defined 'a number of schools which were in varying degrees unorthodox' which came to be called the 'progressive schools', schools which were considered radical at the time of their foundation and since. The orthodoxy against which they made their protest was that of the traditional public schools.

By contrast, in their study of 1975, Sharp and Green took for their object progressivism in a state primary school, proposing a paradox which they set out to explore:

> the radicalism of the 'progressive educator' may well be a modern form of conservatism and an effective form of social control in both the narrow sense of achieving discipline in the classroom and the wider sense of contributing to the promotion of a static social order generally.[12]

Ken Jones, more recently, has mounted a political critique based on the observation that

> Progressive education ... developing from the fringes of the educational system, eventually received official endorsement and

> was promulgated by institutions of teacher education and the leading agencies of curricular reform ...
>
> It has variously been represented as the educational salvation of the working class and as the most efficient means of reproducing through the school the qualities required by a developing capitalism.[13]

Jones' own view inclined more towards the latter. Although he found that no progressive manifesto existed which tried to codify the aims of the movement, looking back at the condition of society in the years of the first world war he saw that

> some kind of intervention beyond the merely repressive was necessary, to create and maintain social unity.[14]

He considered that progressivism had to be discussed not simply as pedagogy, curriculum and teaching methods, but also in terms of its context, its motivating philosophy, and its strategies for gaining influence.

Silver noted, by contrast, that progressive thinking and practice often implied a relatively autonomous social context for education. Although Jones was correct to observe that there had never been any universal codification of progressivism, many individual 'progressives' had expressed quite explicit sets of aims. Silver contrasted two (deliberately oversimplified) models of the purposes of education as being education '*for*' and education '*against*', and cited the 'progressives' along with utilitarians, Christians, theosophists and other groups, as proponents of education '*for*'.

> The history of education in the nineteenth and twentieth centuries abounds with pronouncements and movements which in one way or another have pursued positively expressed aims, and have sought to reform the system or the classroom or the curriculum or the teacher and teacher training in order to achieve such aims.[15]

The aims of such movements tend to assume a consensus and to express their ideals in terms of the child and its personality and creativity, and the intimate and responsible relationship towards it maintained by the teacher; they tend to view the school as a relatively closed institution.

Curriculum History

'What did you learn in school today, dear little boy of mine?' The refrain of a folksong written by Tom Paxton in 1962 and made popular in a recording by Pete Seeger is the familiar opening gambit to a daily interrogation by anxious parents at the school gates or over tea. Parents nowadays may be most immediately concerned with 'basic skills' but Tom Paxton's verses implied a broader curriculum:

> I learned that policemen are my friends,
> I learned that justice never ends,
> I learned that murderers die for their crimes,
> Even if we make a mistake sometimes.
>
> I learned our government must be strong,
> It's always right and never wrong,
> Our leaders are the finest men,
> And we elect them again and again.

An illustration from popular culture is deliberately chosen here to suggest a heightening popular consciousness at this period, of the school curriculum and its implications. Education was gaining prominence on the political agenda in Britain, through concern about educational opportunity and the 'untapped pool of ability'; 1963 was an 'annus mirabilis' for education with the publication of the Newsom and Robbins Reports, and launching of the Plowden enquiry, and in the following year's General Election education played an unusually large role.

At about the same time as Seeger's song hit the airwaves, Raymond Williams was arguing in *The Long Revolution* that a society and its culture were expressed not simply in the distribution of education, the types of institution available and length of courses, but

> It is also that the content of education which is subject to great historical variation again expresses, both consciously and unconsciously, certain basic elements in the culture, what is thought of as 'an education' being in fact a particular set of emphases and omissions.

He went on to identify the threefold nature of the curriculum, embracing not only the skills to earn a living and contribute to the welfare of society, but also the pattern of culture or accepted behaviour and values of the society, as well as the general knowledge and attitudes appropriate to 'high culture'.[16]

Contests over the school curriculum may be traced back in history to the dissenting academies of the eighteenth century and to the classic judgment by Lord Eldon in 1805 when he ruled against the governors of Leeds Grammar School in their desire to extend the basic curriculum of Greek and Latin grammar to include mathematics and modern languages.[17] Recent historical writing has clearly revealed a resistance to elementary schooling based partly on the perceived irrelevance to nineteenth century working class consumers of the state-provided curriculum,[18] and in our own times we have witnessed a distinct challenge from a concerned and articulate middle class clientele, and political debate about the content of schooling has forced the curriculum into the limelight from 1976.

The purpose of the present study is an historical account of the dissemination of a set of ideals and ideas for practice, its central focus being the definition and promotion of curriculum. A feature of curriculum change is its predominantly gradual and continuous nature, especially so in the case of the long evolution of progressivism. Student teachers in 1987 (who themselves received their primary schooling after Plowden) may still be found to refer to these 'new methods' when confronted by 'informality' in curriculum or classroom organization, a pedagogy widely promoted from the first years of this century, acknowledged and endorsed by a government report of over fifty years ago and identified by Bernstein as a 'semi-official' ideology, following the Plowden Report thirty years later. Such a phenomenon calls for historical analysis of the forces of continuity:

> We are left in the position of needing after all to examine the emergence and survival of all that is seen as traditional.[19]

It is not the purpose here to codify a theory or theories defining the relationship between curriculum and its context, but rather to identify and elaborate through empirical study some of the particular features of this relationship in the spread and implementation of progressive ideals and practices in the post-war period. In identifying patterns of development and recurring constraints on change, curriculum history may contribute to curriculum theory. Reid (1986) has elaborated this point by demonstrating the practical application of curriculum history insofar as it depicts curriculum change in terms of action in context, studies concrete and particular instances as opposed to general or universal propositions, and because it enables curriculum theory to be evaluated pragmatically rather than by its internal logic, enabling us to see the partiality and temporality of theories. Thus what Reid calls 'the discovery and articulation of traditions and biographies' constitutes one aspect of the chapters below.[20] Silver has written of the need to establish a sense of the main issues identified by those involved in educational provision. Historians do not have to agree with participants about priorities, but may not ignore them: 'Contemporary perceptions of reality are part of the reality'.[21]

Curriculum theory may be of use to the historian in selecting and organizing evidence. Broadly speaking, in studying curriculum change we have to distinguish between, on the one hand, the operation of what have been termed 'external constituencies', agencies and forces outside the educational system, and on the other, the negotiations between various interest groups within the profession of teachers and educators. A framework for considering curriclum change which focuses more closely on the professional actors has been provided by Cooper, who adapted a working model from Bucher and Strauss. With regard to secondary school subject communities, Cooper provided a description which is both flexible and sufficiently suggestive to merit application to the progressive primary teachers; subjects are not to be regarded as

> monoliths, that is groups of individuals sharing a common consensus both on cognitive norms and on perceived interests, but rather as shifting coalitions of individuals and variously sized groups whose members may have, at any specific moment, different and possibly conflicting missions and interests.[22]

For his working model, he saw as requiring study not only the make-up of these groups but also other factors: their alliances inside and outside the profession; their relative power in respect of resources available to them; changes in the distribution of resources and climates of opinion (including the opinions and influence of extra-professional interest groups such as industrial and political); competition for control over syllabuses and textbooks; career interests of groups and individuals; diffusion of ideas and materials and the reaction to them, partially accounted for by 'subcultural conflict of perspective and interest'; and finally the continuing vulnerability to attack of any powerful group and its prevailing ideals.

Dissemination

Alexander (1984) has argued that conceptualization of curriculum and pedagogy is to a large extent a function of the nature of the assumptions and discourse of primary teachers, mediated through teacher education and professional interaction. The discourse consists of a cluster of issues, which relate to political and social categories. Hamilton (1980) observed that 'educational practice lies at the intersection of economic history and the history of ideas', that 'taken independently neither technologies (material resources) nor beliefs (ideological resources) are sufficient to account for the practices of schooling.'[23] In examining the process of dissemination, we consider 'technologies' in the variety of media by which ideas were conveyed, as well as the prevailing 'beliefs' themselves. Processes of dissemination are significant, because the medium was a considerable part of the message. For example a film produced with the intention of promulgating primary progressivism, which conveyed in its imagery and style, a clear implication of the superiority of the rural over the urban school;[24] an influential book on progressive primary practice which embodied in its format and presentation the ideals of children's work as highly finished product, and the high value placed on a good-looking classroom.[25] Progressivism as a 'faith' seemed encapsulated by an innovating cadre who followed the teachings of a retired HMI, whilst the processes of curriculum development within a handful of LEAs created an aura of dogmatism and elitism.[26] Patterns of dissemination also reveal the authority structures and the informal networks within which curriculum and teaching methods are defined.

The professional environment in which teachers work is the product of a multiplicity of agencies and their interaction. Vehicles of dissemination can be identified and examined. They include in-service courses, literature in the form of periodicals and books, and other media such as video and film. Impinging on the teacher is both a professional and popular culture of schooling, the latter comprising educational debate in the media at large. This wider discourse is constantly subject to change in social conditions and in political debate.

Aspects of progressivism in elementary school teaching had already been well established before the war by certain renowned 'pioneers' whose work in the earlier part of the century has been described by Selleck.[27] Chapter 1 below considers the nature of progressivism as promulgated in terms of ethos, curriculum content and teaching methods in the primary school, but as the second chapter makes clear, new factors, social, educational and professional in the post-war period were significant for curriculum development. Chapter 3 looks at the work and influence of prominent individuals who contributed to dissemination of progressive ideals in the post-war era. The following chapters then examine in turn three important vehicles specific to the period, by which the dissemination of ideologies and practices occurred: professional training, especially the growth of in-service training, professional organizations, and developments in school architecture. Attention paid by the media to educational matters in these decades contributed significantly to a public image of progressivism, and this is considered in chapter 7. Chapter 8 looks at the way these factors worked in one local education authority, Oxfordshire, with particular reference to the role of the advisory service. The last chapter returns to the wider context in which curriculum development took place, and again attention paid by the media to educational matters played a considerable part in the 'backlash' of the 1970s.

Notes

1 Rowland, S. (1986) 'Where is primary education going?', *Journal of Curriculum Studies*, 19, 1, p. 88, a review of DES (1985) *Education 8 to 12 in Combined and Middle Schools*, London, HMSO.

2 Blyth, W.A.L. (1965) *English Primary Education, Vol. 2,* London, Routledge and Kegan Paul, pp. 20–43.

3 Golby, M. (1982) 'Microcomputers and the primary curriculum', in Garland, R. (Ed.) *Microcomputers and Children in the Primary School*, Lewes, Falmer Press.

4 Alexander, R. (1984) *Primary Teaching*, London, Holt Rinehart and Winston, p. 13.
5 Richards, C. (1984) *The Study of Primary Education, A Source Book, Vol. 1*, Lewes, Falmer Press, p. 62.
6 Sharp, R. and Green, A. (1975) *Education and Social Control: A study in Progressive Primary Education*, London, Routledge and Kegan Paul; Centre for Contemporary Cultural Studies (1981) *Unpopular Education: Schooling and Social Democracy in England since 1944*, London, Hutchinson, pp. 65 and 129.
7 Lawton, D. (1981) 'The curriculum and curriculum change' in Simon, B. and Taylor, W. (Eds.) *Education in the Eighties: The Central Issues*, London, Batsford.
8 Armstrong, M. (1980) *Closely Observed Children: The Diary of a Primary Classroom*, London, Writers and Readers; Rowland, S. (1984) *The Enquiring Classroom: An Approach to Understanding Children's Learning*, Lewes, Falmer Press.
9 Blyth, W.A.L. (1984) *Development, Experience and Curriculum in Primary Education*, London, Croom Helm.
10 Schiller, L.C. (1969) 'The progressive ideas in state schools' in Ash, M. (Ed.) *Who Are the Progressives Now?*, London, Routledge and Kegan Paul, p. 153.
11 Stewart, W.A.C. (1986) *The Educational Innovators, Vol. 2, Progressive Schools 1881–1967*, London, Macmillan.
12 Sharp, R. and Green, A. (1975) *Education and Social Control: A Study in Progressive Primary Education*, London, Routledge and Kegan Paul, p. viii.
13 Jones, K. (1983) *Beyond Progressive Education*, London, Macmillan.
14 *Ibid*, p. 23.
15 Silver, H. (1983) *Education as History*, London, Methuen, p. 5.
16 Williams, R. (1961) *The Long Revolution*, Harmondsworth, Penguin, pp. 145–7.
17 Tompson, R.S. (1970) 'The Leeds Grammar Schools case of 1805', *Journal of Educational Administration and History*, 3, 1, December.
18 Gardner, P. (1984) *The Lost Elementary Schools of Victorian England*, London, Croom Helm; Humphries, S. (1981) *Hooligans or Rebels?*, Oxford, Blackwell.
19 Goodson, I. (Ed.) (1985) *Social Histories of the Secondary School Curriculum: Subjects for Study*, Lewes, Falmer Press, p. 3.
20 Reid, W.A. (1986) 'Curriculum theory and curriculum change: What can we learn from history?' *Journal of Curriculum Studies*, 18, 2, p. 159.
21 Silver, H. (1983) *op. cit.*, p. 241.
22 Cooper, B. (1985) *Renegotiating Secondary School Mathematics*, Lewes, Falmer Press, p. 10.
23 Hamilton, D. (1980) 'Adam Smith and the moral economy of the classroom system', *Journal of Curriculum Studies*, 12, 4, p. 282.
24 see chapter 8 below.
25 see chapter 1 below.
26 see chapters 3 and 8 below.
27 Selleck, R. (1972) *English Primary Education and the Progressives: 1914 to 1939*, London, Routledge and Kegan Paul.

1 *The Nature of Progressivism*

Definitions

When the first edition of the *Oxford English Dictionary* was published in 1909, the word 'progressive' was not apparently recognized to have any particular significance for education, though the following year, G.K. Chesterton considered that George Bernard Shaw's disregard for convention arose from 'that progressive education of his'. In the sphere of late nineteenth-century municipal politics, the term had become attached to those who were liberal and favoured progress or reform in political and social matters, broadening to mean advocacy of change, innovation or experiment, signifying the 'avant-garde'. In 1908 H.G. Wells wrote of 'these progressive times'.

In 1839 a translation of Madame Necker de Saussure's classic work had introduced the term 'progressive education' into the English language, and as lately as 1976 an article in *The Listener*, reporting Neville Bennett's research, concluded that 'anxious children did particularly poorly in a progressive classroom'. These examples were considered representative enough by the lexicographers to find their way into the *OED Supplement* in 1982. Progressivism has thus been a long-lived concept. It has had many detractors, — as well as many adherents who actually disowned the label. Though some teachers may have rejected the label, a variety of developments in primary school curriculum and practice at a particular historical period constituted far more than a disparate and unconnected set of coincidences, and though individual actors may have seen their contributions to change as independent and personal responses to the educational needs of the young children for whom they were responsible, the term 'progressivism' provides an appropriate concept within which to examine the interrelatedness of events.

Selleck (1972), in his study of *English Primary Education and the Progressives 1914–1939*, noted that advocates of the 'New Education' about the turn of the century were united more by opposition to the old ways of narrow curriculum and rigid methodology than by any common creed, but that out of a confusing mixture of theories, beliefs and practices, evolved a view which could be labelled 'progressive'. That fluidity still applied more than half a century later and reforming primary teachers in the period since 1945 were often extremely reluctant to be branded by any sort of 'ism'. Alec Clegg, a leading promoter of progressivism in post-war education, in reflective mood on the abolition of his West Riding LEA in 1974, predicted that future educational historians would probably write about 'open education', 'activity methods' and 'free choice',

> the verbal shorthand of those who started it all and knew what they were doing, but which more recently have become the jargon of those who . . . have jumped on the bandwagon but cannot play the instruments.[1]

In a lecture at Goldsmiths' College the same year he criticized 'unthinking cliché-mongers' and 'mechanical techniques'.[2] Yet, to the curriculum historian, the jargonizing itself is evidence of the power of organizing concepts within the discourse, however mechanical or insincere their subsequent application.

Selleck (1972) proceeded by identifying influential texts and experiments that assumed importance as points of reference in the discourse, such as those of Edmond Holmes, who in 1911 shocked the complacent by damning the schools he had lately inspected, Homer Lane, who added a touch of Freudian theory, and Maria Montessori, who helped to realize new approaches within the realms of the possible and the normal. Selleck cited experimental schools such as A.S. Neill's Summerhill, Dartington Hall and the Malting House School at Cambridge, where Susan Isaacs taught, observed and recorded; and he described new methods, such as the 'Play Way', the 'Dalton Plan' and 'Eurhythmics'.

> The progressives were not a disciplined army marching, united, on a particular town. They were a group of travellers who, finding themselves together on the road, had formed a loosely united band.
>
> They shared not a dogma or a doctrine, but a tendency of thought. . . . They shared a general attitude to children and teaching (but not uniformly), they were preoccupied with a similar set of problems (but not all progressives worried equally about all of them); they reached similar conclusions; they agreed that the old education was bad (but not always for the same reasons).[3]

Moreover, the path from theory to practice was difficult and complex. Yet, though the new ideas and experimental methods were not reducible to a neat pattern, there were certain common themes: a reduction in the traditional authoritarianism of the teacher, alternatives to the dominant pedagogical form of the class lesson, removal of harsh punishment and unnecessary drill and discipline, with a preference for self-government by pupils, dissolution of the formal timetable, and a shift in curriculum emphasis from the routine of the 3Rs to more creative and expressive activities. 'Individuality', 'freedom' and 'growth' were key concepts found embodied especially in Percy Nunn's textbook *Education, Its Data and First Principles*, which went through twenty-three reprints and one revision between 1920 and 1945.

Those key concepts, modified by time and circumstances, continued to run through the tapestry of curriculum change in the post-war primary school. Often apparently unconscious of all their precursors, post-war innovators in primary education worked within a professional culture which had developed along such lines. Taken to extremes, these concepts eventually threatened the central consensus of primary progressivism which had held through the 1950s and 1960s, as a more radical line of development led to the deschooling movement, whereupon a deeper cultural tide turned against the values of individuality and freedom; but that theme will be developed at the end of this book.

Texts

A variety of texts, some now quite neglected, might be used to chart the dissemination of progressivism and to help define the various creeds and practices over time. Of an official nature, two which filled the long gap between the 1937 *Handbook of Suggestions for Teachers* published by the Board of Education, and the Central Advisory Council's reports on *Primary Education* for England and for Wales (the Plowden Report and the Gittins Report) thirty years later, were a Report of the Advisory Council on Education in Scotland, published in 1946 and the Ministry of Education's *Primary Education*, a handbook published in 1959.

Though Scottish primary education does not come within the remit of the present study, the Scottish Report aroused attention south of the border.[4] It put the child in the foreground and defined primary education as continuing the work of the child's earliest educators, its parents; it counselled teachers to see the child as an individual and introduced the principle of 'compensatory' education:

> There is one purpose of primary education which in any forward looking and logically developed programme is apt to be under-emphasized. These seven years are among the most vivid of our existence....
>
> We must above all respect this ... on behalf of children, whose happiness is a good deal at the mercy of circumstances and people beyond their control. This purpose, if accepted, involves

> important consequences. The teacher has to recognize differences of capacity and temperament and give all a fair deal. She must recognise and compensate for difference of home background; she must not impose any artificial pattern of life by an over-dominant personality; and she must so help her pupils to coordinate their mental and physical powers as to allow these to develop through disciplined and purposeful activity.[5]
>
> We believe that the object to be achieved is to awaken interests in the child, or make him [sic] aware of needs already demanding fulfilment, so that he will either spontaneously or with suitable encouragement persevere along profitable lines of activity suitable to his stage of development and his native genius.[6]

As for the curriculum, the Advisory Council accepted a number of criticisms of prevailing practice, namely: that the hard division between 'subjects' was an adult conception justified neither by life experience nor as a natural way of learning; that the atmosphere of schools was too 'academic', verbal rather than real, and cut off from the living interests of childhood; that emphasis was laid on passivity rather than activity, children being required to sit still, listen, accept and reproduce either orally or on paper; and that the long tradition of class teaching was seriously questioned, resting on the baseless assumption that all or most can be brought up to a certain standard of attainment in a given time.[7]

The need for research of these problems on a wide basis, national and international, was acknowledged, but the teacher herself was also seen as a researcher:

> The impulse to experiment springs not only from the unresting intellectual activity of the well-endowed teacher, but from the love and concern she has for the pupils in her charge. The ways by which children learn cannot be reduced to a set of rules of universal application.... So the good teacher will always be 'trying something new', and such an attitude will always appeal to the lively minds of children.[8]

Primary teachers were seen as needing wide social contacts and sympathies; their closer association in future with parents and with the world outside school would be accompanied by a rise in social prestige for the teacher — a factor seen as of the highest importance in the improvement of the school curriculum and in the best interests of the pupils.[9]

In 1959 the Ministry of Education took pains in titling its publication for primary school teachers. *Primary Education* was the short title; its lengthy sub-title, though diminutively printed, was: *Suggestions for the Considerations of Teachers and Others Concerned with the Work of the*

Primary Schools. As the Minister, Geoffrey Lloyd, stated in his foreword, the former '*Handbooks of Suggestions*' no longer accorded with the present status of the teaching profession, or with the broader view now taken of what constituted good education.

> Fortunately, we have in this country a tradition of independence and vitality amongst the teachers which guarantees that new knowledge and experience is quickly translated into new courses, new ideas about the way schools should be run, and new teaching methods.[10]

On this premise, the authors (HMI) chose to adopt an approach which informed the work of the Plowden Committee five years later, not to overtly *prescribe* but to selectively *describe*:

> It seems more appropriate in the circumstances of today to describe the arrangements and practices which are to be found in *the more successful* schools [my emphasis] ...
>
> To many teachers much that is described may be familiar.... What is now to be found in the schools has gradually evolved out of the free working and independent initiative of teachers....[11]

Such assertions and assumptions about the pattern of curriculum development seem questionable in retrospect. Moreover the underlying philosophy of contemporary primary education was taken to be increasingly child-centred:

> the ever-deepening concern with children as children ... has gradually spread from the nursery and infant schools to the junior schools. This concern shows itself especially in the awareness of the child as a whole, with inter-dependent spiritual, emotional, intellectual and physical needs, and in the appreciation of the wide range of aptitudes, abilities and temperaments which any class of children presents.[12]

The plan of the book reflected a child-centred approach, beginning with the pre-school years and describing the subsequent stages of the system, nursery, infant and junior, but beginning at each stage with a brief consideration of the characteristics of children at those stages.

On the other hand, the balance of content was firmly weighted towards curriculum rather than child development; part 3 dealt with nine 'Fields of Learning' and occupied two-thirds of the book. Religion, physical education, language, maths, art and craft and needlework, handwriting, music, history, geography and natural history were identified 'to reflect the headings that have become familiar in schools', but it was pointed out that these fields 'merge and overlap' and were not intended for a timetable. Furthermore, education in school was to be considered as more than the sum of subjects or activities, because

> the ultimate criterion of the quality of ... education is the quality and balance of the personality which results.[13]

A balanced attitude towards 'activity' and 'methodical teaching' was advocated — the 1937 advice that tables should be learned was omitted, but 'ultimately, facts must be learned'. In explaining its development, there prevailed a 'Whig view' of curriculum history which had been 'gradually enriched an liberalised as more generous and enlightened views have prevailed' and as material conditions had improved. Public opinion was now considered to have accepted the principle that education should be concerned with the all-round development of each child. There was also a sanguine view of the uniformity of curricular provision (a picture which came to be discredited following widespread classroom-based research in the later 1970s):

> Because tradition is so strong, and because the process of education in this country has always been a slow evolution, not subject to sudden change, and because teachers as a body are in close touch with each other, and with others concerned in the education of children, the curriculum is fundamentally the same in all primary schools.[14]

As well as its general picture of progressivism in the primary schools, then, the *Suggestions* embodied a number of points which will be returned to in the following chapters; the idea of teacher-centred development through teachers' own networks; the role of HMI and local advisers ('Others concerned with the work of the primary schools'), and the notion of infant methods 'filtering up' to the junior stage.

However, the texts most frequently mentioned as influential by those trained and teaching in progressive primary schools in the post-war decades, were not the 'official' documents, but a variety of independently written works, four of which, as a fairly representative sample, are now discussed.

M.V. Daniel's *Activity in the Primary School* was first published in 1947, reprinted the same year and again in 1948, 1949, 1953 and 1955, no doubt responding to demand from the increasing numbers of primary teachers in training as the post-war bulge in birth-rate took hold. The author, Principal of Hereford Training College, hoped that it would 'give encouragement to those fearful of breaking new ground' and that it might 'prove the need for a different approach to those who still adhere to the traditional formal methods of primary school education'.[15] Acknowledging the historical development of the primary school, she referred especially to the recent attention given to theory and practice of education, as a result of the Hadow Report on the Primary School (1931), the experience of the evacuation of school children during the war, experiments in methods and subjects, and research into the psychology of junior age children which had been instigated in the years after 1945.

Daniel defined the primary school as having four main functions: development of physical and mental abilities of each child; the establishment of standards of social behavior (citizenship was a priority on the educational agenda in the post-war years); preparation for everyday life (interpreted as the 'the three Rs'); and classification of children for secondary education. The last of these, she argued optimistically, did not affect the content of education. Her principle throughout was the need for learning through activity. Part 2 of the book offered written descriptions of activity methods in operation, fully illustrated with photographs. One activity depicted was children selecting books in a local bookshop, and reading in school, seated casually on the floor; in another picture, girls were engaged in household tasks, serving tea, cleaning silver, and polishing shoes (men's shoes!), whilst boys were shown inspecting the school boiler with the caretaker. Elsewhere the children were shown gardening, painting and model making, making musical instruments, or engaged in 'self-government' — debates and public speaking. Large classes, confined space and unsuitable furniture had presented teachers with difficulties, yet much progress had been made towards an active approach to education and some of the experiments that had been made to break away from the formal methods of pre-war years were described, including a practical approach to reading, writing and arithmetic, 'subject days', and 'experiments in citizenship' such as a children's parliament and electioneering. She stressed that material factors such as buildings and equipment should be *determined* by teaching method, rather than constraining it, but noted that those concerned with education were now recognizing the need to build new primary schools on a different pattern. Moreover, buildings should be more 'home-like' to reinforce desirable links between school and home.

The underlying principles of these curriculum developments, set out in part 1 of the book, ranged from an awareness of continuing historical change in the structure and methods of schooling, to a new understanding of the nature of children. In this respect she observed that, apart from Cyril Burt's note for the Hadow Committee's Report of 1931, psychological study had tended to concentrate on the under-7s and over-11s. Characteristics of the 7–11 age-range were their vigour and delight in activity, their natural curiosity and desire for experience, and their great interest in their surroundings. It followed from this that teaching must involve action and movement, and discovery by the children for themselves; their reasoning was to be developed through concrete experience, their aesthetic appreciation was to grow from inside rather than be imposed from outside, and the scope of activity must cater for the wide range of intelligence found at this age.[16]

As for the content of the curriculum, Daniel faced the argument put foward by some teachers that schemes of work might be incompatible with the activity methods which should follow the natural growth and development of the children. On the other hand, she argued, teachers needed a sense of direction, and children required some common ground of knowledge as a basis for their post-primary schooling, which meant introducing them to the universal classification of knowledge as subjects. Curriculum categories drawn up by her consisted of:

I	Physical activities	Physical training, games, dancing, rest, meals, hygiene
II	Environment activities	Local geography, local history, local nature study
III	Constructional activities	Handwork, simple physical and biological science
IV	Creative activities	Art, craft, music, movement, creative writing
V	Imaginative activities	Literature history, geography, drama, religious knowledge
VI	Tool subjects	Reading, writing, arithmetic
VII	The school setting	The basis and background of the whole process of education, and of the formation of moral, social and aesthetic standards.[17]

Sybil Marshall's *Experiment in Education* created a good deal of interest on publication in 1963, though some progressive teachers expressed doubts about its usefulness. A blend of autobiography and teacher's handbook (as the publisher described it), it was indeed a compelling and moving account of her eighteen years as teacher in a tiny Cambridgeshire village school. A preference for the rural over the urban was a theme which recurred frequently enough in progressive primary texts, where the ideal was often expressed of transferring the best values and practices of the village schools to their urban counterparts. Significantly, when Marshall entered university at the age of 49 on the closure of her village school, the essay on which she gained entrance was 'The decline of rural idiom and its effect on literature'.

The leitmotifs of her book were child-centredness and the integrated curriculum. As for the former, she was emphatic on the primacy of thinking and feeling over reading and writing, and that the process of education should be concerned with engaging the children and their interests.

> We have passed, quite rightly, from the era of being taught to the era of learning for oneself.[18]

Marshall was aware too of the need to steer a difficult course between the adult's view and the child's view of the world; it was

> absolutely impossible for most people to see anything as a child

> sees it, unclouded by maturity, and not through the mirror of assimilated experience.[19]

Ability to see the world through childish eyes, without adult whimsy, was given to very few (she cited the literary geniuses Lewis Carroll and Kenneth Grahame). In particular she advocated a study of each child's art as a means of learning about them as individuals, and it was art that gave a unity to her curriculum. Self-expression and communication through art was her leading principle. In 'free-writing' books, her children drew first, then wrote about their pictures, and a cooperative frieze from her school won first prize in a *Sunday Pictorial* exhibition in 1957. Marshall's book was richly illustrated with photographs of children's paintings and paper mosaics. Through her developing career as a teacher, she described in one chapter how art and nature study were brought together, in the next, how art, language, religious education and music were integrated, the climax of her final chapter describing a term's work which revolved entirely about Beethoven's *Pastoral Symphony*, introduced to the children on a new record player given to the school.

This climactic ending introduced a sub-theme which was most important in progressive discourse, that of change:

> The symphony is over, now. The giant, Progress, has removed the disc from the player, and closed the lid; for in the name of Progress, aided by his henchmen Economy and Expediency, the school has been closed.[20]

Marshall's account had in fact opened, as so many progressivist texts opened, with an account of the bad old days, of the strict and dull regime she had experienced as a pupil and in her early days as a certificated teacher. But as in much progressivist writing, future change tended to be seen with gloom and foreboding, the onset of accountability and the pressures of economy.

Fundamentals in the First School (1969) was written by seven members of staff at the Froebel Institute, chaired as a group by Molly Brearley, Principal of the College. Robinson (1971) has cited this book as prominent on the reading lists of colleges which he researched.[21] Although it covered the ages 5–9 (where Daniel dealt with 7–11, and Marshall with the entire primary age range), as a text commonly used by teachers in training, it provides some illuminating comparisons. The authors acknowledged the multidisciplinary nature of the study of education, but grounded their own approach on the principles of developmental psychology which they shared, citing the work of Piaget, Bruner and of Susan and Nathan Isaacs as their guiding lights. A select bibliography, shedding further light on their sources, was dominated by those names, but included also Friedrich Froebel himself, John Holt, Rudolf Laban, Suzanne Langer, Herbert Read, Karl Popper and others, —

a broad spectrum of writers representing humane, liberal and creative values. The 'generalizations from psychological knowledge and professional experience' on which they affirmed were six:

(i) children are unique persons and their individuality is to be acknowledged and respected;
(ii) each person constructs his own mind as a result of interaction with things and people in his environment;
(iii) learning is continuous and knowledge cumulative;
(iv) the concept of 'stages' in intellectual development is useful in helping to understand some distinguishable phases of development in a child's thought;
(v) children encouraged in co-operative efforts with other children and with teachers will collaborate in the search for and the sharing of knowledge;
(vi) the mental processes involved in the search for knowledge and understanding contain their own self-expanding and extending propulsion.[22]

From this foundation the book was ordered into seven curriculum areas with their associated physical and mental activities:

Science: expectations, conjectures and validations.
Art: representation and expression.
Literature: impression and reflection.
Movement: action, feeling and thought.
Mathematics: ordering, relating, measuring.
Music: hearing and making sound.
Morality: values and reasons.

Emphasis was laid on the continuous process of learning, so that the school, in its main work of fostering and developing mental life, 'enabling children to experience more fully and consciously all that life has to offer', had to capitalize on the massive volume of experience acquired by the child before school. School was to use the natural energy and curiosity of the child, offering love and appreciation to build up confidence, helping them influence the personal growth and learning in each other through facilitating group work. If the 'community pattern of learning' could not be distilled into formal lessons, nor could it be just left to happen, and the planned intervention by professionally trained teachers must be based on clear principles.

In arguing for careful observation and communication with parents in the early stages of children's development, the authors referred to a precept of Froebel himself, that the parents should practice keeping simple records of children's growth; this would have the dual purpose not only of enlightening the parents about their children but of communicating the sense of care for its unique personal life which the child needs.

(This practice of recording observations of children, is traceable back to Rousseau, and was the basis of Piaget's scientific method; it was practised also by HMI Christian Schiller).[23] The teacher's relationship to the child should be one of 'warm objectivity'; her role was complex and no stereotype would fit it, but a threefold description was offered: as the provider of material, stimuli and 'climate' for individual and social growth, as a mediator of experience who sees every aspect of the child's living as a means of learning, as a teacher, whose professional knowledge and skill enables her to teach at the moment of willingness and ability to learn. Of the four books examined here, Brearley's was thus the most like a scientific treatise, its scientific basis being in Piagetian psychology.

Alongside the Child in the Primary School, written by Leonard Marsh and published in 1970, was illustrated with photographs. A salient characteristic of progressivist texts, like the three previous books (and like the Plowden Report itself), this use of photography in progressivist texts focussed attention on the photogenic child, often viewed with a tinge of romanticism, and heightened the emphasis on classroom environment and on activity methods. But the entire presentation of *Alongside the Child* carried significance in the fusion of medium and message. Produced by Adam and Charles Black, a publishing house with a reputation for high standards of design in books for primary schools, Marsh's book was beautifully set in a fine type on textured suede paper, elegant and technically polished photographs of children in action were interspersed with coloured plates of their art work. A sense of romanticism about primary education and a high regard for craft values were thus conveyed not simply by words on the page, but by the physical quality of the book. Provenance of the children's work and of the photographs, were schools in Oxfordshire such as Finmere, and Tower Hill, Witney, the schools which so impressed Vincent Rogers on his visit to the county,[24] and from the West Riding of Yorkshire.

Beginning with an account of 'The child's world', Marsh described his own sense of the child's 'essential and already established personal integration' which seemed to nullify both the idea of 'subjects' or 'forms of knowledge' and adult attempts to integrate these subjects in artificial 'projects'; thus, it was argued, the primary school curriculum should have a 'psychological basis'. The book continued by discussing children's learning, painting and talking, learning through discovery, using books and writing, before considering school organization through themes such as 'personal relationships', 'the rhythm of the day', and 'the importance of detail'. Though considerable reference was made to Piaget, the book was essentially a descriptive account of 'good practice', instinctive rather than analytical. This approach may be seen as a major *theme* of the work, for at the very outset he stated his guiding principle:

> in this period of dominance by experimental and physical

> sciences, we need to remind ourselves that the basic techniques of the educationalist must be observational, not experimental. We are closer to the biologist than the physicist, and it is the close observational approach of the naturalist that should be our research model in the coming years.[25]

The author's acknowledgments to Christian Schiller, former Chief HMI for Primary Education, and to Lady Plowden, Chair of the Central Advisory Council which reported on primary schools in 1967, clearly linked this progressivism to the formal agents of primary curriculum development in the post-war period. Yet its tinge of romanticism seemed to some teachers removed from the more problematic reality of many classrooms.

In this varied sample of texts, the practical, the inspirational, the scientific and the romantic, a mood of idealism and optimism prevailed throughout. Little attention was paid to problems such as those of children with learning difficulties or emotional disturbance. A telling episode from Sybil Marshall may illustrate this: she wrote eloquently of an educationally sub-normal boy, of his worth and achievements, observing that reading and writing were only secondary to thinking and feeling as objects of education, yet a violent boy who wrought havoc with the smooth running of the school was simply removed by the parents, to her evident relief. It was characteristic of a reaction against a certain rosy idealism that writings such as the American Philip Jackson's *Life in Classrooms* should have more frankly faced up to the complexities and uncertainties of the teacher's role, which demanded the ability

> to tolerate the enormous amount of ambiguity, unpredictability and occasional chaos created each hour by twenty-five or thirty not-so-willing learners.[26]

Certain themes recur in progressive rhetoric. Running throughout was a significant spectre of the bad old days, progressivism thus seeking to define itself by what it rejected. Tales of past rigidity and harshness were important to those who wished to highlight the advances that were being made. Edmond Holmes introduced this theme into educational literature with his influential book *What Is, and What Might Be* (1911) contrasting the 'Path of mechanical obedience' represented by the traditional elementary schools, with the 'Path of self-realization', typified by Harriet Johnson's village school in Sussex. This approach was adopted from nineteenth-century classics of social criticism such as A.W.N. Pugin's *Contrasts* (1836), Thomas Carlyle's *Past and Present* (1842), or William Morris's *How We Live, and How We Might Live* (1888). However, the caricature of past practice offered by some progressivist writers as a foil to new ideas, was often historically imprecise, for not only had there been some individualistic and caring teachers under the codes, such as Harriet Johnson herself, but the codes themselves were not unequivocally harsh. The reviled Elementary School Code as revised in 1883 by Mundella, included the following:

> There must be cheerful and exact discipline, without harshness or shouting. The premises must be clean and well-ordered. The timetable must provide a proper variety of mental employments, physical exercise....
>
> Above all the teaching and discipline must be such as to ... awaken in them a love of reading that is expected to last beyond school life.[27]

Coupled with the reassuring picture of a deplorable past against which innovation could be described,was an obsession with 'making the change'. Some progressivists spoke of their own 'Damascus road' conversions, a theme found in Edmond Holmes' own autobiography *In Quest of an Ideal* (1920), and taken up again by Arthur Razzell in *Juniors: A Postscript to Plowden* (1968).[28] Others argued that they simply taught according to their best instincts and only later discovered progressive ideology:

> As is the case with so many other junior schools in Britain, our way was pragmatic and not, at first, guided by any conscious theory. Yet in surveying our activities, principles emerge which are quite clear to us now. Possibly, also, with greater time to reflect and read, we are able to trace the sources of several ideas which we thought at the time were our own.[29]

There was a strong sense of identity for some, of being in the company of an 'enlightened few'; a paradigm of pioneers working against a traditional and bureaucratically imposed curriculum. Sybil Marshall, in discarding her LEA's official timetable as unnecessary where education 'goes forward with enthusiasm and freedom', argued that those who saw this clearly must count themselves as *enlightened* beings — for evey one of them there are still fifty who worship at the shrine of the fixed and the dependable.[30]

Some early post-war articles in *Teacher's World* on 'modern methods' referred to the process of 'making the change' from 'formal' to 'activity' methods. Advice on effecting change was an important feature of the literature in forthcoming decades: the NUT Consultative Committee Report on Nursery-Infant education contained an account of the 'change-over' from formal to activity methods based on three heads' experience, two Froebel Society pamphlets offered some advice on 'making the changeover', as did one of Molly Brearley's television programmes in the series *Teachers and Children*; and later Moira McKenzie and Wendla Kernig (both heads of well-known progressive primary schools in London) offered students and young teachers advice on the process of 'making the change'.[31]

Marsh illustrated his model of the process of change as usually requiring

> a delay of some two decades (it is often more) between the work of the pioneers and the filtering downwards of experimental work.[32]

The chapters below will argue that such a model, adopted from Schiller's image of the 'progress of the worm' is oversimplistic; it embodies the notion of change through 'pioneers' followed by their disciples, and ignores the continual shifts in the social, cultural and professional contexts of primary schooling. A great deal of ambiguity resided in the progressivist obsession with change, for whilst progressive writers did sometimes acknowledge the need for constant change, there was also frequent reference back to events such as the Hadow Report of 1931 or latterly the Plowden Report, as ideological fixed points[33], coupled with a sense of resistance to contemporary cultural developments.[34]

A significant underlying theme of much progressivist writing was the superiority of country to city. The deep cultural divide between rural and urban has been explored in literature by Raymond Williams (1973) [35], and its impact on educational discourse requires further examination. As early as 1887, Mr. Courthope Brown, Chairman of the Joint Board for Froebel Examinations, questioned the suitability for urban children of the rural imagery of Froebel's kindergarten songs.[36] Concern for the health of school children encouraged open-air schooling in the inter-war period, and more generally an appreciation of the countryside, sunlight and fresh air, was reflected in the growing pastimes of hiking and cycling, and flourishing organizations such as the Youth Hostels' Association; with the coming of the family motor car, petrol advertising in particular mediated a certain image of rural England. For primary education, the countryside was not an unmixed blessing, and the rural school presented problems through its isolation, size and lack of resources.[37] Nevertheless, films such as the wartime Central Office of Information production, *Ashley Green Goes to School*, and Oxfordshire County Council's *Village School*, reinforced the value of family atmosphere and environmental study made possible in the village school,[38] and an open-plan school such as Eveline Lowe School in Southwark, was seen as bringing the qualities of the village school into the town.[39] This rural idealism was, perhaps unconsciously, reflected in a frequent curricular emphasis on nature study and on craft, in which respect the progressive curriculum sometimes appears to have been resisting aspects of cultural change associated with urbanization and mass production.

Fields of Learning

Though the progressive curriculum is not to be defined principally by subject matter, and though curriculum integration was an important feature, yet there were certain characteristic emphases.

Mathematics occupied a favoured place in the progressive primary curriculum. Lancelot Hogben's hugely successful *Mathematics for the Million* (1936)[40] had engendered a popular interest in mathematics and was reprinted and revised throughout the 1950s and 1960s, but it was the close relationship between Piaget's developmental stages and the growth of mathematical concepts which made its application so clear in the child-centred primary classroom. Work by Catherine Stern, the Mathematics Association, Dienes and others provided a wealth of structural apparatus and schemes. The launch of the Russian Sputnik in 1957 provoked new initiatives in maths at secondary level,[41] and Geoffrey Matthews, who directed the Nuffield Maths 5–13 project which began in 1963, recalled:

> the beginning of the end of the 11+ was leaving teachers with the feeling that much of the old stuff was obsolete and that here was an opportunity to teach something more relevant and palatable.

The Nuffield Maths Project provided an effective lever for encouraging a more activity-centred approach to the whole of the curriculum, and in its dissemination through pilot projects based in teachers' centres, for many primary teachers it instilled a new habit of in-service participation.[42] When published, Nuffield maths was given a title drawn from the Chinese proverb so beloved of progressivists:

> I hear and I forget; I see and I remember; I do and I understand.[43]

Christian Schiller, HMI, a leading protagonist of primary progressivism, was himself a mathematician, as had been his teacher Percy Nunn, and Thyra Smith's book, *Number*, contained an acknowledgement to his inspiration. Two of Schiller's students contributed to the literature on primary mathematics.[44]

Art, or self-expression through scribbles, visual symbols and the representation of objects appears to come more instinctively to children than many other activities defined by the school curriculum; progressivism, not unnaturally, accorded it considerable status. The work of Sybil Marshall has already provided one example, and a professional and popular interest in children's visual expression can be traced back to the practices inspired by the Viennese teacher Cizek and exhibitions of his pupils' work in the 1920s, promoted by Marion Richardson in her role as lecturer at the London Day Training College from 1925 and later as an inspector for the London County Council Education Authority. R.R. Tomlinson, Senior Inspector of Art for the LCC, wrote a book on *Children as Artists* published in the prestigious King Penguin series in 1947.[45]

Neglected agents of curriculum development are the firms of educational suppliers. Though many teachers struggled with poor materials in the immediate post-war years, great improvements in the supply of art materials helped to meet demand and served to encourage practice. Firms such as Dryad, Osmiroid and Berol employed the services of teachers to advise on and promote their products, but such promotion could have undesired effects: Sybil Marshall, whose own pupils won a *Sunday Pictorial* competition, wrily described how distorted and mechanical art could become when disseminated insensitively:

> There can surely be very few teachers now who have not heard or read of the modern methods in art, nor seen one of the ubiquitous exhibitions by means of which certain newspapers and artists' suppliers have tried to 'cash in' on the new movement. It has been going for so long now that it can hardly be called new any longer, and it is quite time that teachers understood what they were trying to do.[46]

There were distinctive trends to art in the progressive curriculum; whilst interest in expression derived from the impact of Freudian psychology in the visual arts, a deeper seated native tradition was that of the arts and crafts. An important protagonist of the latter was Robin Tanner, HMI, with his interest in William Morris, and in a tradition which stemmed from Ruskinian ideas of the morality of design. As Morris himself put it:

> The condition of the arts in any age must be sought in the state of the crafts of design.

The educational problem of craft is that it could overshadow individual expression:

> That talk of inspiration is sheer nonsense. I may tell you flat — there is no such thing: it is a mere matter of craftsmanship.

(Morris's attitude was predictive of the poetry writing process at its worst extreme, in some primary classrooms:

> If a chap can't compose an epic poem while he's weaving at tapestry, he'll never do any good at all.)

So it was that the craft tradition sometimes encouraged art work produced to a formula, with an emphasis on technique and presentation. It corresponded with the craft ideal that calligraphy should have a prominent place in many primary school curricula.

Sybil Marshall found that the awareness of art as a medium for the understanding of other subjects led her on to a new interest in nature study, and Leonard Marsh's stated preference in scientific method for biology over the physical sciences was matched in many primary school curricula, where nature study played a prominent part.

In the progressive scheme of things, nature study had a special significance. It was at the core of the 'Utopian' curriculum in Edmond Holmes' (1911) *What Is and What Might Be*. For the Froebelians perhaps it was a means to understanding the unity of creation, and there were strong links between the Froebel Foundation and the School Nature Study Union. The arguments for it were well expressed in a Froebel Foundation pamphlet, worth quoting at length as it also rehearsed the disadvantages of the town child compared to the country child: Recognizing that 'nature' was not the 'natural environment' of the urban child, however, the argument displayed a sensitive balance:

> There are so many difficulties in the way of teaching nature study in town schools that one may be tempted to wonder if it is worthwhile to attempt a subject that has become almost foreign to the environment of city children. Would not derricks and levers, electricity and locomotives be more in keeping with their interests and experiences?
>
> Yet, when we consider that our very existence depends upon *things that grow* — on plants and animals — surely it is right that we should all have some understanding of these things without which we could not live. However useful electricity and the like are in our modern way of life, we still expect to have flowers to decorate our houses, or to keep a budgie or a cat in an effort to satisfy a deep craving within us for contact with nature.
>
> Let us first think what country children have that is denied to their town cousins. Country children grow up in an environment of farms and gardens where there is birth, life, death, life re-born year in, year out in a wealth of examples . . . the whole seasonal rhythm of nature that mirrors the rhythm of life itself.
>
> This, in its wholeness, is not experienced by the city child. We cannot recreate it in the classroom, but we must seek whatever instance we can to illustrate this cycle of life . . . to develop an appreciation of the beauty, purposefulness and slow sureness of natural growth.[48]

There was also a recognition that transport had changed the relationship of town and country:

> in these days of easy travel there are few who do not sometimes penetrate to the countryside and many among teachers who spend most weekends there.[49]

However, the author emphasized that nature study in town schools was not to be a poor imitation of that which was possible in a village school, but something rich and beautiful in its own way. Children must *do* nature, and not just listen to or watch programmes; the example was given of a school within sight of Big Ben which used window boxes, tubs, sink gardens, a bomb-site, and visits to park, zoo or country. Science in the primary school was the focus of growing interest in the later 1950s as a vehicle for working from the child's own experiences and for learning by discovery, reflected in a growing number of publications from the National Froebel Foundation (1958) *Scientific Interests in the Primary School*, the Educational Supply Association (1960) *Approaches to Science in the Primary School*, and the British Association for the Advancement of Science (1962) *The Place of Science in Primary Education.*

Blackie (1967) saw PE and art the spearheads in primary curriculum change.[50] Physical education had a long tradition in the curriculum, going back to concern for the nation's fitness, and to a fairly liberal tradition with the introduction of Swedish Drill in the Code of 1895, and a new syllabus from 1909 incorporating games and recreational activities. But more recently it had been the influence of Rudolf Laban, the German emigre, who set up a dance school at Dartington in 1938, and introduced the idea of creative personal development through movement.

Laban had some notable followers, such as Lisa Ullman who ran the Art of Movement studio in Manchester, recognized by the Ministry of Education for one-year courses for women, and Diana Jordan, an adviser in the West Riding LEA, and author of *Children and Movement.*[51] Alec Clegg had met Laban when working as Deputy Education Officer in Worcestershire, and was instrumental in bringing Diana Jordan to work in the West Riding.[52] It was appropriate that the Laban Centre for Movement and Dance should eventually in the 1970s have found a home in Goldsmiths' College, an institution which became noted also for its training of progressive primary teachers. Salt (1982) has observed that Piagetian concepts of thought as internalized action also served to reinforce a curriculum connection between movement and intellectual activity.[53] Official encouragement of a developmental and creative approach to movement came through the work of Ruth Foster, HMI, and the publication in the early 1950s of two Ministry of Education handbooks of physical education in the primary school: *Moving and Growing* and *Planning the Programme*; which replaced the previous Board of Education syllabus of 1933.

These few aspects of the curriculum reveal some features of progressivism in practice, the process of curriculum development, and the variety of means by which ideas were disseminated. Developments in other fields of learning such as language, where the work of the Rosens stemmed from their literary instincts and the influence of Christian Schiller, as well as from new directions in sociological and linguistic research, could be further explored to show how they mediated an increasingly progressive stance and how they added to a more progressive whole in the primary school curriculum. Notable absences from the curriculum could also be considered, such as civics, or modern languages, where the experiemental inclusion of French in the primary curriculum foundered partly on its conflict with the organization of an integrated day.[54]

Notes

1 Clegg, A. (1974) 'A subtler and more telling power', *Times Educational Supplement*, 27 September.
2 University of London, Goldsmiths' College (1974) *The Changing School: A Challenge to the Teacher*, report of a conference, p. 13.
3 Selleck, R.J.W. (1972) *English Primary Education and the Progressives, 1914 to 1939*, London, Routledge and Kegan Paul, pp. 60 and 61.
4 Scottish Education Department (1946) *Primary Education: A report of the Advisory Council on Education in Scotland*, Cmd 6973, London, HMSO; comment on the Report is found, *inter al*, in *Teacher's World* no. 2148, 22 November 1950.
5 Scottish Education Department (1946) para. 24.
6 *ibid*, para. 109.
7 *ibid.*, para. 79.
8 *ibid.*, para. 81.
9 *ibid.*, para. 103.
10 Ministry of Education (1959) *Primary Education, Suggestions for the Considerations of Teachers and Others Concerned with the Work of the Primary Schools*, London, HMSO, p. iii.
11 *ibid.*, p. 10.
12 *ibid.*, pp. 10–11.
13 *ibid.*, p. 115.
14 *ibid.*, p. 114.
15 Daniel, M.V. (1947) *Activity in the Primary School*, Oxford, Blackwell, p. 5.
16 *ibid.*, pp. 40–1.
17 *ibid.*, pp. 83–4.
18 Marshall, S. (1963) *An Experiment in Education*, Cambridge, Cambridge University Press, p. 24.
19 *ibid.*, pp. 107–8.
20 *ibid.*, p. 211.
21 Robinson, P. (1971) 'Ideology in teacher education', unpublished MSc (Econ) thesis, University of London, Institute of Education.
22 Brearley, M. and others (1969) *Fundamentals in the First School*, Oxford, Blackwell, p. 159.
23 see chapter 3 below.
24 Rogers, V. (1970) *Teaching in the British Primary School*, London, Macmillan.
25 Marsh, L. (1970) *Alongside the Child in the Primary School*, London, A. and C. Black.
26 Marshall, S. (1963) *op. cit.*, pp. 30 and 62; Jackson, P.W. (1968) *Life in Classrooms*, New York, Holt Rinehart and Winston Inc., quoted by Richards, C. (1978) *Education 3–13*, Driffield, Nafferton Books, p. 238.
27 PP 1883 [C.3738] liii, 91
28 Razzell, A. (1968) *Juniors: A Postscript to Plowden*, Harmondsworth, Penguin, p. 31; Probert H. and Jarman, C. (1971) *A Junior School (British Primary Schools Today)*, London, Macmillan for the School Council, p. 7.
29 Probert, H. and Jarman, C. (1971) *op. cit.*, p. 74.
30 Marshall, S. (1963) *op. cit.*, p. 42.
31 *Teacher's World*, No.2098, 9 December 1949; NUT (1949) *Nursery-Infant Education: Report of a Consultative Committee Appointed by the Executive of the National Union of Teachers*, London, Evans/NUT; Mann, B. (1962) *Learning Through Creative Work*,

Froebel Foundation Pamphlet, p. 24; Walters, E.H. (1965) *Activity and Experience in the Junior School*, (5th edn) Froebel Foundation Pamphlet, p. 8; McKenzie, M. and Kernig, W. (1975) *The Challenge of Informal Education*, London, Darton Longman Todd, pp. 157–60.

32 Marsh, L. (1970) *op. cit.*, p. 40.

33 Blenkin, G. and Kelly, A.V. (1981) *The Primary Curriculum*, London, Harper and Row, pp. 35 and 36; Alexander, R. (1984) p. 18 noted: 'Primary discourse abounds in throwbacks — the vocabulary, the sentiments, the saints and villains are the same now as a century ago' — not entirely accurate, but the sense of the argument is true.

34 Blackie, J. (1963) *Good Enough for the Children?*, London, Faber, pp. 45, 130; see chapter 3 below.

35 Williams, R. (1973) *The Country and the City*, London, Chatto and Windus.

36 Lawrence, E. (1952) *Friedrich Froebel and English Education*, London, Routledge and Kegan Paul, p. 64.

37 See, for example, NUT (1959) *The Curriculum of the Junior School, Consultative Committee Report*, Schoolmaster Publishing Co. Ltd., pp. 78–85.

38 See chapters 7 and 8 below.

39 See chapter 6 below, and Cunningham, P. (1987) 'Open-plan schooling, last stand of the progressives?', in Lowe, R. (Ed.) *The Changing Primary School*, Lewes, Falmer Press.

40 Hogben, L. (1936) *Mathematics for the Million* (2nd ed.) 1937; 3rd ed. 1951, 4th ed. 1967). Hogben, a radical Cambridge scientist whose career reflected great breadth of learning, was also author of books for primary school children such as Hogben, L. (1955) *Man Must Measure*, London Rathbone.

41 Moon, B. (1986) *The 'New Maths' Curriculum Controversy, An International Story*, Lewes, Falmer Press.

42 Matthews, G. (1973) 'A beginning of teachers' centres', in Thornbury, R.E. (Ed.) *Teachers' Centres*, London, Darton Longman Todd, pp. 50 and 62–3.

43 Nuffield Mathematics Project (1967) *I Do and I Understand*, London, W. and R. Chambers and John Murray for the Nuffield Foundation. A penchant for the oriental may be traced in some progressivist attitudes, from Edmond Holmes' interest in Buddhism onwards.

44 Smith, T. (1954) *Number: An Account of Work in Number with Children Throughout the Primary School Stage*, Oxford, Blackwell; Holloway, G.E.T. (1967) *An Introduction to the Child's Conception of Space*, London, Routledge and Kegan Paul; Holloway, G.E.T. (1967) *An Introduction to the Child's Conception of Geometry*, London, Routledge and Kegan Paul; Marsh, L. (1967) *Children Explore Mathematics*, London, A. and C. Black.

45 R.R. Tomlinson's *Picture Making by Children*, first published in 1934, was revised in 1950; Carline, R. (1968) *Draw They Must*, London, Edward Arnold, chapter 13.

46 Marshall, S. (1963) *op. cit.*, p. 104.

47 Hyndman, M. (1980) 'Utopia reconsidered: Edmond Holmes, Harriet Johnson and the school at Sompting', *Sussex Archaeological Collections*, 118, p. 351.

48 Hutchinson, M.M. (1961) *Practical Nature Study in Town Schools*, London, National Froebel Foundation p. 1.

49 *ibid.*

50 Blackie, J. (1967) *Inside the Primary School*, London, HMSO, p. 7.

51 Jordan, D. (1966) *Children and Movement*, Oxford, Blackwell.

52 Parkin, P. (1985) 'Lady Mabel College: Its origins and development until 1972' *History of Education Society Bulletin*, 35, p. 37.

53 Salt, E. (1982) 'A comparative study of the teaching of dance in the primary school', unpublished dissertation, Froebel Institute College.

54 Burstall, C. (1974) *Primary French in the Balance*, Slough, NFER, p. 245.

2 *Context of Progressivism*

Progressivism was a blend of the traditional and the innovatory. At times it accompanied what might be described as progressive attitudes in society at large; its regard for the individualism of children, and especially for ensuring educational opportunity for deprived children, went hand-in-hand with broader social tendencies in the post-war decades. Yet in teaching method and curriculum it often appeared to be resisting developments in popular culture and mass communications; examples documented elsewhere in this book are the emphasis laid on craft values, curricular bias towards 'nature' and the rural, resistance in some quarters to the use of television in school, and attacks on the 'commercialization of childhood'.

However much the progressivist literature concentrated its attention on activity within the classroom, it was also a product of changing social and economic circumstances in the years between the 1944 Education Act and the Plowden Report, for example the status of children, standards of living, and developments in technology, communications and popular culture, all of which had important bearings on primary school curriculum and teaching methods. It seems appropriate then to distinguish social and professional contexts in considering developments which coloured the progress of progressivism.

Social Context

From the 1944 Act to the Plowden Report, the population of England and Wales rose from 42.5 million to 47.1 million.[1] Birth rates fluctuated over the period with peaks of 18.0 per thousand in 1946–50 and 1960–65, having a significant impact on school population: in 1951 there were 3.5 million 5–10-year-olds at school (97.2 per cent of them in the state sector), and in 1968 4.5 million (95.5 per cent in state schools).[2] The net effect on the balance of population was a rise in the percentage of the young (0–14) from 22 per cent in 1951 to 23 per cent in 1966 (continuing to rise to nearly 25 per cent in 1971), though these figures are worth comparing with the 32 per cent of 1901 and 24 per cent of 1931. Mean family size rose marginally from 1945 until the early 1960s, when it began to fall, but remained at about two children.[3]

Qualitative evidence reveals a picture of changing relationships between parents and children. In a post-war essay on 'The spiritual foundations of the family', the Rt. Rev. E.J. Hagan expressed the view that the declining birth rate, decay of parental control, increase in juvenile delinquency and the growing prevalence of divorce were ominous indications of a widespread revolt against the restraints, sacrifices and duties of family life, whilst a survey by Geoffrey Gorer for *The People* newspaper published in 1951 found that 68 per cent of his sample believed children to need more discipline, and discovered little belief in the innocence or innate goodness of children.[4]

Ronald Fletcher's more optimistic view in 1962 was that widespread evidence existed for an ever increasing parental concern for their children's education and welfare.[5] Writing in 1965, D.C. Marsh observed that changes in the status of married women had probably encouraged a greater degree of genuine affection between husband and wife than ever before, and that reduction in family size had reflected this change; control over family size had become firmly accepted as a normal feature of married life.[6] Marwick (1982) has argued that the limitation of family size encouraged a view of children as objects to be enjoyed; wartime evacuation of children and separation of families and the loss of young lives through aerial bombing, seemed to have put a new premium on the importance of children and the need to provide them with loving care. Widely published research on child rearing in the late 1940s and early 1950s seemed to emphasize a more indulgent attitude towards children, notably John Bowlby's work arising from a study of the adverse effects of maternal deprivation and the relation of mental health to maternal care. The new interest was more than philanthropy, as social self-interest was also involved:

> Deprived children, whether in their own homes or out of them, are a source of social infection as real and serious as are carriers of diphtheria and typhoid.[7]

Even in so-called advanced societies, according to Bowlby, conditions of bad mental hygiene in nurseries and institutions were tolerated, which, if found in the field of physical hygiene, would have led to public outcry. This book, first published in 1953, reached a very wide readership through the relatively new means of paperback publishing; it was reprinted six times before 1965, and its second edition that year was reprinted annually for the next decade. In the second edition (1965), Bowlby noted that the years since 1953 had seen new evidence and scientific debate, and

> an ever-widening recognition of the need to ensure that children receive the care and affection now known to be necessary for their healthy development.

Other examples of this phenomenon included the works of Dr. Benjamin Spock; his *Baby and Child-care*, which appeared in Britain in a pocket edition in 1956, was boasted by his publishers to be one of the greatest best-sellers, and *Dr. Spock Talks With Mothers*, concerning children from 5 to adolescence, was reprinted annually in the USA from 1954 to 1961; its first British edition was published in 1962.

With increasing prosperity, the family was also becoming an important unit of consumption in the 1950s, and advertising did much to construct a set of values and child-rearing practices in the popular domain. In the *Radio Times* for 20 April 1954, accompanying details of an afternoon television broadcast by a teacher, Margaret Mann, about her teacher training course, were advertisements for Dettol, the Morphy Richards toaster, and Cow and Gate:

> Wise mummy, to buy this *real* cream, that's sealed to keep fresh for a month of Sundays.[8]

Elsewhere, Katie was busy giving meals 'man-appeal' for her sons and her husband — and someone else's Mum wasn't using Persil. At the same time, however, children may be identified as independent consumers. Pulling in the opposite direction from the cohesive nuclear family was a new independent youth culture. War gave children new freedoms and post-war economic conditions fostered their independence. In the early 1950s the figure representative of this detachment of youth from the rest of society was the Teddy Boy.[9] A further contributory factor to the independence of youth was National Service, breaking family links and opening new horizons for teenage boys. Though 'youth culture' was a teenage phenomenon it gradually filtered down the age-range, creating a precedent for treating younger children too as potential consumers.

A rising standard of living directly facilitated a more widespread application of progressive ideas and practices in school. In the early years of the century a major preoccupation of state elementary schools had been the provision of school dinners to tackle undernourishment of children, and the development of school medical and dental services to identify and deal with endemic conditions such as tuberculosis, inner ear disease and dental caries, which impeded many children's capacity for learning. As a dramatic measure of improved health, by the 1950s infant mortality had fallen from the level of 1930 by 50 per cent to thirty per 1000, compared with sixty in 1930, and by 1968 the figure had fallen to eighteen.[10] From 1948, 98 per cent of school children were drinking one-third of a pint of free milk daily, and children were taller and heavier in 1950 than they had been before the war.[11] The development of penicillin and new antibiotics (such as streptomycin, curing the tuberculosis which had so affected the inter-war generations), disinfectants and detergents, synthetic fibres, and plastics all represented a considerable advance in maintaining the hygiene and health of society.

Children were also increasingly better housed and physically more comfortable at home. Although a significant amount of sub-standard housing remained, standards generally improved. For example, the proportion of households sharing a dwelling in England and Wales fell from 14.3 per cent in 1951 to 7.3 per cent in 1966, and owner occupation rose from less than 30 per cent in 1951 to 40 per cent in 1961 and 50 per cent by 1971.[12] In 1947 68.3 per cent of dwellings had been built before 1919; by 1967 this had been reduced to 38.4 per cent.[13] In 1951, 21 per cent of households lacked sole use of a WC, reduced in 1966 to 7.8 per cent; in 1951 45 per cent cent lacked sole use of a fixed bath, by 1966 19 per cent (and by 1971 12 per cent).[14] For those lacking sole use of hot water tap, the percentage for 1951 is not available, but for 1961 was 24 per cent, and for 1966, 15 per cent; a later measure of physical comfort which became pertinent was that of central heating: by 1964 11 per cent, and by 1971 35 per cent of houses had it.[15]

The 'white-hot technological revolution', a concept popularized by Harold Wilson in his election campaign of 1964, contributed in various ways to this process. Products such as detergents have already been mentioned. Processes such as freezing and drying enhanced the diet available although the long-term nutritional effects of these processes and the use of additives, has yet to be fully understood. Wilson's description was particularly appropriate to nuclear power; work had begun on the Windscale nuclear processing plant in 1946, and by May 1956, Britain's first nuclear power station at Calder Hall began operation. This helped generate the electrical power consumed by refrigerators, washing machines, spin driers and dishwashers; in 1956 8 per cent of households had a refrigerator, rising to 69 per cent by 1971, by which year 64 per cent of families also had a washing machine. These domestic appliances perhaps contributed marginally to further improvement of health and hygiene, but more significantly to leisure. Purchase of these appliances was afforded by a rise in real earnings over the period, of about 50 per cent: at constant (1975) prices, the real gross average earnings for male manual workers rose from £31 to £45 between 1951 and 1967, and for women from £17 to £25.[16]

Leisure time available to many workers increased over the period: normal weekly hours declined by nearly 14 per cent over the years 1938–1968, although weekly hours actually worked seem to have decreased less dramatically:[17]

	Normal weekly hours	*Weekly hours actually worked*
1945	47.5	47.4
1951	44.6	46.3
1968	40.5	44.5

In 1938, three million workers had agreements for an annual one-week holiday; in 1952 two-thirds of agreements were for twelve days or two weeks, and by 1969 a similar proportion were for two or three weeks.

It might be argued from such indices that as the physical comfort of a large proportion of the population improved, so more attention could be paid to elaborating a curriculum concerned with mental culture. Official provision for leisure constitutes an important feature of the social and cultural context of the school curriculum. A wartime Council for the Encouragement of Music and the Arts became in 1946 the Arts Council, whose architect and first chair was John Maynard Keynes who advocated state subsidy for the 'civilizing arts of life'; amongst the Arts Council's early members were Sir Kenneth Clark, Director of the National Gallery, and Sir John Maud, who was shortly to be appointed Permanent Secretary at the Ministry of Education. Its first annual grant-in-aid from the Treasury of £0.25 million in 1945–46 grew to £5.7 million by 1966/67.[18] About the same time, section 132 of the Local Government Act (1948) allowed the levying of up to 6d on the rates for the arts. Later the Libraries and Museums Act of 1964 broadened the role of local authorities with libraries, museums and art galleries, to sponsoring and promoting cultural events.

As in the progressive primary curriculum, so too in state-sponsored leisure, physical culture was given a prominent role alongside artistic culture. The Peak District was designated Britain's first national park in 1949. This process had begun before the war with a Physical Training and Recreation Act (1937) which allowed expenditure by councils and local education authorities on the provision for the general public of facilities such as gymnasia, playing fields and swimming baths, and in 1958 a further Act extended this provision to capital loans for voluntary organizations. Capital loans to local authorities sanctioned by the Ministry of Housing and local government in the later 1950s offer some measure of expansion; as shown in the Table below. A Central Council for Physical Recreation had been formed in 1935 from national associations of teachers of Swedish gymnastics and of organizers and lecturers in physical education, and this voluntary body had been officially recognized by the government, and through grant aid from 1937. After the Second World War, its functions had been agreed by the Ministry of Education as being to develop all forms of post-school physical recreation.

	Swimming baths	*Playing fields, tennis courts, etc.*	*Public parks, open spaces, children's playgrounds*
	£	£	£
1955/56	580,797	819,664	1,229,673
1959/60	1,938,139	1,301,099	2,538,125

In 1960/61, grants to national voluntary bodies under the 1937 Act totalled £409,000, of which the CCPR received £140,000, and, amongst others, the English Folk Dance and Song Society, £7500.[19]

State-sponsored leisure and cultural activities, then, suggest a widespread official acceptance of curricular assumptions and emphases characteristic of progressivism, such as education for self-fulfilment with particular reference to physical exercise and the arts. Leisure, however, also embraces popular culture, and it seems that the progressive curriculum, despite its professed child-centredness, took little account of the more commercialized aspects of the child's life outside school, especially the child as a consumer. Central to commercial popular culture, was the development of communications over the period since 1945. Print and publishing, the media of radio, film and television, and road and air transport became ever more significant features of the changing cultural context in which progressive ideals were adopted in primary schools; they merit close attention also because they impinged on the dissemination of ideas and practices in a variety of ways.

Books were a traditional form of communication, yet fundamental changes were still occurring in the supply of, and access to reading material. The cheap paperback, pioneered by Allen Lane and the Penguin press in the inter-war period became a common feature of the 1950s, and together with public libraries finally killed off in the 1960s the old commercial 'circulating' libraries such as a Mudie's and Boots'. The quantity of books published rose rapidly in the 1960s, especially in fields such as popular history and sociology and in 'cultural criticism', and the new methods of retailing increased sales of books. The number of titles published stood at 15,000 in 1939, 18,000 in 1951 and 32,400 in 1969 (and of these the total of fiction titles fluctuated but remained at just over 4000). Book sales rose from about seven million in 1939, to twenty-and-a-quarter million in 1946, and subsequently by 1969 to about seventy-seven million. This near four-fold increase in the quarter of a century after the Second World War must be seen against a population increase of less than 10 per cent over the same period.[20]

One consequence was the circulation and impact of works such as Richard Hoggart's *The Uses of Literacy* in 1957, a key text, which aroused serious interest in and respect for working class culture.[21] Like John Blackie, Chief HMI for Primary Education, who figures largely in chapter 3 below, Hoggart attacked the trivialization of commercial entertainment but for different reasons: for Blackie it offended the high cultural traditions of classic literature, and demeaned the child, whereas for Hoggart it undermined traditional working class culture. The liveliness of contemporary debate on this issue was reflected in a conference held by the National Union of Teachers in 1960 on 'Popular culture and personal responsibility'. In a subsequent publication, Denys Thompson observed:

> While the market is the test of what shall be disseminated, the controllers appear to the tools of impersonal forces, and in their subservience they are bound to provide us with worse fare than we deserve or than the media are capable of.[22]

Together with the novels and films produced by a variety of 'angry young men' in the later 1950s, Hoggart's work laid the foundations for later attacks on the middle class cultural supremacy which was so evidently endorsed in the school curriculum. Karel Reisz's film *Saturday Night and Sunday Morning*, which won the best British film award for 1960, was based on Alan Sillitoe's (1958) novel of working class life in Nottingham; Sillitoe's next novel, *The Loneliness of the Long-distance Runner* (1959), was also produced as a film in 1962, directed by Tony Richardson, another notable example of the genre being Lindsay Anderson's (1963) film of the David Storey novel, *This Sporting Life*.

Developments in public broadcasting were even more spectacular than those in publishing. The starting point in our period was the three state radio networks: the Light Programme, with its comedy and light entertainment, Home Service for news and current affairs, and Third Programme, broadcasting music and high culture. The Third Programme was the most recent arrival, having been established by the post-war Labour government, as one of a number of measures aimed at patronage of the arts. At the risk of oversimplifying a complex situation, it might be observed that this provision reflected a three-tiered view of society in the same way that Norwood's proposals for the tripartite organization of secondary education had done. State broadcasting as a bulwark of social and cultural standards was the legacy of Lord Reith, who had been Director-General of the BBC from 1927 to 1938.

Commercial radio competed with state broadcasting, especially in the provision of popular music for the young. Outlawed in this country, it was transmitted from the Duchy of Luxembourg, and later, from 1964 onwards, from 'pirate' ships, demonstrating the power of telecommunication to undermine state control of culture. Eventually the establishment conceded by launching, in 1967, Radio 1 as a channel for pop music and ultimately, in 1972, allowing commercial radio broadcasts within these shores. The significance of pop music in the present context was in its contribution to 'youth culture', creating a separate identity for youth.

Though at first this applied more to the teenager than to the primary school child, the target age of the pop music audience gradually lowered, and it at least set a precedent for a separate commercial culture aimed at the under-11s as consumers.

In the earlier 1950s relatively few homes had a television. Fewer than 10 per cent of households had current TV licences in 1951, but by 1966 this proportion had grown phenomenally to nearly 80 per cent.[23] The BBC Audience Research Department estimated that in 1952, 5.8 per cent of the population over 16 years of age watched some TV; significantly, in 1960, their categories changed to include all over 5 years of age, by which time 28.7 per cent constituted the evening audience, and this rose to 32.9 per cent by 1968.[24] Qualitatively, change included the introduction of commercial television, allowed by legislation in 1954; *Coronation Street*, broadcast by ITV, and one of the most successful serials ever for audience ratings, began in 1960. Young children were soon, through the medium of television, bringing to school a very different cultural background from the children of their parents' and teachers' generation. Moreover, television also served as a medium for conveying images and expectations of school into the home. Discussion of television is not intended to ignore the importance of film as a means of communication, especially in the earlier part of the period; it will be considered in chapter 5 below as a significant medium in the diffusion of progressive practice amongst teachers, but in the arena of popular culture it was hard hit by television, cinema admissions in Great Britain falling from over 1600 million in 1946 to under 300 million in 1966.[25] Moreover, coming direct into the home, television was to have much more of an impact than cinema on the primary school child. This new element of the young child's experience helped to fuel a fierce debate about the moral effects of broadcasting institutionalized in the campaign of Mrs Mary Whitehouse from 1964. The issue figures little in progressive discourse, though, and then mostly insofar as the function of the school was thought to be a necessary counter to the trivialization of mass culture by television.

Other technological advances which were gradually altering the child's cultural experience, were developments in road and air transport in the form of family car ownership and foreign holidays, but little acknowledgement is to be found in the progressive pedagogical literature of these aspects of the child's changing world.

Professional Context

> What a wise and good parent would desire for his (sic) own children, that a nation must desire for all children.[26]

These words from the 1931 Hadow Report embodied a philosophy appropriate to progressivism: the quality of parenting, it implied, was open to evaluation, and was associated with wisdom; the community, and thus the educational system, was assumed to adopt a quasi-parental responsibility towards children in general. This preamble might also be seen as a portent of consumers' rights, which pressed more closely on the profession in later decades. Legislation is the means by which dominant values prevailing in society take form in terms of provision and compulsion. Laws, such as the 1944 Act, have subsequently to be interpreted through an administrative structure, and it was within this structure, defined here as the 'professional context', that advocates of progressivism sought to disseminate and to implement their principles and practices in the years after 1945.

The Act enshrined for the first time in law, a principle that had gradually informed administrative thinking during the decades previous to the war, namely that 'primary education' was to be seen as a distinct phase, a common experience of schooling for all children from 5 to 11. The description of a 'common experience' was limited, however, by the dual system of provision by state and church, and by the continued existence of an independent sector which resulted in a distinct and separate curriculum for children of the 'upper classes' from the age of seven. On these grounds, as well as on the maintenance of selection for secondary schooling (which itself had a considerable impact on the primary school curriculum) the Act has been described by many recent historians as a typically Conservative measure.[27] Simon (1986) has called it 'not a "New Order" but the old older in disguise'.[28] A more extreme criticism has been that Beveridge and Keynes masterminded the welfare state as a settlement to protect capitalism, though such an interpretation has to be judged in the light of the popular welcome shown for these measures. The national enthusiasm for reconstruction had been identified early by civil servants responsible for drafting the Education Bill, who had seen that the war was

> moving us more and more in the direction of Labour's ideas and ideals.[29]

It has been argued that these civil servants from largely public school and Oxbridge backgrounds, planned a careful compromise in order to preserve their influence and their interests;[30] certainly the state system of education continued to be administered from 1945 to 1952 with an Old Etonian, Sir John Maud, at its head, and it is in this context that progressivism, which became a quasi-official orthodoxy in the new Ministry of Education, was propagated.

Debate has been joined over the role of Ellen Wilkinson, the new Labour government's first Minister of Education. Dennis Dean, defending her difficulty in the implementation of a Conservative Act against the criticism of the radical Left, has documented her conviction that the working class youngsters who had grown up during the depression and war deserved an education which would show them how life, with a higher standard of living and improved social and leisure facilities, could be used to its full advantage.[31] In the secondary modern school, she favoured cooperative project work and freedom from exams, not as inferior to the narrow traditionalist curriculum of secondary grammar schools, but as a preferable alternative to vocationalism. In this she stood out against Herbert Morrison, the senior Labour politician and Lord President of the Council who, in a government increasingly obsessed with industrial productivity, was suspicious of education producing too many black-coated workers and insufficient manual labour. Wilkinson saw county colleges as having priority over the further raising of the school leaving age to 16, so that people would learn not to see the end of their school life as the end of education, and in this policy she was in conflict with R.H. Tawney, the veteran proponent of Labour education policy and with the Council for Educational Advance.

The post-war Labour government's policy shared with some strands of progressivism the aim of 'raising the cultural level' of the population, which it attempted by such means as the establishment of the Arts Council in 1946 and the Third Programme on BBC radio in 1948, coupled with its opposition to commercial radio. But it has been argued that intellectual leadership, which had been occupied by the Left, was taken over by such figures as T.S. Eliot with his vigorous defence of traditional Christian values, or F.R. Leavis and the scrutiny group, with its upholding of a minority culture in a mass civilization; had constant war propaganda contributed to a sense of national superiority coupled with introspection and anxiety?[32] The external threat against which war had been fought was totalitarianism; now peacetime reforms were directed at maintaining traditional values against the threats posed by commercial entertainment and by rising juvenile delinquency. The great increase in public concern about juvenile delinquency during and immediately after the war has been documented by Marsh (1965).[33] Thus, the determination to reconstruct, to create a better environment for all, included the patronage of high culture, as well as features of educational reform such as the provision of youth services and the teaching of civics in schools. Ambiguity of this kind must be seen as underlying the promotion of progressivism.

The 1944 Act included provision for a Central Advisory Council for Education, the first chair of which was Sir Fred Clarke, Principal of the London Institute of Education from 1936 to 1945. To include Clarke amongst the progressivists is to adopt a broad definition, for Clarke had opposed the individualism of Sir Percy Nunn (his precursor at the Institute) and attacked William McDougall's theory of instincts which had held sway over progressive thinking in the inter-war years.[34] But it may be argued that in Clarke there begins to be a synthesis of the 'liberal romantic' and the 'social democratic' strains (to adopt Richards' 1984 taxonomy), a combination of concerns which coloured the Plowden Report twenty years later. Under the influence of the war, and of Karl Mannheim, Clarke addressed himself to the clash of ideologies that was the 'crisis of Western civilization'. *Education and Social Change* (1940) set out his ideas within a Christian framework: social planning was necessary, but compatible with freedom only if one could assume a people whose trained critical intelligence encouraged enlightened self-discipline. Britain's mission at this time was to realize the 'middle way' of 'planning for freedom'. Between the ideologies of Plato (the 'closed' society) and of Rousseau (the 'open' society'), he opted for the latter, quoting Nunn approvingly:

> Nothing good enters into the human world except in and through the free activities of individual men and women.

But he criticized Nunn and others for dealing with education either in speculative philosophies, or in quasi-scientific abstractions, whilst taking insufficient notice of the *social* factors conditioning human behaviour.[35] In the 'All Souls Group' founded in 1941 to discuss educational reform, he met, amongst others, R.A. Butler and two of the younger innovating chief education officers, John Newsom of Hertfordshire and Douglas Cooke of Buckinghamshire. He was openly critical of Cyril Norwood's divisive proposals for secondary education, and supportive of Butler's proposed alteration of the emotionally restricting term 'elementary' to 'primary'. In a retrospective look at the work of the Central Advisory Council, he offered a curiously accurate adumbration of the Plowden Report, noting a great need in primary education

> for a group of experienced and sympathetic people, enjoying some detachment and independence, to sit down and contemplate the primary school child in himself (sic).[36]

The concern for 'the whole child', so characteristic of progressivism, was well reflected in the early work of the CACE. Its first report, *School and Life*, published in December 1946, argued that the curriculum was not to be narrowly vocational but to serve industry by developing personal qualities; more attention was to be paid to primary schools, and in particular many unhealthy and obsolete school buildings should be replaced; methods of cooperation between parents and school were suggested, and local studies of the school's neighbourhood should be promoted in the curriculum.[37] The second report, which followed in 1948, was also of a progressive tendency in its consideration of 'the natural interests and pursuits of school children out of school hours', and 'the extent to which school work and activities can and should be related to, and develop these interests'. Amongst its recommendations was that LEAs should increase facilities for play, that more library facilities should be provided, and that the newly established Arts Council should help provide concerts and exhibitions out of school.[38]

The 1944 Act gave a wide role to local education authorities whose duty, according to Section 7, was

> so far as their powers extend, to contribute towards the spiritual, moral, mental and physical development of the community ...

by securing efficient education to meet the needs of the population in their area. Thus the Act itself reflected progressive thought in its definition of public provision in terms of a holistic view of the child. LEAs became responsible for school meals, the school health service, child guidance and youth clubs.[39] Hence, too, LEAs of necessity became ever more highly organized bureaucracies, and the example of the West Riding is described in the following chapter.

A salient factor in the professional context of progressivism was the rising professional status of teachers. Recent research by Nias has shown primary teachers to be variously motivated, for example by altruism or by individualism, some seeing their work as a calling, others as a career.[40] Apart from self-perception, however, a generally perceived professional status for the primary teacher was a necessary basis on which curriculum experiment and innovation could be conducted. The responsibility of individual class teachers was part of official policy as far back as 1905 when the *Handbook of Suggestions for Elementary School Teachers* had stated:

> The only uniformity of practice that the Board of Education desires to see in the teaching in public elementary schools is that each teacher shall think for himself (sic) and work out for himself such method of teaching as may use his powers to the best advantage and be the best suited to the particular needs and conditions of the school.... But freedom implies a corresponding responsibility in its use.

Ronald Gould, General Secretary of the NUT, addressing the education section of the British Association in 1954 on the subject of *The Teacher in the Twentieth Century*, referred to this claim to professional freedom in the teachers' work, and acknowledged the 1905 statement as a 'charter of liberty'.[41] In the post-war era, the faith in education for restructuring society coupled with a new breed of recruits to the profession encouraged the development of this professional independence. Teachers were increasingly insistent on their authority in matters of curriculum and control, exemplified by the NUT's establishment of its own Research Department and Consultative Committee,[42] and at the same time the Ministry appeared willing to delegate responsibility for curriculum matters, a position expressed by the famous disclaimer attributed to George Tomlinson, Minister of Education from 1947 to 1951:

'The Minister knows nowt about curriculum'. Within the profession, it has been suggested that demobilised ex-servicemen were less likely to accept dogma, though it is not difficult to argue that the reverse might have been true. R.A. Butler later blamed the left-wing influence of the Army Bureau for Current Affairs for gaining the forces' vote in the 1945 election, and a number of primary teachers recruited from the armed forces have testified to the sense of idealism and purpose which they derived from various aspects of their war experience. Despite the War Minister's initial veto on ABCA's publicizing of the Beveridge Report, it was eventually reported fully through this channel.

Clement Attlee, as Prime Minister, publicly enhanced the status of the profession by addressing the NUT at their conference in 1949 on 'The teacher's part in the post-war world'.[43] The effects of disruption in home life and the demand for skills created by new technologies, placed a responsibility on teachers. But above all it was what he called 'the spiritual nature' of the teachers' task in preparing children for citizenship in a democracy that placed a premium on cultivating individual initiative, despite the difficulties of doing so in classes of forty or even thirty. Furthermore, he called on teachers to develop what he called 'a university outlook', in the liberal sense of seeing their own training as training for life. He implied acknowledgement of professional status and drew an example from the legal profession in pleading with teachers to reject a narrow 'over-professionalized' approach to their task, though he side-stepped the question of low salaries in education, which was a live issue at the time.

Ronald Gould's speech at the 1954 Oxford conference of the British Association, already mentioned above, went on to quote at length from A.N. Whitehead's assertion that although the state might exercise general control and public opinion imposed certain restrictions, the community at large was incompetent to determine subject matter and method, and in this the individual teacher should refer to a consensus of professional opinion. To support his argument, Gould made frequent reference to earlier apostles of progressivism such as Rousseau, Pestalozzi, Sir John Adams, Whitehead, Nunn and Clarke. But he criticized some attempts at democratic control in schools, made in the aftermath of a war against authoritarianism, when children had been given 'too much freedom and responsibility for their immature minds'. Teachers were not to regard every established school practice as sacrosanct, but an openness to new ideas was not to be uncritical, and in this respect he voiced a demand for more continuing education for teachers.

Gould also identified a dilemma which may be seen as lying at the heart of progressivism, namely assumptions about the power of the school; for he considered that Fred Clarke's views about the educational power of the media, cultural institutions and society as a whole, were in danger of overlooking Pestalozzi's faith in the transforming power of the teacher. Nevertheless, Gould felt that teachers should regard the education service as a developing partnership. The concept of partnership with parents was to be found increasingly in progressivist discourse, and had conflicting implications for teachers' professional status; in one respect, the idea of professional concern for the whole child heightened the concept of professional responsibility, yet the sharing of this responsibility with 'unqualified' parents might be seen to undermine professional expertise and autonomy. According to a Gallup Poll enquiry undertaken for the *News Chronicle* in 1959, teachers were accorded a considerable degree of respect by parents and by the population at large: 58 per cent of the former and 53 per cent of the latter 'admired' them and only 3 per cent and 4 per cent respectively were derogatory. The poll did not distinguish between primary and secondary teachers. About 30 per cent of all respondents believed that teachers were amongst the most able graduates from university, although half of them could not express an informed opinion on this issue. Only 6 per cent of parents thought that teachers were seeking an easy job and although a small majority considered that teachers' holidays were too long, 44 per cent opposed this view. Fifty-nine per cent of parents felt that education was as much the concern of parents as of teachers; but only 16 per cent thought it should be left entirely to the latter. Seventy-two per cent of parents believed that the parent-teachers' associations could play a useful role.

Supporting teachers' claims to professional status, was the exponential growth of social science research relating to education in the 1950s. But at the same time, wider publicity given to this research also raised lay people's understanding of educational issues. Psychology and child study had already enjoyed a well established influence on educational policy, through figures such as Cyril Burt and Susan Isaacs, and their evidence to the Hadow Committee in its enquiries into primary and infant education in the early 1930s is well known.[44] After the war, a National Foundation for Educational Research was established with the ubiquitous Fred Clarke as its first chair (as well as chairing the Central Advisory Council he was also Adviser on Educational Developments and Research to the NUT from 1945). Its early research projects included studies of rewards and punishments in schools, cumulative records of pupils' progress, and the use of audio-visual aids. Early funding came from the Carnegie and Leverhulme trusts, the major teachers' unions, and all but one of the universities; 140 of the 147 LEAs became corporate members, subscribing ¼d per pupil on the school roll (rising to 1d by 1958). The President of the NFER was *ex-officio* the Minister of Education, and despite David Eccles' allegation during his first presidency, that educational research was an activity 'imposed by the long-haired on the long-suffering', the Foundation prospered and grew. In 1950 it had a staff of fourteen, which by 1962 had increased to forty-six. Ironically perhaps, a lucrative source of income was the publication of intelligence tests, whilst one of its most significant pieces of commissioned research was that of Alfred Yates and Douglas Pidgeon, published in 1957 under the title *Admission to Grammar Schools*, which demonstrated the misallocation of about 70,000 children in an average year at 11+. In the same year Philip Vernon, for the British Psychological Society, identified a variability of 20–25 per cent in IQ test scores, attributable to environmental factors.[45]

The growing importance of sociology had been anticipated by the work of Karl Mannheim and Fred Clarke and sociological research began to make a considerable impact in the 1950s. It was something of a newcomer in the post-war academic world, 1945 seeing the first allocation of public funds to universities for the study of sociology. The founding of a new journal, the *British Journal of Sociology*, based at the London School of Economics, was an event of particular historical importance; the fourth volume in 1953 carried its first major article on education, research by Halsey and Gardner on selection for secondary education, which indicated under-representation of working class children in grammar schools. It was to take some time for this research to be mediated into professional discourse and to find its way into syllabuses of teacher education.

The CACE reports on *Early Leaving* in 1954 and *15 to 18* in 1959 gave official recognition to the methods and insights of sociological research.[46] Not only did this provide another scientific dimension to the profession of teaching, but emphasis on environment rather than heredity implied an enhanced importance for the teacher's role. Introducing the CACE report *Half Our Future*, Edward Boyle, Conservative Minister of Education, adopted a phrase coined by the Labour politician and writer on socialism, Anthony Crosland:

> The essential point is that all children should have an equal opportunity of *acquiring intelligence*, and of developing their talents and abilities to the full. (my emphasis).[47]

These sociological findings therefore presented the challenge of increasing educational opportunity and imposed upon teachers the role of distributing social justice; in the subsequent Robbins Report on Higher Education, their role was also officially enhanced as of national economic importance in tapping the wasted pool of ability. In the pre-Plowden era, sociology made a particular impact through the publication in 1964 of the third volume of a longitudinal study of 5000 children born in 1946. *The Home and the School: A Study of Ability and Attainment in the Primary School* was written by J.W.B. Douglas, Director of the Medical Research Council Unit at the London School of Economics, and revealed an 'interlocking network of inequalities'. Thus the teacher's professional role was highlighted as a necessary agent of social amelioration, grounded on the evidence of scientific research.

Notes

1 The first figure is a mid-year estimate for 1944, and the second figure is for the intercensal year 1966. Some statistics in the section which follows are taken from the decennial census of 1951, where the period of immediate post-war recovery might represent something of a distortion, and choice of date is sometimes restricted by available data.
2 HALSEY, A.H.. (Ed.) (1972) *Trends in British Society Since 1900*, London, Macmillan. pp. 31 and 165.
3 *ibid*; CENTRAL STATISTICAL OFFICE (1980) *Annual Abstract of Statistics, 1980 Edition*, London, Central Statistical Office.
4 HAGAN, RT. REV. E.J. quoted in MARSH, D.C. (Ed.) (1965) *The Changing Social Structure of England and Wales, 1871–1961*, London, Routledge and Kegan Paul, p. 57. GORER, G. (1951) *Exploring English Character*, quoted in MARWICK, A. (1982) *British Society Since 1945*, Harmondsworth, Penguin, p. 72.
5 FLETCHER, R. (1973) *The Family and Marriage in Britain* (3rd edn) Harmondsworth, Penguin, pp. 178–9.
6 Significant factors included the reintroduction of the IUD as a means of contraception in the mid 1950s (widespread use of oral contraceptives dated only from the late 1960s). Also a higher material standard of living was attainable from a joint income and was not offset by tax-relief in favour of the family; tax advantages moreover would not compensate a young mother for withdrawal from the increasing number of social activities available. MARSH, D.C. (Ed.) (1965) *The Changing Social Structure of England and Wales, 1871–1961*, London, Routledge and Kegan Paul, p. 56.
7 BOWLBY, J. (1965) *Child Care and the Growth of Love* (2nd edn) Harmondsworth, Penguin p. 239. First published in 1953, the book had six reprints in its first decade; the 2nd edition was reprinted annually 1966–74.
8 *Radio Times*, 20 April, 1954.
9 MARWICK, A. (1982) *op. cit.*, pp. 75–6.
10 HALSEY, A.H. (1972) *op. cit.*, p. 338.
11 MARWICK, A. (1982) *op. cit.*, p. 74.
12 CENTRAL STATISTICAL OFFICE (1979) *Social Trends No. 10, 1980 Edition*, London, HMSO p. 28; HALSEY, A.H. (1972) *op. cit.*, p. 302.
13 HALSEY, A.H. (1972) *op. cit.*, p. 303. The earlier figure is for Great Britain, the later for England and Wales.
14 *ibid*, p. 305; MARWICK, A. (1982) *op. cit.*, p. 73.
15 *Social Trends 1980*, p. 29.
16 *Social Trends 1980*, p. 14–16.
17 Collated by Halsey, A.H. (1972) *op. cit.*, p. 120 from Ministry of Labour Gazette and its successors.
18 WHITE, E.W. (1975) *The Arts Council of Great Britain*, London, Davis-Poynter, pp. 63 and 311.
19 CCPR (1960) *Sport and the Community: Report of the Wolfenden Committee on Sport*, London, CCPR, pp. 20–2.
20 HALSEY, A.H. (1972) *op. cit.*, pp. 564–5.
21 MARWICK, A. (1982) *op. cit.*, pp. 128 and 132–3; Hoggart's book was reprinted thirteen times by Penguin books over the next twenty years.
22 THOMPSON, D. (Ed.) (1960) *Discrimination and Popular Culture*, Harmondsworth, Penguin, p. 11. Another contemporary cultural dilemma was that of the 'gulf of mutual incomprehension' between literary intellectuals and scientists, voiced by C.P. Snow first in the *New Statesman* in 1956, and three years later in his Rede Lecture: 'The Two Cultures'.
23 *Social Trends 1980* p. 33 (by 1978 it was more than 90 per cent).

24 HALSEY, A.H. (1972) *op. cit.*, p. 556.
25 *ibid.*, p. 559.
26 BOARD OF EDUCATION (1931) *Report of the Consultative Committee on the Primary School*, London, HMSO, p. xxiv.
27 ADDISON, P. (1975) *The Road to 1945*, London, Cape; KOPSCH, H. (1970) 'The approach of the Conservative Party to social policy during World War Two', unpublished PhD thesis, London; WALLACE, R.G. (1981) 'The origins and authorship of the 1944 Education Act', *History of Education*, 10, 4, December.
28 SIMON, B. (1986) 'The 1944 Education Act: A Conservative measure?', *History of Education*, 15, 1, March.
29 R.S. WOOD, Deputy Secretary, Board of Education, quoted in GOSDEN, P. (1976) *Education in the Second World War*, London, Methuen pp. 248–9.
30 SIMON, B. (1986) *op. cit*; SAVAGE, G.L. (1983) 'The civil service and secondary education during the inter-war period', *Journal of Contemporary History*, 18.
31 DEAN, D.W. (1986) 'Planning for a post-war generation: Ellen Wilkinson and George Tomlinson at the Ministry of Education 1945–51', *History of Education*, 15, 2, June.
32 *ibid.*
33 MARSH, D.C. (1965) *op. cit.*, pp. 258–9.
34 SELLECK, R. (1972) *op. cit.*, pp. 104 and 127.
35 MITCHELL, F.W. (1967) *Sir Fred Clarke, Master-teacher, 1880–1952*, London, Longmans, pp. 94 and 166–7.
36 *ibid.*, pp. 112–3.
37 MINISTRY OF EDUCATION (1946) *School and Life*, [First] Report of the Central Advisory Council for Education (England), London, HMSO. (The LCC Education Committee had produced a report under this title in March 1943).
38 MINISTRY OF EDUCATION (1948) *Out of School*, Second Report of the Central Advisory Council for Education (England), London, HMSO.
39 Although LEA services were extended in the favourable climate of 1946, however, the Home Office retained responsibility for children in care, despite Ellen Wilkinson's attempts to gain this task for the Ministry of Education.
40 NIAS, J. (1981) '"Commitment" and motivation in primary school teachers', *Educational Review*, 33, 3, p. 181; NIAS, J. (1985) 'Reference groups in primary teaching: Talking, listening and identity' in BALL, S. and GOODSON, I. (Eds.) *Teachers' Lives and Careers*, Lewes, Falmer Press.
41 GOULD, R. (1954) 'The teacher in the twentieth century', *Advancement of Science*, 11, 4, June.
42 see chapter 4 below.
43 NUT (1949) *The teachers' part in the post-war world, an address delivered by the P.M. the Right Hon. Clement Attlee CH MP to the Annual Conference of the National Union of Teachers*, London, NUT.
44 SELLECK, R. (1972) *op. cit.*, pp. 125–6.
45 VERNON, P. (1957) *Secondary School Selection: A British Psychological Society Inquiry*, London, Methuen.
46 MINISTRY OF EDUCATION (1954) *Early Leaving: A Report of the CACE (England)*, (Chair: Sir Samuel Gurney-Dixon), London, HMSO; MINISTRY OF EDUCATION (1959) *15 to 18: A Report of the CACE (England)*, (Chair: Sir Geoffrey Crowther), London, HMSO.
47 MINISTRY OF EDUCATION (1963) *Half our Future: A Report of the CACE (England)*, London, HMSO, p. iv.

3 *Promoters of Progressivism*

This chapter is about promoters and not about pioneers. Accounts of progressivism have run the risk of isolating and even idolizing the work of a few individuals, and hagiography can easily usurp history. Van der Eyken (1969), for example, wrote of 'adventures in education'; his chosen few 'adventurers' were courageous innovators in their own way, but his account falls short of critically assessing either their impact or the means by which they gained influence.[1] It has been a tendency of the progressive movement to make saints. Examination papers for the Froebel Certificate in the late 1940s, for example, required candidates to reproduce in uncritical fashion the ideas of a select list of 'pioneers' such as Rousseau, Pestalozzi and Froebel; Dorothy Gardner reputedly kept a little shrine to Susan Isaacs at the London Institute of Education, and a picture of Olave Bates, progressive headteacher of Finmere village school in Oxfordshire, is reported to have graced the walls of the 'Plowden wing' at Goldsmiths' College.

In studying the phenomenon of dissemination, we must look at the position in the educational structure of 'promoters' and at the platforms they used. Many of the early pioneers like A.S. Neill and Susan Isaacs, made their experiments outside the state system, but for these ideas to be implemented more widely required the operation of organizational change. The idealism of Percy Nunn, who worked within the state system as Principal of the London Day Training College (from 1932 the London Institute of Education), began to colour official policy as early as 1927 in the *Handbook of Suggestions for Teachers in Elementary Schools*. Official acknowledgment of progressivism became clearer with a Report of the Consultative Committee of the Board of Education on the Primary School, under the chairmanship of Sir William Hadow, in 1931. But the educational philosophy espoused there hardly tallied with the structure of elementary schooling then still in force, and the full realization of its philosophy was preempted by the same Committee's earlier proposal in its

1926 report on education of the adolescent, for a selective system of secondary education.

Curriculum development and the changing institutional structure can only be described as erratic. No machinery existed for curriculum appraisal and innovation, and administrative roles were not clearly defined. What follows is not a study of the role of chief education officers or of the national inspectorate, but rather of three individuals: Alec Clegg, CEO for the West Riding of Yorkshire, Christian Schiller, HMI, and John Blackie, HMI: yet their respective contributions have to be seen against a continuously evolving interpretation of the official roles. All three men had been educated at Cambridge in the 1920s, and their careers intersect at various points, such that the promotion of progressivism may be located in a particular social and cultural context.

Chief Education Officer: Sir Alec Clegg

The 1944 Act brought no change to the system whereby local education authorities were given the responsibility (and the freedom) of planning provision. Hence the key role of the chief education officer. The post-war period saw a number of CEOs who encouraged innovation, such as Newsom in Hertfordshire and Mason in Leicestershire. The example taken here, as a significant promoter of primary progressivism, is Alec Clegg. He was not typical of chief officers, but his work provides a significant instance of the diffusion of progressive ideas and practices, and it is instructive to consider the influences upon him and his own ways of working.

The West Riding of Yorkshire became noted as an LEA in which a new identity was established for primary education in the post-war years, a challenge to many traditional underlying assumptions, which was described by one who experienced it as a revolution in the classrooms.[2] Much of the credit for such changes as took place was due to the idealism and administrative skill of Sir Alec Clegg, CEO in the county from 1945 to 1974. Progressive principles such as child centredness, curriculum integration and concern for the school environment, ran through his administration colouring its development and innovations. It might be said that Alec Clegg had schools in this blood, as his grandfather and father had both been teachers, and so indeed was his wife and one of his sons. Nurture, as well as nature however, played an important part in his professional formation, and after an upper second degree in French and German at Clare College, Cambridge, he followed a one-year postgraduate course at the London Day Training College in 1931/32, acknowledging thirty-five years later that

> those of us who had the privilege of working with the Nunn, Burt,

> Dover-Wilson trinity were probably the most fortunate intending teachers to have been trained in this country so far.[3]

Contact with Percy Nunn at this early stage in his career may well have contributed to the development of his progressive philosophy, but there is no doubt too that as a character he was innately individualistic. Paying tribute after his death, one of his former Deputy Education Officers, Jim Hogan, wrote of Sir Alec's disregard for conventionality, whilst another, Len Browne, described him as

> the Puck of the educational world. To work with him was occasionally exasperating but never dull or mechanical.[4]

He began his career as a grammar school teacher at a time when, by his own admission, the curriculum had become ossified by examinations and 'people no longer had to think why they were teaching what they were teaching'. He claimed to be most interested in secondary school children, or 'the fourth quartile', and in this connection he served on both the Crowther and the Newsom committees. However his fervent commitment to the problems of social deprivation and educational disadvantage entailed a natural progression from the compensatory ideal to a progressive philosophy of education:

> Schools should be, for the less fortunate, what the home is for the more fortunate, a place where there is work but where there is also laughter; a place where there is law but where there is also grace; a place where there is justice but where there is also love.[5]

Thus the education of the spirit took precedence for Clegg over the education of the mind, a priority which had been illustrated by some developments in the primary sector:

> The richer understanding of a child's needs has made the best of our primary schools places of beauty, and communities in which eager activity and loving concern prevail.[6]

Clegg's influence as a promoter of progressivism was exerted through his work both as a local educational administrator and as a national figure in his writing and public speaking. He had started in educational administration in Birmingham, where the CEO, Lionel Russell, was a model of the efficient administrator whose main concern was procuring and distributing resources, but later worked as a Deputy Education Officer in Worcestershire, where his chief, Robert Logan, had been touched by the idealism of Henry Morris, Director of Education in Cambridgeshire. During his stay in Worcestershire from 1942 to 1945, he had contact with Christian Schiller, working in that area as HMI. He moved to the West Riding as Deputy Education Officer in January 1945, and in September of the same year he took over as Chief Education Officer, remaining in post for thirty years. His predecessor in the post, A.L. Binns, had been a national figure, highly regarded at the Board of Education and consulted both formally and informally during the drafting of the Butler Education Act. Clegg's main interest was in improving the practice of education, and administration was simply a means to this end.

As a skilled administrator, Clegg was able in addition to imprint his personal idealism on the education service of the Riding. In his first year of office he worked with Walter Hyman, Chairman of the Education Committee, to simplify the policy-making process and concentrate the decision-making in one Policy Sub-Committee (later Policy and Finance Sub-Committee), leaving himself free to spend more time in schools and colleges and to keep himself more fully acquainted with their development.[7] Attendance at other sub-committees he delegated to the trusted deputies he had gathered around him. He also delegated to advisers whom he had attracted to the West Riding, such as Diana Jordan and A.L. Stone; in a letter of 1950 to Brown, CEO for Warwickshire, he commented on the colleagues of outstanding ability who had come to the West Riding because he was there and they wished to work with him.[8] The circumstances of the time and place were also favourable insofar as national population grew over the next decades, and a drift of commuters from the boroughs to the Riding imposed expansion and thus opportunities for change and innovation.

Personality and administrative style are not divorced. His way of exerting influence on the schools through policies of in-service education and promotion, his care in the appointment of advisers and heads, his practice of keeping in touch with schools and courses, provide a particular model which may be described in the abstract. But in visiting schools and in addressing courses, it was Clegg's charisma which made the lasting impression. On 17 June 1955 he recorded *A Day in the Life of a CEO*; it was a long day which lasted well into the evening but notable events included, at midday a visit to Carlinghow School, where a discussion took place between the Deputy Education Officer, the headteacher and others about 'the best way of spreading ideas which the headmaster had worked out', at 7.00 pm a meeting with the staff of a course at Woolley Hall to help coordinate it, followed by an address to the 'Brighter School Environment' course.[9] He was sometimes criticized for favouring particular schools which happened to be 'on the way to Castleford' but his classroom visits counted for a great deal and would be remembered years later. The impact of his visits was such that for the vast majority of teachers who knew that the event was most unlikely, the idea that Clegg might at any moment walk through the door was still a powerful myth.

On matters of primary curriculum and teaching methods, Clegg appears to have had particular areas of interest, but was not dogmatic. A personal letter written in 1952 recounted how

> Last week at a teachers' course I told our teachers I could not care less how they taught arithmetic or reading or writing; all I was concerned with was that the child of ordinary ability leaving the junior school should do sums accurately, should write legibly and read fluently, and that if teachers could not achieve this they could not teach and they were bad. These were the words I used.
>
> I think it is quite absurd to talk about activity methods as if they were equally suitable for all subjects of the junior school curriculum and as if all the teachers in any particular school taught all the children all the time by these methods.[10]

In his evidence to the Plowden Committee, he set out clearly and concisely what he saw as the distinguishing features of 'informal' and 'formal' primary schools, but pointed out that nearly all schools showed a mixture of these teaching methods; though both types of school produced similar results as far as basic skills were concerned, he suggested that informal teaching was likely to increase because of its concern for the individual ('important in these days when so much is done to and for the mass'), the happier and better behaved communities that seemed to result, and the superior quality of work which they produced; the latter points were not entirely subjective judgments, he claimed, and could be demonstrated.

Paramount was Clegg's concern for the individual, typified by his considerable interest in the longitudinal study from J.W.B. Douglas, published as *The Home and the School.* He considered the book of such educational significance that he prepared a digest for the Policy and Finance Sub-Committee on 12 May 1964, at which it was resolved that a copy of the report be sent without comment to each school.[11] In a memo later the same month, he noted: 'Streaming surely is on the way out. Can it long survive the Douglas Report?', but as early as 1953 in a letter to Hyman he pointed out that his opposition to selection at 11+ was an opinion which he had personally held for ten years.[12] Clegg's primary concern for children's progress and the effect of schooling is vividly illustrated by the personal interest which he took in Mrs Pyrah's class at Airedale School, Castleford. A disproportionately high number of her class gained grammar school places and he initiated an extensive investigation, checking the results of the Moray House tests normally used by having the children also take the NFER tests. The results correlated so well that he wrote to Sir Cyril Burt in August 1967 asking for his observations, making the point however that during his twenty years in the West Riding he had been

> troubled by the correct use and misuse of intelligence and standardized attainment tests. We have tended in this county to come down against their use as a criterion of selection but have

> encouraged teachers to use them to get to know more about their pupils.[13]

The case became celebrated and was published in the *Sunday Times Magazine* in the following year.[14]

Clegg's own curricular interests included a specific concern for the arts, passionately argued in a memorandum on the proposal to establish a training college for teachers of art and music in 1946:

> It might not unreasonably be claimed that the catastrophe of the last six years was due to the failure of man's sensibilities to temper the use of the forces placed at his disposal by his highly developed intellect. It is undoubtedly true to say that in the schools, we tend to teach what can be tested and memorized to the neglect of the more civilising subjects and activities of which Art and Music are two. There is thus a case for strengthening the teaching of these subjects and raising their standard and status in the schools.

He pointed out that it was usual for teachers to be specially trained in physical training, in handicrafts and in domestic subjects, and that the Ministry prescribed a special course for intending teachers of art. For music teachers there was no corresponding pedagogical training — the lack of which was all the more dangerous since a native aptitude on the part of talented musicians could interfere with their comprehension of pupils' lack of ability. Moreover there were sound educational arguments for an element of integration in the arts:

> Music and Art are almost invariably taught as isolated subjects despite their common purpose, which is to stimulate and train the child's sensibilities and, furthermore, the training in each subject, particularly in Music, is apt to be narrow.

The intention of the proposal was therefore that

> each student may leave the College with a wide conception of the Arts generally and their effect on the education of the child.[15]

A liberal policy towards book provision was implemented through the West Riding Bookroom, a reference library which teachers were given every encouragement to visit regularly.

Peter Newsam observed that Sir Alec's achievements stemmed from a rare ability to understand and trust the relationship between teacher and taught, and he used the resources of the education authority to support and enhance that relationship in every possible way.[16] It might be said that his own progressivism enabled a similar philosophy and practice to prevail in the classrooms within his authority. His acknowledgment of the professionalism of teaching is reflected in many details of his administration. Thus, in making recommendations for selection processes, he proposed a school record card on which the teacher could note attainments in arithmetic and English together with an assessment of personal qualities, and commented that the card could be expanded as teachers became familiar with its use and were able to advise the authority on its shortcomings. He added:

> It will be necessary, if this scheme is to succeed, not only to rely completely on the integrity of the junior school teachers but to make them very clearly aware that diagnosis of the child's capacity and interests must more and more become a part of their professional duties.

Nearly twenty years later, on the experimental introduction of foreign language teaching in the primary schools, a report of the Education Officer included the condition that teachers recruited 'should not only have a command of the language, but an insight into good primary school practice'.[17]

Clegg attached great importance to improving both the initial and the continued education of teachers. Gosden and Sharp (1978) have noted the circumstantial factors which assisted him in this: a widespread sense of the need for improvement created by the McNair Committee, the advantages for enterprising authorities created by the new system of pooling training college expenditure from 1946, and a well-established precedent in the Riding of in-service provision through the Annual Vacation Course which dated back to 1912 and was traditionally under the control of the CEO. Clegg found the Ministry very supportive of his efforts at setting up new training colleges after the war.[18]

Most telling of all Clegg's achievements however was the foundation of a further education college for teachers, a somewhat unusual institution at the time, in Woolley Hall; the special atmosphere of Woolley Hall and its courses, both consonant with Clegg's progressivism, are considered further in chapter 4 below. Gosden and Sharp have observed that it was at Woolley Hall that 'the Ark of the Covenant of West Riding education was kept during the Authority's last two decades', and they consider that the concept which governed its foundation was perhaps the most significant single development in the county's education service after the war.[19] Anticipating possible objections, Clegg foresaw that this project would be thought an expensive addition to the already costly development plan for new school buildings, but pointed out that good teachers are more important than good buildings, and to neglect the teachers would be to put the cart before the horse.[20] The scheme was publicly announced at a meeting of the Yorkshire Federation of the National Association of Head Teachers (NAHT), where it was stressed that this new type of training college would be 'a pioneer in the country' where teachers could reside for a fortnight or a month to take a refresher course not of the type to which they were accustomed at Bingley but one 'as purely cultural as could be conceived'.[21] A letter to Mrs Bland (County Alderman) somewhat later revealed that Clegg was sensitive to a permanent need within the teaching profession, not one created simply by wartime conditions:

> Once a teacher has been appointed and has taught for five years possibly the same subjects to the same type of child during these five years, he tends to get in a rut, and, though he may manage to instruct, he can no longer educate in the best sense of the word.
>
> The only way I know of combating this kind of professional lethargy is by refresher courses conducted by our staff and by some of the best minds that we can bring in from outside, and for these refresher courses to be followed up by some of the staff at any rate who have responsibility for the course.[22]

One means of improving the quality and professionalism of teaching was the judicious use of an advisory service, and here again Clegg was able to benefit from a well-established tradition in the West Riding. Although the Plowden Committee found in 1965 that less than one-third of LEAs employed their own inspectors, the West Riding had appointed its first inspector back in 1891, and its first adviser in 1906.[23] The latter were originally appointed in subjects such as art, music, drama, gardening, woodwork and physical education, subjects which the training college courses tended to neglect. Clegg's most inspired appointments to the advisory service were in the field of the arts and included individuals whose work he had come to know personally, for example Arthur Stone, the Head of Steward Street School, Birmingham, whose varied art work with children was documented in the Ministry of Education pamphlet *Story of a School*, and Diana Jordan, a pupil of Laban, who had been on the staff in Worcestershire. Clegg expressed the view that their most valuable work was in the organizing of courses.[24] His philosophy was that the advisers, like teachers, would work most effectively not by instruction in technique, but by interest, encouragement and enthusiasm, and this bore fruit in the 'family feeling' which was said to characterize the West Riding:

> a feeling of belonging as an individual to a large body of people linked by a common attitude towards children and learning.[25]

Clegg's concern for the professionalism of his inspectorial and advisory staff is well illustrated amongst the West Riding papers. In a letter to the Chairman of the Committee in 1955 he listed the total number of engagements over a fortnight of his twenty-nine inspectors and advisers, showing that 163 sessions of engagements had taken place outside office hours, with only twelve sessions of time taken off in lieu, and following an anonymous letter of complaint he sent a circular letter to all inspectors reminding them of their professional duties, expressing confidence in the majority and hoping that one or two would not bring the whole team into disrepute.[26]

Clegg's educational philosophy was also apparent in his attitude to subject specialism amongst the advisory staff. When under pressure from his committee in 1965 to appoint specialists in mathematics, he corresponded privately with a local HMI, seeking advice. Whilst recognizing the need in particular specialisms where teachers may be incompetent or may have failed to change with the times, he also saw that

> the message of the last ten to twenty years is of the folly of fragmenting the learning process more than we need (see paragraph 448 of Newsom); yet the specialist dealing with a general subject is likely to do just this. Indeed I have been very hesitant about suggesting an adviser in modern languages, but the number of folk who can tackle a modern foreign language below 11+ is so small that we must get some help.[27]

Clegg's ideal of a more integrated approach to the job which put the child and the school as a whole before the subject was realized when the advisory service was eventually reorganized in 1969 and 1970. Inspectors were now to be known as advisers, and with an appropriate hierarchy, the teams were given responsibility for geographical areas, individual advisers offering their subject expertise within this framework.

Like John Newsom, another contemporary and very influential CEO, Clegg was conscious of the value of publicity. In October 1963 he supplied copies of his memorandum on the three-tier system to the educational correspondents of national newspapers, to many leading educationists and to other chief education officers. *The Excitement of Writing*, the first of his anthologies of children's work, was originally produced as 'a report by the West Riding Education Committee' edited by C.T. Broughton and A.B. Clegg, and circulated amongst West Riding schools as a means of disseminating good practice and encouraging a more creative approach to children's language learning. Its enormous success when published commercially is shown by its printing history: eight impressions were produced in the first six years. Royalties from this and later books were paid into a special educational fund at the disposal of the Education Officer for educational amenities.[28] Personal ideals and skills as a raconteur lent force to his public talks; one, entitled 'Attitudes' and delivered before the North of England Education conference at Southport in 1962 revealed Clegg's interest in history and changes in society and social behaviour.[29] His talks were also marked by their range of references to educational thinkers and writers as diverse as Bacon, Locke, Thring and Sampson. A submission of evidence by Clegg to the Plowden Committee on the age of transition from primary to secondary school included a long quotation from Richard Mulcaster, the sixteenth century schoolmaster.

Thus Clegg used the role of CEO to facilitate the dissemination of progressivism amongst his own teachers, and contributed himself to the discourse.

HMI: Christian Schiller

Edmonds (1962) quoted a current definition from the International Bureau of Education of the role of national and local inspection as

> a service to interpret to teachers and the public the educational policies of the authorities, and also to interpret to the competent authorities, the experiences, needs and aspirations of teachers and local committees.[30]

Though the Ministry was legally obliged under section 77 of the 1944 Education Act 'to cause inspections to be made', a House of Commons Select Committee in 1967/68 recognized that the balance of work was shifting away from full inspections followed by formal reports, and would continue to do so. Commenting on HMI's duties in 1979, Sheila Browne noted that as well as reporting to the Secretary of State on the condition of education, they also sought 'by long-standing tradition' to contribute directly or indirectly to the improvement of education in the institutions they visited.[31] As far as dissemination was concerned, Edmonds referred to their role since 1944 in compiling pamphlets for publication by the Ministry, described in one instance as

> a new anthology of the ideas and practices which teachers are successfully developing in their schools.[32]

And by 1979 Browne was proposing that HMI needed to use its voice publicly through television, radio, film and the printed word, for its knowledge and opinions to reach those who influence education or consume its product. In the dissemination of progressive ideals and practice an important role was played by national refresher courses organized by HMI for teachers. Before the war, residential courses for elementary teachers had been organized, and some of these began to be aimed at teachers of the primary age-groups from the mid-thirties. Such courses proliferated from 1945 onwards.

At the centre of a most influential network of 'promoters of progressivism' lay the HMI Christian Schiller. Alec Clegg considered that history would judge Schiller to be the most powerful influence exerted on the junior schools of Britain after the first world war, yet Robin Tanner has written of the 'universal ignorance' of Schiller's influence. The general ignorance speaks volumes about the particular way in which

Schiller's influence was exercised. He became the very first Staff Inspector for Junior Education following reorganization under the 1944 Education Act, but the network of heads, advisers and college principals who practised and propagated his gospel were those, relatively few in number, who attended the in-service course which he ran from 1956 to 1963 after his retirement from the Inspectorate.

Schiller's rapid elevation to HMI seems redolent of Victorian practice whereby the inspectorial task was the prerogative of the middle and upper-class guardians of culture rather than of those whose own experience lay in state education. Education at Gresham's School in Holt, a commission and Military Cross in the First World War, a mathematics scholarship at Sidney Sussex College, Cambridge, graduating in 1921, followed by a teaching post for two years at the progressive public school Rendcomb comprised his career up until the age of 28. That year he attended the postgraduate teaching course at the London Institute, after which he was appointed directly to the inspectorate.[33] As District HMI in Worcestershire from 1937 to the end of the war, he would have had dealings with Alec Clegg, who was Deputy Director of Education in that county from 1942–45. Their common Cambridge background, and more certainly their shared experience of studying under Percy Nunn at the London Day Training College, are also likely reasons for mutual interest.

Certainly Nunn's philosophy of individualism shone through Schiller's lectures and also informed the war-time residential holiday courses for teachers which he organized. With the somewhat ill-defined nature of HMI's role, one which has grown up by custom and practice is that of participation in in-service training. As an HMI in Worcestershire, Schiller ran residential courses, and as Staff Inspector for Junior Education from 1946, and often in collaboration with Robin Tanner HMI, he used these as a means of 'scouting for talent' and 'fostering excellence'. These courses created an important precedent and set a pattern which was followed in later years; teachers would be encouraged to paint, write poetry and perform, and through this process of realizing their own potential, it was hoped that their expectations of their pupils would be heightened. Schiller saw the HMI's task as encouraging primary teachers in the post-war world to see their role differently from that of the old elementary school teachers.

Most notable of his courses, however, was one conducted after his retirement, a one-year course at the University of London Institute of Education which ran from 1956 to 1963. This course was facilitated by new regulations issued in 1955 which allowed a one-year secondment by LEAs to be reimbursed. The impact of the course was considerable in that many of the teachers who passed through it subsequently achieved influential positions as heads, advisers and teacher trainers. Course members were personally selected and often through known contacts; true to his dislike of 'systems' Schiller resisted attempts by the Institute to expand his course and restricted it to a dozen a year, so that the 100 or so products of the course appear as an innovating cadre. Amongst their number were John Coe, later senior primary adviser in Oxfordshire, Arthur Razzell, author of *Postscript to Plowden* and senior primary adviser in East Sussex, Connie Rosen, writer on children's language and director of a Schools Council project on language development in the primary school, and Leonard Marsh, leader of an innovating postgraduate course for primary teachers, and author of books on primary education. Any suggestion of elitism in this way of running a course was countered by Schiller's insistence on the need to select promising specimens and carefully to foster 'growing points', a botanical analogy which became common in progressivist rhetoric. In the course of an uneasy relationship with the Institute he firmly refused to include assessed coursework or exams, or to offer certification such as a diploma. The course was to be worthwhile for its own sake.

Central authority and local authority are interdependent in educational innovation and selective recruitment to Schiller's course reinforced a particular geographical concentration of primary progressivism. The secondment of individuals and their subsequent career advancement depended largely on LEA sympathy and backing. In the subscription list for the memorial volume published after his death, of 240 subscribers the seven most frequently represented counties were: Yorkshire (54), London (27), Essex (24), Oxfordshire (20), Kent (18), Hampshire (9) and Hertfordshire (8), offering an accurate picture of the innovating and progressive authorities, whilst Surrey, Sussex, Bucks and Berks were also represented by several subscribers, suggesting that geographical factors of proximity to London were also of importance.

Schiller was clearly an inspiring lecturer and teacher. A strong sense of conviction expressed in straightforward language is the hallmark of his posthumously published lectures.[34] They were highly anecdotal, a marked characteristic of much progressive writing. Keeping diaries of his own children's actions and sayings, and notes of children whom he saw in schools, his lectures were prolifically illustrated with stories which would reappear in a variety of guises. In seminars he was remembered by many of his students for his powerful silence; his way of sitting back, observing and listening. His interventions were sparing and apt. Certainly the model of learning espoused in his lectures was one not of forcing, but of facilitating and encouraging the growth of the individual; there was an almost oriental, self-effacing quality to his teaching. The role of HMI as seen by Schiller was one of cross-pollination. His own model of change was that of the progress of the worm, much quoted, for instance by Marsh (1970):

> The movement of change is not a steady advance on an even front; nor is it a series of changes after brilliant ideas. The major force

> in the movement is the patient and persistent pulling of pioneers, scattered far and wide, each at work in his or her school, determined to find a way in which their children shall live and learn more abundantly.[35]

Christian Schiller was an individualist, who sat uncomfortably within a 'system' and reputedly had enemies in the Inspectorate and amongst more conventional academics. His own formative influences included Whitehead, whom he knew and quoted a great deal, and Nathan Isaacs. He was a follower of A.S. Neill and Bertrand Russell, and had once, with Robin Tanner, inspected the school at Dartington Hall. Thus he had well-established links with the classic 'progressives' of the inter-war period. In the course of a discussion at the schools Broadcasting Council, he revealed his respect for P.B. Ballard, who had been a leading figure amongst 'progressive' educationists before the war.[36]

An important function of HMI was that of advising other educational bodies. Representing the Ministry of Education, Schiller was a member of the Primary II (7–11) Programmes Sub-Committee of the Schools Broadcasting Council. It might reasonably be guessed that these meetings were not his favourite official commitment. Robin Tanner has commented that Schiller was no great enthusiast for schools broadcasting, which by its nature seemed to undermine the individualism and flexibility required of a progressive curriculum; a letter of apology to the secretary, R.C. Steele, excusing himself for absence on the grounds of prior holiday commitments, suggests a certain coolness towards the topic:

> I always enjoy the meetings, partly because of their intrinsic interest, but also because they seem to me a model of their kind.[37]

His interventions at these meetings provide some unusual but vivid illustrations of his character and his educational philosophy; there was sometimes a certain prickliness in his exchanges, as minuted. On 11 February 1949, a syllabus of broadcasts on world history was being discussed. Schiller asked whether 'modern times' could not be a little more modern, as some of the subjects proposed were old when he was 10

> I know that the war has occupied the whole of these children's lives, but things do happen now — penicillin and chloroform for example....
>
> The Easter Island Raft story. What we want is subjects 'on the tongue' now.[38]

Discussion of a music series for children of 8 and 9 took place in October 1950 and turned to the question of musical notation, which Schiller considered an ulterior purpose, and

> an ulterior purpose is off-putting and you lose all you are out for. The statement that listening is too hard is an indictment of

> present teaching. The remedy is not to have notation teaching but more listening to sharpen the powers. . . .
>
> Music is bogged down in notation. There are schools giving a musical education up to nine without notation. Why shouldn't we have a start?
>
> Skills should keep pace with creativity. Skills should follow listening. . . . In other arts, impulse first, skills follow.[39]

During a discussion, when the title of an English programme was being considered, Schiller's viewpoint is delightfully contrasted with a range of opinions from his fellow committee members: John Spencer, a training college representative from Harrogate, one Miss Marriott, a teacher, and a Mr E.C. Wright (other member):

ASEO:	Should the title be altered?
Wright:	Junior English I or Junior English II
Schiller:	Why call it English?
ASEO:	Stories and Rhymes. Stories and Verses.
Schiller:	Tales — stories —
Marriott:	The word stories might induce teachers to bring out their knitting.
Spencer:	I don't see why children shouldn't acquire the word literature — if it is literature.[40]

Though he acknowledged the improvements which had taken place over fifty years in the quality of teachers and of children's learning, given his individualism it is not surprising that towards the end of his life he found himself ill at ease with current developments in education. He came to believe that there were too many advisers, that the government's Inspectorate should have diminished as local advisory services expanded. He deplored the introduction of middle schools on the grounds that adolescents and pre-adolescents required different approaches. He was disdainful of educational research. A slightly Olympian and unrealistic view of teachers' influence in society was perhaps reflected in his optimistic conviction that the 11+ would be doomed once a large number of teachers were sufficiently confident to decide for themselves how to organize and assess their children's learning; in reality it was popular and political pressure, backed by evidence from the social sciences, that achieved this end.[41]

But it was his powerful influence on a dynamic elite that counted. Schiller inspired veneration in some of his students; the annual memorial lecture and his posthumously published lectures convey an air of reverence, and reflect the model of diffusion as that of magisterial wisdom passed on by word of mouth to a chosen few (just as the name with which he had been endowed curiously combined the notions of faith and enlightenment). Lacking was any sense of argument or debate, or of education as a science; the unproblematic view of education may have been to some extent a reflection of the political consensus of its time, yet as such it was an approach unsuited to achieving widespread innovation within the educational system.

HMI: John Blackie

John Blackie's name is closely associated with the Plowden Committee, on which he served as an assessor (non-voting member) at the end of his official career in the Inspectorate, as Chief Inspector for Primary Education from 1963–66. He was aware that certain HMI had a reputation as radical advocates of progressivism, and that some teachers had a view of 'airborne inspectors' who advocated 'licence' in the classroom. Yet he himself was, chronologically, 'an Edwardian, almost a Victorian'. Born in 1904, son of a Bishop of Grimsby, he had been educated at Bradfield and Cambridge, returning to Bradfield to teach for five years before joining the Inspectorate at the age of 29. His experience of primary schools to which he often referred was therefore, like Schiller's, that of observing rather than of doing. He was no specialist in this phase of education, having been Chief Inspector for Further Education from 1951 to 1958, before his translation to CI for Primary Education in the closing years of his career. He summarized the values in which he believed as 'Christian, progressive, and founded in art, literature, music and craftsmanship as the highest achievement of the human imagination', and he saw teachers as 'guardians and transmitters of culture'.[42] Blackie's concern for 'quality' reputedly led him to demand from his colleagues written English that was incisive and polished, but also provoked him to demand that children should be offered 'neither the childish nor the superficial, but the very best possible'.[43]

Blackie's association with primary progressivism reached its fruition in his role as an assessor to the Plowden Commmittee. But his influence did not cease with his retirement in 1966. Like Schiller, he also continued to teach after retirement, as a part-time lecturer at Homerton College. He was commissioned by the Department of Education and Science to write a popular guide 'for parents and grandparents' as well as for college of education students, its chatty style and its brevity no doubt contributing to its success for many years as an introductory course book. We have in printed form some of the speeches delivered to teachers' courses, two of which were originally privately printed for circulation in the West Riding LEA, and which appear to have served as a powerful vehicle of progressive ideas.[44]

Blackie was an articulate advocate of progressivism. His approach was child-centred. He considered that Christians and humanists could accept, on different grounds, that each individual child mattered (though he accepted that Communism, Islam and Hinduism would not be prepared to underwrite it as a principle — in a talk of 1954 he referred with disapproval the racial discrimination exhibited towards immigrant workers in the Midlands).[45] He believed in good relationships and mutual respect between teacher and taught — what he called 'creative authority' — as the basis of discipline. He was for doing away with dull and banal reading schemes, for the introduction of school libraries and 'real books', and for teachers 'sharing' their favourite literature with children. He was for learning to write through self-expression. Mathematics was a way of thinking to be acquired through practical applications. Above all, he was not dogmatic about curriculum and teaching methods, which should derive from principles and convictions:

> crafts ... are not just a matter of 'how-it's-done' but ... have their roots in the oldest needs and preoccupations of man; mathematics, a glimpse at least of the art and the beauty; language ... which is the vehicle for the hopes, longings and sorrows of the human heart....[46]

Though these talks were sensitive, well argued, constructive and entertaining because so well illustrated by literature and everyday observation, at the same time they effectively convey the image of an Inspectorate drawn from a cultural elite and promoting an elite culture.

On popular culture there is a sense of humour in Blackie's comments; (he once quoted Bill Haley as saying 'If this is Rock'n 'Roll give me Bach every time') but ultimately he was disparaging:

> 'Thankyou for the world so sweet' is for 'the kiddies', not for the children whom we love and respect.
>
> I am desperately afraid of superficiality, of threadbare feeling, of callous indifference, of sloppy romanticism, of enthroned mediocrity ... all of which we may find upheld, under the flag of democracy, in many respectable quarters.[47]

On another occasion he borrowed a phrase of Milton's to refer to 'the hungry sheep', and was scathing about their culture of football, dog-tracks and television.[48]

Given his social and educational background it is not surprising that his talks were larded with classical and literary allusion. Reading in retrospect, one can sense a dissonance of cultures showing through, as when, addressing teachers in the West Riding, he took for his text an old schoolmaster and colleague from Bradfield. As for the growth of psychological investigation and child-study, which he was concerned not to denigrate, he saw this as lagging behind intuition, though intuition needed 'a sound theoretical base to support it'.[49] The anecdotal style which Blackie and Schiller had in common, whilst no doubt inspiring to a live audience, seems less satisfactory in retrospect as a basis for curriculum and pedagogical development. The anecdotal approach has to be considered in the context of hostility shown by Schiller towards the development of educational science and research. Griffin-Beale has described how Schiller would frequently repeat certain stories about children using different names. There was it seems, almost a trade in anecdotes: Blackie in 1954 quoted a piece of writing which he had read in the composition book of a 9-year old boy, the very same piece which had been cited ten years earlier by Schiller in a lecture to emergency training students at Harrogate.[50] The crucial point, however, about this style of rhetoric as a means of transmitting educational ideas, is its limitation; inspirational it may have been, but a groundwork for educational advance, it was destined to be found wanting in the long term.

Blackie gained a degree in English at Magdalene College, Cambridge, just three years after F.R. Leavis had earned his at Emmanuel College. By the time Leavis published his *Mass Civilization and Minority Culture* in 1930, Blackie was back at his old public school as a schoolmaster. Three years later, he joined the Inspectorate and was posted to Manchester where 'he identified himself with the problems of deprivation and squalor'.[51] This combination of events illuminates his later writings. Recent work by Francis Mulhern and Terry Eagleton in the history of English criticism enables Blackie to be accurately placed in a particular historical and cultural tradition. The work of the Leavises and other English scholars in Cambridge in the inter-war years produced the journal *Scrutiny* which was, however, much more than a journal, — it was a moral and cultural crusade.

> English was not only a subject worth studying, but *the* supremely civilizing pursuit, . . . English was an arena in which the most fundamental questions of human existence — what it meant to be a person, to engage in significant relationship with others, to live from the vital centre of the most essential values — were thrown into vivid relief.[52]

Leavis's faith in the uplifting effect of culture through education made him a true inheritor of Matthew Arnold, and a significant effect of Leavis' teaching was its all-pervasive hold within the educational system. This was manifest in the secondary school curriculum, but it may also be observed informing the rhetoric of primary progressivism, especially in lectures by Blackie.

Eagleton might have been referring to Blackie when he wrote of *Scrutiny's* belief that the quality of society's language was the most telling index of the quality of its personal and social life, and of the journal's campaign against the philistine devaluing of language and traditional culture blatantly apparent in 'mass society'. Adherents of

Scrutiny aimed to nurture the study of literature to equip individuals to survive in a mechanized society of trashy romances, alienating labour, banal adverts and vulgarizing mass media. Francis Mulhern, writing within the framework of historical materialism, saw the objective cultural function of 'Leavisism' in the mid-twentieth century as two-fold: to mediate the establishment of a new discourse on literature in the national culture, and to mediate the large-scale entry of a new society into the national intelligentsia.[53] In the 1920s Leavis and his colleagues represented a new entry of lower middle class origin to Cambridge, a social phenomenon of particular relevance for his subsequent appeal to a new breed of teachers and an expansion of higher education in the decades after the Second World War. There is more than an echo in the later period of the earlier response of Leavisite scholars to the 1914–18 war, for whom:

> Literature would be at once solace and reaffirmation, a familiar ground on which Englishmen could regroup both to explore, and to find some alternative to, the nightmare of history.[54]

A necessary background to understanding their influence is the composition and status of the Inspectorate, and in relation to the careers of both Schiller and Blackie, the traditions of HMI are of some significance. The model of school inspectors as 'guardians of culture' was epitomized in Matthew Arnold. But Edmond Holmes, HMI, who stands as an important source of progressivism, reflected later that the criterion of selection had been a first class degree from Oxford or Cambridge, 'as a guarantee of industry and decent ability'.

> I was ridiculously young, ... and I had, I need hardly say, no qualification for the difficult and responsible job of inspecting schools.[55]

Yet Holmes himself had been responsible for the notorious circular of 1910 which created a political storm by accusing local inspectors drawn from the ranks of elementary school teachers as being generally 'uncultured and imperfectly educated ... creatures of tradition and routine'. Unease about the relationship to working-class, elementary and later primary schools, of an Inspectorate drawn predominantly from a privileged educational background and with little or no experience of the schools in question, had been expressed by the National Union of (Elementary) Teachers since at least 1870, whose evidence to the Royal Commission on the Civil Service 1912–14 resulted in a strengthening of the 'Elementary Branch' with recruitment of more experienced teachers. Fifty years later dissatisfaction again expressed through the teachers' unions helped once more to force an enquiry.[56]

In 1968 the House of Commons Select Committee on Education and Science decided to enquire into the Inspectorate. Its report was largely concerned with identifying and approving the change that had taken place from an inspectorial to an advisory role, but recognizing also that the growth of local advisory services had reduced the need for a central inspectorate.[57] The Schools Council had assumed the former HMI role of advising on curriculum content, and the increasing professionalism of teachers gradually obviated the need for traditional forms of inspection. Several comments and recommendations of the Committee acknowledged a certain remoteness on the part of HMI. Whilst they were no longer recruited almost entirely from public schools, there was still underrepresentation of non-graduate teachers from primary and secondary schools. Many witnesses had suggested a change of title to express the increasingly advisory role of HMI, but the inspectors themselves did not want this, and the fact of appointment by Her Majesty in Council, though 'of no great significance, . . . clearly delights the people who enjoy it'.[58]

The need for a smaller, perhaps more highly specialized inspectorate, more closely related to its changed functions and 'more in touch with social developments affecting education' was noted, and provision was recommended to allow and encourage inspectors to refresh their teaching experience in schools and colleges, 'to be embodied in their contract of service'.[59] Blackie, in his book on inspection reflected his own independent school origins in a partial account of this committee, choosing to lend more credence to the plaudits from HMI given by the Headmasters' Conference than to Michael Duane's criticisms.[60]

Of course, even as he wrote, the structure of the Inspectorate was changing, but the historical fact, of considerable significance when considering the diffusion of particular ideologies in the 1950s and 1960s, is that two senior and influential inspectors had received their own professional formation in an educational world strikingly different from that which they were addressing. Their message was heard and willingly applied to considerable effect by a new generation of primary teachers, but perhaps in its origins and its manner of mediation lay the seeds of a later discontent. The irony is that two key promoters of a philosophy of 'learning through doing' were not themselves 'doers' but only 'observers' in the field of primary education. There is a marked difference between the careers of Schiller and Blackie, and later Chief Inspectors for Primary Education such as Norman Thomas (1973–81) and Geoffrey Elsmore (1981–85), who were both primary teachers of long experience. The later incumbents had both come from progressive authorities, Thomas having been a Hertfordshire headteacher from 1956–61 and Elsmore a headteacher in Oxfordshire from 1956–63, but as Chief Inspector, neither proselytized in the way that Schiller and Blackie had, for by then the nature of the task had changed.

Notes

1 EYKEN, W. VAN DER (1969) *Adventures in Education*, London, Allen Lane.
2 TATTERSALL, E. (1976) 'The West Riding philosophy' in OPEN UNIVERSITY *The West Riding: Changes in Primary Education*, E203 Case Study 2.
3 WEST RIDING EDUCATION COMMITTEE PAPERS, Brotherton Library, University of Leeds MS 731 (WREC Papers) Box 15/0063; letter from Clegg to Sir Cyril Burt, 16 August 1967.
4 Obituary for Clegg, *Education*, 24 January 1986, p. 82.
5 CLEGG, A. (1974) 'The shadow and substance of education' in UNIVERSITY OF LONDON, GOLDSMITH'S COLLEGE, *The Changing School: A Challenge to the Teacher* (Report of Conference 1974) p. 14.
6 *ibid.*
7 GOSDEN, P.H.J.H. and SHARP, P. (1978) *The Development of an Education Service: The West Riding 1889–1974*, Oxford, Martin Robertson, p. 33.
8 WREC Papers, Box 2/B5: letter from Clegg to Brown, 18 March 1950.
9 WREC Papers, Box 2/G8: 'A day in the life of a CEO', 17 June 1955.
10 WREC Papers, Box 2/D10: letter from Clegg to C.A. Knowlson, Swansea, 11 August 1952.
11 WREC Papers, Box 15/LT41: Policy and Finance Sub-Committee, 12 May 1964.
12 WREC Papers, Box 2/U2: Comments on Plowden Working Paper re middle schools, 28 May 1964; and /E7: letter from Clegg to Hyman, 5 August 1953.
13 WREC Papers, Box 15/0063–0073: documents concerning Mrs Pyrah's class.
14 WREC Papers, Box 15/LT22.
15 WREC Papers, Box 2/BB1: Sub-Committee: Post-war education, 19 February 1946, agendum 3, memorandum re proposal to establish Bretton Hall. This predilection for the arts is interestingly one shared by a number of innovative CEOs of the period, including Henry Morris, Stewart Mason.
16 Obituary for Clegg, *Education* 24 January 1986, p. 82.
17 WREC Papers, Box 15/LT25: Policy Sub-Committee, 19 November 1946; and LT42: Policy and Finance Sub-Committee, 13 October 1964.
18 GOSDEN, P.H.J.H. and SHARP. P. (1978) *op. cit.*, pp. 101–15.
19 *ibid*, pp. 120–1; see also MILNE, I.R. (1965) in *Froebel Journal*, 3 October.
20 WREC Papers, Box 2/G1: Sub-Committee: Post-War Education, 16 October 1945, Agendum 4, Memorandum.
21 WREC Papers, Box 2/G10: Press cutting: *Yorkshire Observer*, 6 May 1946. A description may also be found in the *Times Educational Supplement*, 7 September 1946, p. 425.
22 WREC Papers, Box 2/DD2: letter from Clegg to Mrs Bland, 13 October 1947.
23 GOSDEN, P.H.J.H. and SHARP, P. (1978) *op. cit.*, pp. 122–3.
24 WREC Papers, Box 2/G1: Sub-Committee: Post War Education, 16 October 1945, Agendum 4, Memorandum.
25 TATTERSALL, E. (1976) *op. cit.*, p. 16; the West Riding *Schools Bulletin*, in which teachers were encouraged to write, was one manifestation of this policy.
26 WREC Papers, Box 2/Y5: letter from Clegg to Chairman, 1 July 1955, and M10 Circular letter to inspectors, 1 June 1961.
27 WREC Papers, Box 2/01: letter from Clegg to C.G. Hayter HMI, 19 March 1965.
28 WREC Papers, Box 15/LT56: Policy and Finance Sub-Committee, 11 June 1972.
29 WREC Papers, Box 2/X: 'Attitudes', talk given to North of England Education conference, Southport, 5 January 1962.
30 EDMONDS, E.L. (1962) *The School Inspector*, (International Library of Sociology and Social Reconstruction), London, Routledge and Kegan Paul, p. 150.
31 BROWNE, S. (1979) 'The accountability of Her Majesty's Inspectorate' in LELLO, J. (Ed.) *Accountability in Education*, London, Ward Lock Educational, p. 35.

32 Edmonds, E.L. (1962) *op. cit.*, p. 153.
33 Biographical details and accounts of his opinions which follow are taken from Schiller, C. (1979) *Christian Schiller in his Own Words*, (Ed.) C. Griffin-Beale, published by private subscription through A and C. Black. Reprinted by NAPE 1983.
34 *ibid.*
35 Marsh, L. (1970) *op. cit.*, p. 41.
36 BBC Written Archive R16/334/2: Note of a meeting 9 October 1950. P.B. Ballard, a Welshman trained at Borough Road, had been an Inspector for the LCC from 1906–30, and a President of the Child Study Society, and had a number of publications to his name covering the fields of mental testing, and English and maths teaching. He had also been an amateur painter and a President of the Chiswick Group of Artists. He died on 1 November 1950. Ballard was author of influential books in the inter-war years such as *Thought and Language* (1934).
37 BBC Written Archive R16/334/1, and Robin Tanner in an interview wth the author, June 1986.
38 BBC Written Archive R16/334/2 Notes on meeting 11 February 1949.
39 BBC Written Archive R16/334/2 Notes on meeting 10 October 1950.
40 BBC Written Archive R16/334/2 Note of a meeting 9 October 1950.
41 Schiller, C. (1979) *op. cit.*
42 Blackie, J. (1963) *Good Enough for the Children?*, London, Faber, p. 132.
43 *The Times*, 11 April 1985, obit. J. Blackie.
44 Blackie, J. (1963) *op. cit.*
45 *ibid*, pp. 51 and 144.
46 *ibid*, p. 140.
47 *ibid*, pp. 53 and 45.
48 *ibid*, p. 130.
49 *ibid*, p. 51.
50 *ibid*, p. 16; and Schiller, C. (1979) *op. cit.*, p. 12. Schiller cited it as the work of a 9-year-old boy in Salford, so one can assume that the anecdote had been transmitted to him by Blackie, who had been District Inspector in Manchester from 1936–47.
51 *The Times*, 11 April 1985, obit. J. Blackie.
52 Eagleton, T. (1983) *Literary theory: An introduction*, Oxford, Blackwell, p. 31.
53 Mulhern, F. (1979) *The Moment of Scrutiny*, London, New Left Books, p. 313.
54 Eagleton, T. (1983) *op. cit.*, p. 30.
55 Holmes, E.G.A. (1920) *In Quest of an Ideal*, Richard Cobden-Sanderson, pp. 16–17.
56 NUT (1960) *Annual Report*, London, NUT, p. 54.
57 House of Commons Select Committee on Education and Science, *Her Majesty's Inspectorate (England and Wales)* PP 1967–68 (400-I) vii.
58 PP 1967–68 (400-I) vii, para. 41.
59 PP 1967–68 (440-I) vii, paras. 42, 43.
60 Blackie, J. (1970) *op. cit.*, pp. 50, 62 and 65.

4 *Professional Education and Training*

Demography had its part to play in the dissemination of progressivism, in so far as developments in teacher training responded to shifts in the birth rate. Most obviously, the first and second 'bulges' in the primary school population required more teachers and hence more colleges, and a larger system of teacher education increased the scope for innovation. But also, subsequent dramatic falls in the birth rate reduced the demand for initial training and left spare capacity for in-service work. Furthermore, as the bulges reached their later teens, the larger cohorts of students passing through higher education increased the supply of potential teachers and allowed for a raising of entry qualifications. However, supply and demand are only two elements in a complex network of interlocking factors which affected the nature of professional training; structural change in the higher education sector, developments in educational research, shifts in educational and social values, the vagaries of economic performance and public finance, and latterly conflicts of political ideology relating to the role and status of teaching, all had a part to play.

This chapter will consider some of the ways in which teacher education became a vehicle for the diffusion of ideals and practices. It will outline the model of a teacher defined in progressive writing, and will continue by considering one particular example of an initial training institution; thereafter the all-important role of in-service courses, as provided by a variety of agencies will be described.

With these factors in mind, a brief outline of the most significant institutional changes provides a necessary backcloth. As a result of the McNair Committee's report on supply, recruitment and training of teachers, published in May 1944, area training organizations were set up in the years between 1947 and 1951. These were diversely organized groups of colleges most of which centred on a particular university institute of education, giving form to the not uncontroversial view that teacher training should derive its authority from a source which enjoyed 'recognized standards' and 'established independence ... powerful enough to resist the encroachment of centralization'.[1]

Other developments in initial teacher education included the Emergency Training Scheme, which provoked a good deal of thought about the curriculum of professional training, and produced 35,000 new teachers in the space of six years; rapid growth of the college sector from ninety-one colleges in 1939 to 146 in 1960, and in college students whose numbers almost doubled from 25,000 in 1952 to 48,000 in 1960 and doubled again to 95,000 in 1968; extension to three years of the Teacher's Certificate course in 1960, and introduction of BEd degree courses from 1965 with the raising of minimum entrance requirements to courses and eventual establishment of an all-graduate entry to the profession. Such a growth in the college sector created scope for innovation, and, together with the increasingly academic content of courses, a lucrative market for publishers! Validation of BEd courses by the Council for National Academic Awards from 1968 loosened the traditional relationship with universities, and the mergers and closures of colleges in 1975, 1977 and 1982 considerably altered the picture of provision. Most recently the White Paper *Teaching Quality* in 1983 and the subsequent establishment of a Council for the Accreditation of Teacher Education (CATE) has moved significantly towards centralization. Development of in-service work included the introduction of secondment in 1955, and the establishment of teachers' centres in the later 1960s.

Against this background, features relevant to the diffusion of progressivism include: the status and model of the primary school teacher; the role of individual colleges; the content of courses, especially with their increasing length and higher academic status; and patterns of in-service training.

Progressive Model Teacher

The model of the progressive primary school teacher, and consequent approaches to training, are well illustrated in the series entitled *British Primary Schools Today*, published for the Schools Council in 1971/72. Ann Cook and Herb Mack, who were co-directors of the Community Resources Institute at the City University of New York, were authors of two titles in this series: *The Teacher's Role* and *The Headteacher's Role*. Both had experience of English and American schools, and based their accounts on periods of observation in selected primary schools and on interviews with selected teachers.

Their selection of the class-teachers was significant. Four who were working within the framework of an 'open classroom' philosophy were chosen for interview after classroom observations and consultations with headteachers to ensure not uniqueness, but 'soundness as professionals who might well speak for numerous other colleagues'. Something of a contradiction is evident here, alongside the claim that these were skilled and experienced practitioners 'such as must be fairly rare, even in British schools that have made advances'.[2] Was the progressive teacher a common phenomenon, or not?

All four 'talked modestly about their personal growth as a teacher'; all felt that they were constantly learning, and stressed that one of the strengths of the system was that they were able to expand their own interests and abilities as well as those of the children. They were

> introspective, continually evaluating their effectiveness in providing children with a challenge, extending their interests, and in providing meaningful experiences.

The fundamentals on which they basically agreed, included a powerful respect for the individual. Their practice was marked by much thought and planning outside school hours, especially time spent in making the classroom efficient and exciting as a learning environment. None of them followed a prescribed curriculum, being prepared instead to provide learning experiences prompted by the children's interests and needs, and all regarded education as a dynamic process in which they were always learning from the child.

Alongside the ideal of the teacher held out by primary progressivists has to be considered the general status of the primary teacher. It was a problem perceived by Plowden.[3] A slowly but perceptibly increasing proportion of graduate teachers in primary schools (3.2 per cent in 1951 and 4.8 per cent in 1971) rose more sharply during the 1970s as BEd graduates joined primary school staffs; the proportion of women to men (3:1) remained fairly constant and had implications in a period when women were only gradually accorded equal status in the world of work (despite having secured equal pay for teaching from 1961); pupil teacher ratios fell only very slowly and remained inferior to those in secondary schools.[4] Increasingly academic study and 'higher' levels of qualification for the teaching profession, together with more extensive and more sophisticated educational research were developments favouring a rise in professional status. Progressivism seemed to enhance the responsibility of the teacher, yet progressivist writing frequently demeaned most forms of empirical research in education.

Plowden distinguished two models of the primary teacher, a distinction which becomes significant for understanding the diffusion of progressivism through in-service courses. One model comprised those who would 'make education their life work. The innovators, the future heads of schools, the teachers in colleges and departments of education, the advisers and administrators', whose work 'is the spear head of advance'. By Plowden's implication these were mostly male; female students were expected to work only a few years before leaving to raise families, even though the Report's own statistics reveal a fairly marginal difference in the rate of staff turnover as between men and women.[5]

Initial Teacher Education

Selleck (1972) acknowledged the training colleges as one of the principal agents of progressivism in the period to 1939. Courses of initial training were in a position to exert a powerful influence over the work of schools, but the decentralized system meant that no standard practice prevailed. As recently as the late 1960s, the introduction of the BEd degree saw a bewildering variety of models.

Molly Brearley's account of pre-service courses deserves attention for some significant shades of emphasis. Her sanguine description of relationships between colleges and schools described an ideal which, even as late as 1972, probably characterized only a handful of the most progressive primary courses, amongst them the Froebel Institute courses at Roehampton, where Brearley herself had been Principal from 1955 to 1970. The model of collaboration described included headteachers sometimes helping in the selection of students, many teachers invited to colleges for discussion, lectures and social purposes, and a rich variety of school attachments for students, working with children and their teachers in small and large groups, both in college and in school. In 1982, however, the HMI study of 'the new teacher in school' revealed that many college courses failed to achieve this level of collaboration between college and school.

Child study was central to Brearley's description of courses:

> One of the main objects of this course is that students should learn how to observe individual children, and how to use, as their frame of reference, a knowledge of child development in general.[6]

For this purpose, education courses were supported with films, filmstrips, recordings and closed circuit television. Embedded in her description of teacher education courses was an acute awareness of the circumstances of continuous and rapid curriculum change and the professional independence of the teacher:

> in a rapidly changing world, the 'specifics' will be constantly superseded and much will depend on the degree of flexibility, resourcefulness and understanding of principles that the teacher can bring to bear in meeting contemporary needs.

Also, a great decline in the use of textbooks in schools had thrown more responsibility onto the teacher, a responsibility which could only be met by giving the student criteria for selection and presentation.

In a decentralized system of teacher education, no individual college may be regarded as typical. Certain institutions stand out as having played a key role in the diffusion of progressivism; the Froebel Institute was highly regarded by progressive heads as a source for new teachers, as were St John's College at York, Stockwell, and Sidney Webb College. The reasons for a particularly progressive reputation in certain colleges may be peculiar to their providing body, their structure and, of course, their staffing. Goldsmiths' College was pre-eminent for its pioneering post-graduate course for primary teachers from 1961. In the case of Goldsmiths' a tradition had been established which survived and still continues through several generations of tutors and lecturers.

Goldsmiths' College played such an important part in the propagation of progressivism over a period of time that it deserves special consideration. Its individuality lay in its 'most confusing and illogical set-up', as Baroness Stocks described it. Founded in 1890 by the ancient city livery company of Goldsmiths as an unsectarian and undenominational institution for education and recreation, its aim was to promote 'technical skill, knowledge, health and general well-being among men and women of the industrial, working and artisan classes'. Although originally intended as an adult institute, such a breadth of aim itself anticipated later broad interpretations of the primary school curriculum.

Its unique structure, and its contribution to the present story, date from 1904 when, transferred to the University of London as a college for teachers from the metropolis, three distinct departments evolved for training in art, teacher training and adult education. Goldsmiths' offered a two-year scheme of study to intending elementary school teachers, and an early memorandum of 1905 identified the possible value of associating the training department with the School of Art in view of the need for blackboard drawing required by the Board of Education, as well as the desirability of some wider art education within the two-year course. However, it was considered questionable whether drawing from the nude would be appropriate in the training of teachers![7]

Its complement of trainee teachers was always considerable, rising from 330 in 1918 to 576 (241 men and 335 women) in 1930, and in the post-war period from 570 in 1947 to about 1900 in the mid 1960s. It was the association of an art department and teacher training under one roof which lent a unique flavour to the institution, especially in the education of its influential student Robin Tanner (later HMI), who studied for a teacher's certificate in the 1920s and subsequently in the evening art classes. The foundation by a craft company and the resulting ethos had pointed relevance for a progressive view of primary education; the text of the College Hymn expressed this so well that it must be quoted in full:

Goldsmiths' College Hymn

In the vapour of the furnace he must wrestle with his work,
Where amid the unwrought metal countless forms of beauty lurk;

To shape them and adorn them is the task he may not shirk:
The smith is working on.
Sitting daily by his anvil he pursues his ceaseless quest,
His joy is in his craftsmanship, the mystery's touch impressed;
But still the elusive masterpiece will never let him rest:
The smith is working on.
The beating of the hammer in his ear for ever cries,
The heavenly patterned vessel hangs before his dreaming eyes;
His heat is set on perfecting his golden enterprise:
The smith is working on.
We work in richer metal, by a greater anvil stand
As we seek to fashion children for a finer, nobler land;
Till the mystic touch approves them from the Master Craftsman's hand
The 'Smiths are working on.

Though slightly out of accord with the favourite progressive image of biological growth, this hymn yet emphasized the aesthetic, and the craft of teaching with its 'mystic touch'. These words, repeated at the morning assembly, an apparently well-loved tradition in the college, themselves must have infused students with a philosophy of education even before classes began. A verse from Ecclesiasticus gave biblical authority to this ethos:

> The smith also sitting by the anvil and considering the iron work . . . the noise of the hammer and the anvil is ever in his ears, and his eyes look still upon the pattern of the thing that he maketh: he setteth his mind to finish this work, and watcheth to polish it off perfectly.[8]

The Teacher Training Department was notable for its pioneer work and experimentation, much of which was associated with progressive approaches to primary education. In 1918 a College nursery school was established as a demonstration school. Such demonstration schools were not uncommon in the nineteenth century colleges, but here the students were encouraged to visit the children's homes and get to know their background. Although the school was not reopened after the return from evacuation in 1945, careful study of the pre-school child in its home background continued as an important element of the course. Ann Driver's experimental work on music and movement broadcasts for schools was associated with Goldsmiths', being carried out at the Junior Demonstration School in Childeric Road, and in 1932 the BBC set up an experimental studio at the College for broadcast lessons by radio. Film, too, was a medium experimented with for its educational possibilities. At the Kender Street LCC Junior Mixed School in 1937, another of the Goldsmiths' demonstration schools, Catherine Fletcher and George Cons carried out an experimental enquiry into use of neighbourhood resources for educational activity in schools, bringing into the classroom the local dustman, sewerman and other tradespeople. Their published account of the work carried a foreword by A.E. Dean, Warden of Goldsmiths', which pointed out the value to students of giving insight into children's living interests, enabling students to override the prevailing conceptions of subject boundaries, and opening to them fresh opportunities of classroom work through direct personal cooperation with people carrying out essential community services.[9]

Various members of the Training Department staff were remarkable for their activity and their writing in the educational world. Thomas Rayment, Warden from 1915 until 1927, was active in the National Froebel Union. Roger Raven, Vice-Principal from 1929, became Chairman of the 'New Ideals in Education' Conference. Of lecturers appointed in the inter-war years four (including F.J. Schonell) went on to university chairs, six subsequently became principals of other training colleges, and four entered Her Majesty's Inspectorate. One of the latter was Ellen Oakden, author, with Mary Sturt, of many books, including *Modern Psychology and Education*, which went through eight editions from 1926 to 1937, and *Matter and Method in Education* first published in 1928. Ellen Oakden served as Assistant Secretary to the McNair Committee on the training of teachers from 1942–44, and later had responsibility as HMI for the College itself in the period after 1945, supporting further innovations in the Training Department's curriculum.

Egregious amongst such peers, Nancy Catty was remembered by Robin Tanner as an influential teacher, a lecturer from the earliest days in 1905 until 1928 when she retired to continue her writing. An early work, in collaboration with colleagues at the College, was *Training in Appreciation: Art, Literature, Music*. Tenets of progressivism as well as Goldsmiths' bias towards the arts are reflected in her theme that one of the most important functions of a school was developing a love of some form of art for its own sake; the difference between the 'new' teaching and the 'old' was to *motivate* children in their desire for appreciation and intellectual effort.[10] Companion to this volume was one on the application of modern educational theory. It opened with a quotation from R.H. Tawney: though education was seen by Catty as serving the needs of the modern state, those needs were to be defined by the 'socially conscious', and teachers were to inculcate thinking and acting for oneself, rather than blind obedience.[11] Her *Theory and Practice in Education* (1934), was listed by Selleck (1972) as one of the widely read progressive texts. *Learning and Teaching in the Junior School* (1941) was a guide to tried and tested applications of the Hadow Report, and continued in print through the 1950s, as did her *First Book on Teaching*, written in 1929 and still in print in 1961.

Goldsmiths' sense of identity, its high academic standing, professional commitment and above all its association with progressivism persisted in the post-war years. A 'message from the Warden', Richard Hoggart, in the prospectus for 1980/81 claimed that:

> The history of Goldsmiths' is part of the social and educational history of Britain during the last century and a half. To a great many people ... it is known for its range, its readiness to experiment, its openness day and night to anyone who seeks intellectual training.[12]

In 1970 a House of Commons Select Committee chose Goldsmiths' as one of the colleges to examine for its report on teacher education, and the documentation reveals much about the progressivism of the College in the 1960s.[13] Two Schools Council projects were currently centred there: 'Art and Craft 8–13' and 'Language Development in the Primary School'. A 'curriculum laboratory' was at work on curriculum reform, and an educational television unit had achieved useful results which were becoming well known. Of particular interest, however, was its postgraduate training for infant and junior schools which started in 1961, a course which accommodated about 100 students by 1970, anticipating an increase to 120 or 140 (training for graduates was about to become compulsory).[14] For this course, the Department of Education and Science had financed the building of special accommodation; the College prospectus announced significantly that the course had

> recently moved into new purpose-built premises where students are able to experience at first hand the kind of working situation they are likely to meet in the *innovating schools in various local education authorities.* (my emphasis)[15]

Called the 'Plowden' wing, it was modelled on an Oxfordshire primary school.

The course was directed by Leonard Marsh, who had become a follower of Christian Schiller after attending Schiller's course at the London Institute. Books written by Marsh testify to the deep influence upon him of the former Staff Inspector for Primary Education.[16] Certainly the postgraduate primary course embodied many of Schiller's principles, and much of its organization was based on the personal contacts established through the 'Schiller group' and other progressive networks. Marsh made a point of saying that most applicants came as a result of personal recommendations from former students. A particular feature of the course were the visiting teachers 'all personally known to members of the Department'; the intention was to provide examples of 'distinguished practice', the teachers mounting exhibitions of children's work, and reference was made to Oxfordshire and Yorkshire as a source. Marsh had previously come to know Oxfordshire primary schools in his earlier post at St Paul's College, Cheltenham, and much use was made of certain

Oxfordshire schools for visits by Goldsmiths' students, and of selected Oxfordshire heads. Film was mentioned as being used for a similar purpose of conveying progressivism as practised in some local authorities. As in primary school topic work, so in college, each term had main themes: child development and mathematics in the autumn, language and environmental work in spring. The course was classroom based, with a great deal of child contact, and students worked in selected primary schools with experienced heads who had attended in-service courses at the college and so were well-known to the Department.

An interesting addendum to the minutes of evidence was a critical report on the organization of the postgraduate primary course, submitted by a group of students. Whilst approving of the course aims, they felt that too little time was given to discussion of educational principles, and to practical guidance on the teaching of reading, writing and maths, and that minimal assessment was offered of work carried out on teaching practice. At the same time they found too much emphasis on pursuance of the students' own performance at skills. Whilst they recognized the importance of the aesthetic appeal of the classroom, an over-concern with superficialities was identified, such as 'the use of dress pins rather than drawing pins' for display.

On hearing of this report another group of students signed a counter-memorandum dissociating themselves from these criticisms. They praised that close contact between students and tutors which they were encouraged to sustain during their teaching career, and they found that the nature of the course gave students freedom to develop as individuals within the framework of its philosophy, — 'as teachers whose primary concern is for the children'. Significantly, this second memorandum was written at a residential course with school-children from Oxfordshire and Yorkshire 'giving us the inspiration and practical experience to continue our apprenticeship as teachers'.[17] Memories of the course by later students included an appreciation of the 'pursuit of excellence' and an emphasis on the aesthetic environment, but a failure to address the problems of children with learning difficulties.

The relationship of initial to in-service courses was important. An advanced course for 'experienced heads and others' was to enable 'reconsideration of the nature of the curriculum, the role of the head, and the processes of change in education'. Entitled the 'Plowden' course, its Advisory Committee was chaired by Lady Plowden and included Christian Schiller (whom Marsh suggested should be invited by the Select Committee to submit written or oral evidence on the course). Visits to schools were an essential feature, the aim being

> to build up a parish-like pattern of contact between schools that will support the teachers and cause them to set higher professional aspirations and develop adequate processes of evaluation.

The staffing of an annual national course run by the Advisory Centre for Education at Cambridge, and known as the 'Plowden conference' became an integral part of the College's in-service commitment as presented to the House of Commons Select Committee by Marsh in 1969. Similarly, an annual one-day education conference was organized jointly for part-time course members and for teachers in schools by the Faculty of Education and the Goldsmiths' College Association, the explicit purposes of which were: a forum for discussion from representatives of all branches of education and the social services, a lively and up-to-date subject for discussion and practical relevance. In 1974, Sir Alec Clegg was the main speaker.[18] Another significant annual event was the Christian Schiller memorial lecture, and annual weekend conference which had originally begun as a reunion for members of Schiller's in-service course at the London Institute.

Goldsmiths' College continued to maintain its reputation for progressivism partly through the work of two of its lecturers, Geva Blenkin and Vic Kelly who in their published writings expounded progressive philosophy and practice, defending it against what they saw as both political attack in the pressure for accountability and professional subversion in form of statistical classroom research. *The Primary Curriculum*, an important student textbook published in 1981, opened on an embattled and defensive note with its quotation from the Hadow Report of 1931:

> The primary school has its own canons of excellence and criteria of success; it must have the courage to stand by them.[9]

Course Content: Piaget

Not only are the institutions of interest, but also the syllabuses followed by students, together with their prescribed reading. Robinson (1971) surveyed the reading lists of three colleges and identified five titles which were commonly recommended.[20] A markedly progressive approach was reflected in these, which included: Molly Brearley and others' (1969) *Fundamentals in the First School*; Mary Brown and Norman Precious (1968) *The Integrated Day in the Primary School*; Leonard Marsh (1970) *Alongside the Child in the Primary School*; Lorna Ridgway and Irene Lawton (1968 ed.) *Family Grouping in the Primary School*, and Vincent Rogers' (1970) *Teaching in the British Primary School*. Brearley and Marsh figure elsewhere in this chapter, Ridgway in chapter 5 and Rogers in chapter 8 below.

It will be instructive to concentrate on one particular phenomenon, the insertion of Piagetian psychology into teacher education. Edward Blishen recollected Piaget referred to dismissively in lectures in 1949, as the unnecessary intellectual elaboration of commonsense.[21] Child development had increasingly been a feature of professional courses since the 1930s, but Piaget's work was relatively little known amongst the wider public and even professionally in the mid 1950s. A search of the *Times Index* for those years reveals considerable interest in Edith Piaf and Pablo Picasso, but no reference to Piaget! The *Times Educational Supplement* in April 1959 presented his work with the apparent assumption that it was as yet unfamiliar. Reporting the work of the Geneva Institute for Sciences of Education, which combined psychological research into child development with experimental pedagogy, the *Times Educational Supplement* concluded:

> This is an investigation of considerable scope, which is still in the pure research stage. The results, it is hoped, will represent a valuable contribution to knowledge in the field of education.[22]

The wider discovery of Piaget in Britain coincided with the lengthening of initial training from two to three years, the third year regarded very much as for additional academic work, and the first BEd courses were introduced in 1965. Closer study of child development was ideally suited to a more academic but still professionally relevant course.

Those who had worked in progressive primary schools in the 1960s varied considerably in their views as to how far Piaget had influenced their practice, though in many cases he was claimed as having given useful theoretical support to practices already established. How deeply and how widely inscribed were Piagetian theories in professional discourse may be illustrated by typical references in two texts, quite contrasting in nature yet characteristic of the multifarious vehicles through which ideas are informally disseminated and assumptions reinforced. In his presidential address to the NUT Conference in 1967, Dennis Gilbert JP, referred in passing to:

> the great importance of early environmental factors, particularly in respect of linguistic and conceptual experiences,[23]

whilst Christopher Jarman (later an Oxfordshire adviser) in a very practical book on display in schools, employed the rationale that

> by handling and discussing ... real things from the past, children who are still at the stage of concrete thinking may get a little nearer to putting themselves in the place of those who used to handle them.[24]

These references are almost incidental and 'taken for granted'. More explicit was Marsh (1970), who devoted nearly a tenth of his book *Alongside the Child* to a discussion of Piaget, identifying the stage of 'concrete operations' as roughly matching the period of the junior school.

An extensive and challenging account has been given by Walkerdine

(1984) of the way in which developmental psychology and child-centred pedagogy went hand in hand in producing a new kind of practice. Her analysis has revealed how the scientific child-study movement of the late nineteenth century emerged, and how mental measurement and child development later evolved as twin techniques; liberal and radical critiques of the 1960s and 1970s in which concern for the individual child was set against the application of norms of selection and grading, missed the point that child-centredness and developmental psychology similarly relied on systems of classification and regulation, obscured by talk of 'freedom'. Bernstein, she observed, had used the concept of 'invisible pedagogy' to designate a similar relationship. Another point of reference was Bruner's observation in 1980 of the dogmatic approach of nursery teachers to play, based on a narrow interpretation of the 'development idea'. Walkerdine herself considered that

> It is perhaps the supreme irony that the concern for individual freedom . . . should have provided the conditions for the production of a set of apparatuses which would aid in the production of the normalized child. It is the empirical apparatus of stages of development which of all Piaget's work as been most utilized in education. . . .
>
> It is those procedures which form part of the day-to-day running of classrooms, providing the taken-for-granted forms of a pedagogy which teachers frequently do not associate with the name of Piaget, who appears as a dimly remembered figure from college days.[25]

A study of college examination scripts would doubtless provide a depressing picture of what understanding students had gained from their lectures and reading. Walkerdine has made suggestive use of one student's notebook, but a difficulty of researching the decentralized system of teacher training is that colleges and college courses varied widely. Three widely read textbook accounts of Piaget, however, may provide some indication of how his ideas entered professional discourse.

In the dissemination of Piagetian ideas, the Froebel Society had an important role to play, and Nathan Isaacs in particular, through the Society, featured as a frequent interpreter. In *Piaget: Some Answers to Teachers' Questions* (an undated Froebel pamphlet) Isaacs accounted for the confused way in which Piaget's ideas had been received in Britain, both in the sequence of English translations, which did not follow the order of Piaget's original writing, and in the conflicts between established progressive ideals in England on the one hand, and the hypotheses and experimental methods adopted by Piaget on the other.[26] These conflicts had been expounded in the critical reception of Piaget's early work by Susan Isaacs, but subsequently reconciled in Nathan Isaacs' writing. It has to be said that neither in this pamphlet, nor in the earlier and much reprinted *Some Aspects of Piaget's work* (first edition 1955, eighth edition 1965) do Piaget's ideas become very easily accessible to the average teacher, in that Isaacs' style involved close argument about psychological and philosophical principles.[27]

Much more comprehensible to the student in initial training would have been two digests of Piaget, and the printing histories of both indicate that they were widely consumed. Of *A Teacher's Guide to Reading Piaget*, the journal *Teachers' World* offered a somewhat racy comment:

> Deserves to succeed in its object of giving teachers an *aperitif* prior to reading Piaget in the raw.[28]

The authors, Molly Brearley and Elizabeth Hitchfield, former Principal and Lecturer at the Froebel Institute, recorded their own debt to Nathan Isaacs. In their opinion, Piaget's importance for teachers was the counter to an emphasis on quantitative mental measurement, since in his 'open-ended tests' Piaget was examining the *processes* of thought. Moreover, Piaget's work now provided scientific justification for teachers who had adopted a child-centred approach with only philosophical theory and intuitive judgment to guide them. Their accounts of experiments, each followed by a discussion of its theoretical and practical significance, were presented as

> analogous to teachers' daily procedure in the classroom where experience must be followed by reflection in order to plan future work.[29]

Published in 1966, this title was reprinted four times to 1972, and finally went out of print after 1982.

Still selling in 1986, however, was Ruth Beard's outline guide, first published in 1969, reprinted the same year and annually for the next three years.[30] Where Brearley and Hitchfield concentrated on experiments relating to particular concepts, Beard's work was structured around the Piagetian stages of child development:

> To teachers it is of some importance not only to know the order of stages in thinking, if there is an invariable order, but also to known what misconceptions to expect among children of different ages and at what age the majority of children in a given environment reach each stage.[31]

Beard makes no reference in her bibliography to Brearley and Hitchfield (or to Nathan Isaacs' work), but what the two books do stress in common is the concept of 'readiness' which pervaded child-centred teachers' practice, sometimes in a distorted and restricting way. Thus Brearley and Hitchfield:

> It is easy to assume that children are ready to start their learning at the point in a subject at which the teacher chooses to begin, but in fact it is essential to know what particular experiences should have been encountered to prepare them to form the basic concepts of the subject matter involved.[32]

Some of the more rigid interpretations of Piaget were subsequently modified for students in the writings of Margaret Donaldson.[33]

In-service Education and Training

Geoffrey Matthews, coordinator of the Nuffield primary mathematics project, described 'in-service training' as 'a bleak term', and other common nomenclature, such as 'refresher courses' sounds equally barren in retrospect. Whatever name it was given, staff development was of considerable importance in the progressivist scheme, as illustrated by a volume by Brearley and others on the education of teachers, in the Schools Council series *British Primary Schools Today*;[34] in this pamphlet, seven pages describe the system of initial training, whereafter thirty-five pages are devoted to the subject of in-service schemes.

The Hadow Report of 1931 recognized in its introduction that the new conception of the work of primary schools imposed a heavy responsibility for innovation on the teachers, who would need

> imagination and adaptability, initiative to break with routine and ingenuity to devise improvements.[35]

The education of young children was

> in a state of more than ordinarily rapid growth. What is true today will be irrelevant tomorrow....
>
> Are [the schools'] methods of organisation ... the scale on which they are staffed and the lines on which their education is planned, of a kind best suited to encourage individual work and persistent practical activity among pupils, *initiative and originality among teachers*, and to foster in both *the spirit which leaves the beaten path and strikes fearlessly into new fields, which is the soul of education?* [my emphasis][36]

In this context, various means of in-service training were encouraged, such as vacation and weekend courses, guidance from local authority inspectors, peripatetic teachers to give demonstration lessons, and study circles organized by teachers themselves, or branch meetings of teachers' associations which would enable them to pool their experience.

Many new recruits to the teaching profession in the immediate post-war period came from the armed forces through emergency training and it may be argued that the work of agencies such as the Army Educational Corps and the Army Bureau of Current Affairs, in undertaking 'the greatest experiment ever conducted in mass adult education',[37] laid the foundations of a demand for further professional education. Moreover the Emergency Training Scheme included a two-year probationary period during which in-service courses were to be undertaken. Despite criticisms of the scheme, only 40 per cent of applicants were accepted, and an official account paid tribute to the quality of students.[38] This generation of teachers certainly created a much increased demand for in-service courses, and Dent (1977) has described the huge proliferation of short courses provided by LEAs, institutes of education and teachers' associations in the post-war years.[39]

Plowden had significant hopes for the effectiveness of in-service, associated with its model of the 'spear head' teacher. Every teacher should have a substantial period of in-service training at least every five years,

> giving teachers time to become familiar with new content and methods and to try out experiments ... the frontiersmen (sic) of education need opportunities to meet like-minded teachers, to test innovations by the practice of others, and to continue their personal education ... residential courses, where talk can go on into the small hours, have a value of their own.[40]

Phrases such as these, typical of progressive discourse, reveal a 'hidden curriculum' of in-service, a perception of the realities of ideological dissemination. They embody the spirit of 'fire-lighting' advocated by Sir Alec Clegg, a spirit reflected in accounts of HMI courses and the in-service activities of certain progressive LEAs. They also imply the setting up of 'networks' favoured by Marsh at Goldsmiths' and on the local authority level, for example, by Edith Moorhouse in Oxfordshire.

It was no doubt a mark of the increasing professionalism of primary teachers that two-thirds of those in the national survey for Plowden were found to have attended courses for an average of thirteen days between 1961 and 1964. Attitudes of teachers to INSET showed that 80 per cent of certificated teachers and 69 per cent of graduates thought there should be more INSET provision, though only 36 per cent of all teachers thought that courses on offer dealt with the aspects in which teachers needed most help. Assistant teachers were considerably more critical in this respect than heads, a significant fact, when, as we shall see below, heads were a key to professional development in progressive schools.[41]

The variety of in-service provision in the post-war period is daunting, and so is the lack of statistical and qualitative data, although the available information on this topic has been usefully collated by Eraut and Seaborne and Alexander, Craft and Lynch (1984).[42] Interpretation of such statistics as exist is complex, requiring consideration of the proportions of teachers involved and the length of individual courses. The largest number of teachers attended maths and PE courses, but art and craft accounted for the largest number of in-service days, whilst science, and general primary and infant courses ranked low. 'New maths' was recognized to have provided a considerable stimulus to in-service training, and the dominance of movement, and of art and craft, may partly reflect the bias of the progressive curriculum discussed in chapter 2 above. Cane's 1967 survey for the NFER of primary and secondary teachers showed that many believed in-service courses irrelevant to the harsh reality of classroom life, but more primary than secondary teachers were able to put into practice their experience from in-service courses:

> In-service training appeared to have had considerable impact in junior and infant schools, and involvement of teachers in the Nuffield maths project was particularly evident.[43]

Subject emphases were considered to reflect the nature of provision rather than teacher preference, and the uneven distribution of LEA advisers which was most prolific in PE, music, drama and art.

A survey by Townsend for the DES of the years 1964–67 showed LEAs as the largest provider of in-service courses. Plowden's tabulation of courses by sponsor showed that between 1961–64, for primary teachers, LEAs provided about 65 per cent, the DES 3 per cent, institutes of education 14 per cent and 'other' (including colleges and professional associations) nearly 18 per cent.[44]

Three principal modes of in-service will be considered briefly here, namely courses at institutes of education, the work of HMI, and LEA activities. The National Union of Teachers also made a significant contribution to in-service provision.

The new university institutes of education which were established after the McNair Report followed a variety of models. Thus the University of Birmingham Institute built its strength on research, inheriting the tradition established by C.W. Valentine (Head of the University Department of Education from 1919 to 1946) and continued by M.V.C. Jeffreys as Director of the Institute and F.J. Schonell as Head of the UDE. The research work, especially in remedial education, was so successful that by 1958 a Department of Child Study was established. By contrast, the University of Leeds Institute concentrated its early efforts on teaching, offering thirty-five short courses for teachers in cooperation with local education authorities; in 1948 were launched three diploma courses (one year full-time or two years part-time), one of which was for specialists in primary education, and much of the teaching in the Institute was shared between university staff and LEA advisers, schoolteachers, and college lecturers.[45]

Plowden referred to residential short courses as one of the main ways by which HMI had 'influenced the school curriculum and come into informal contact with teachers to their common benefit'.[46] Behind this dry phrase lay a significant process, frequently referred to by progressive teachers who had attended HMI residential courses. They recounted 'inspirational' and 'uplifting' experiences provided by HMI such as Christian Schiller and Robin Tanner. Beautiful country house locations, such as Dartington Hall, were deliberately chosen. A characteristic feature of such courses, noted with approval by Plowden, was the contribution of experts from outside the world of education, such as the potter Bernard Leach, or Phyllis Baron, the printer. The purpose of the courses was often primarily to extend the personal education of the individual teacher, and to provide activity and 'real experience' on an adult level, as a model that might later be translated into classroom practice. As examples of talks given, we have the published versions by Schiller and Blackie. Blackie spoke of the aim of Ministry courses as:

> initially disruptive. We try to pull ourselves out of the ruts which all of us, inevitably and naturally, inhabit, and expose ourselves to every wind that blows. However uncomfortable this may be at first, it is a stimulating experience and ultimately a rewarding one. Even if we return to our ruts, we do so with a better knowledge of where they lead....[47]

This realistic approach must however be tempered by the view that teachers on these courses were often far from being exposed 'to every wind that blows' but rather to a carefully contrived 'hothouse' of high culture.

The expansion of advisory services by LEAs was one aspect of the general drive to increase and improve in-service education. A singular feature of the post-war period was the establishment by LEAs of residential centres for adult education and in-service courses, such as the well-known Missenden Abbey in Buckinghamshire. Another noted example already referred to was Woolley Hall near Wakefield in the West Riding of Yorkshire. Woolley Hall had more than local significance, used as it was for national HMI courses, and a favourite location for in-service courses from Oxfordshire in particular. One can see in the establishment of Woolley, an embodiment of Clegg's progressive approach to education in general and to the teaching profession in particular; his memorandum of 1945 on the need for refresher courses stated:

> It is generally accepted that sound standards in education depend primarily on the quality of the teacher, and lack of inspiration is perhaps the chief obstacle to good work in the classroom.
>
> It follows, therefore, that the first concern, even in normal times, of an authority responsible for education in its area should be to select good teachers and to maintain their enthusiasm and technical proficiency.
>
> This task becomes many times more important today than in

> normal times because of the effect which the war has produced on the teaching profession.
>
> Many thousands of teachers are now tired after five or six years of work with large classes, with inadequate supplies, and with surroundings which of necessity have been allowed to grow dismal. The new Act demands many thousands of new teachers who, though they may as result of their war experience bring something new into the profession, cannot expect to be as well prepared for it as the pre-war trained teaches. In the immediate post-war period the training colleges, where limitations have been openly recognized by the McNair Report, will be overburdened before they can be reformed.
>
> It can hardly be denied, therefore, that the need for the continual training of new recruits and the refreshing and enlivening of older teachers will now be greater than ever before.

In defining the types of course required to meet post-war needs, Clegg pointed to the obvious need to bring teachers up to date in the latest methods of their subjects, but more important, he considered, was the need for a 'direct attack on their general sensibilities and breadth of outlook', which could only be effected by bringing in outside speakers from a range of fields, from industry to the theatre.

There were important considerations regarding the building to house these activities:

> One cannot hope for really good work as long as those attending the courses have to camp out in secondary schools ill equipped with boarding facilities....
>
> The object of the scheme would be the raising of standards and, therefore, the interior design and fitting of the place should be good. The building should house a library of recent school books, reference books and books on pedagogy. There should be a music room and the picture library would display the West Riding collection but in a better setting than the one in which it is now to be seen. A room should be equipped for demonstrating the newest optical aids to teaching, and there would be practical subject rooms. Part of the garden would be set out as a model school garden, and a model classroom should be included for demonstration classes.[48]

Shropshire County Council had its own centre in Attingham Park, a large country house. In a striking film produced under the title of *The Creative Spirit* by Mary Ellison, Primary Adviser, children from three different junior schools are seen on educational visits to Attingham Park enjoying activities which sought to integrate the expressive arts using the environment of the country house. In the final sequence, teachers come to Attingham Park and follow a similar course to that which the children have experienced. Like children, the commentary notes, the teachers are to learn by doing — they are to appreciate what it feels like, as well as learning skills. 'For every individual, child and adult', the film concludes, 'involvement in the creative arts is not something added on, it is at the core of the curriculum'.

Thornbury (1973) citing Cane's research on in-service for NFER in 1967 noted that the county residential centres continued to flourish, as a familiar feature of British in-service, but the trend was found to be towards shorter day courses, and local curriculum groups. The number of teachers' centres set up by LEAs expanded enormously in the 1960s to 270 in 1967, and 617 in 1972.[49] The Schools Council supported a model of teacher-directed in-service in its encouragement of teachers' centres. This model was advocated too by Plowden, recognizing the influence that teachers might have on each other. The increasing availability of personal transport in the post-war decades must be counted an important factor in changing the style of in-service activity, enabling teachers to attend meetings in local authority centres after school, and more easily to visit other schools to compare practice.

Some progressivists saw the the teacher's own school as an appropriate location for professional development. The four teachers studied by Cook and Mack were said to exhibit continual growth in their repertoire of professional abilities, and referred to the support and leadership of their headteachers as well as to the courses they had attended.

> Many factors contribute to the functioning of an integrated day: cultural patterns, historical processes, advisory bodies, development of materials, design of schools and administrative support, to mention a few. Yet, when analyzing the reasons why some schools seem to have developed and sustained the particular philosophy of education upon which the integrated day is based, it is difficult to avoid singling out the role of the headteacher.[50]

Thus Cook and Mack highlighted the critical role of the head. The heads whom they interviewed were from four selected LEAs (unspecified in the text). These, they stressed, were not typical, but were selected on the grounds of sharing a particular philosophy of education and acting to implement this philosophy in practice. Plowden had noted that headteachers were frequently unable to specify their objectives, but those interviewed were quite articulate, and paid more than lip-service to their beliefs, 'apparently shaping their definition of role from their strength as teachers in the classroom'. An interesting point to emerge was that they saw themselves, first and foremost, as teacher trainers — as supports for staff, as catalysts, as innovators, as educationists. All gave priority to their role in the classroom, alongside that of the teacher, subtly communicating style and philosophy.

In criticism of this process was a legitimate fear that school-based professional formation could lead to introversion. John Elliott and the Ford Teaching Project have latterly been at pains to develop INSET with a high degree of school-focus whilst preserving intellectual rigour. Successful school-based INSET

> challenges the capacity of a school's professional community to accommodate appraisals of its practice, to evaluate its own activities, to be open to new ideas, to enable cooperative and coordinated rather than privatized and random approaches to curriculum development.[51]

Although the 'third cycle' of training was given priority by the James Report, and was seen to comprehend a wide range of activities (the extension of personal education, the development of professional competence and the improved understanding of educational principles and techniques), the examples which it elaborated tended to a more pragmatic emphasis on new technology, books and equipment and developments in national and local policies such as first and middle school reorganisation. Research and observation in school, and collaboration with practising teachers was mentioned, but there was lacking the idealistic fervour of Hadow.[52] Progressivists have tended to lament an ever more instrumental view of in-service which has prevailed in the 1970s and 1980s.

The strongest influence on individual teachers was probably that of the school itself. An enthusiastic and strong-minded head, a tendency to recruit young teachers, extensive staff discussion, these were the means by which ethos and policy were created. The ideology was disseminated to individual teachers *within* the school. Taylor's research for the Schools Council showed the school itself to be perceived by teachers as the strongest influence on their practice.[53] The operation of informal communication was assumed in earlier documents, such as *Primary Education* of 1959, which expressed the view that:

> Because tradition is so strong, and because the process of education in this country has always been a slow evolution, not subject to sudden change, and *because teachers as a body are in close touch with each other and with others concerned in the education of children*, the curriculum is fundamentally the same in all primary schools ... (my emphasis)[54]

Yet Taylor's teachers rated the influence of 'other schools' as very low: 'the power of each individual school to influence what is taught is exercised independently of other schools ... an index of the autonomy of each and every primary school'.[55]

Notes

1 BOARD OF EDUCATION (1944) *Teachers and Youth Leaders*, London, HMSO, para. 170.
2 COOK, A. and MACK, H. (1971a) *The Teacher's Role* (British Primary Schools Today), London, Macmillan for the Schools Council, pp. 7–8.
3 DES (1967) *Children and Their Primary Schools*, London, HMSO, para. 1118.
4 DES (1974) *Statistics of Education Vol. 4 (Teachers)*, London, HMSO, pp. 4–5.
5 DES (1967) *op. cit.*, paras. 951, 1016, and Appendix 5, vol. 2 p. 227.
6 BREARLEY, M., GODDARD, N., BROWSE, B., and KALLET, T. (1972) *Educating Teachers* (British Primary Schools Today), London, Macmillan for the Schools Council, p. 11.
7 DYMOND, D. (Ed.) (1955) *The Forge:The History of Goldsmiths' College 1905–1955*, London, Methuen, p. 8.
8 (Ecclesiasticus XXXIX 28); *ibid*, p. [v].
9 CONS, G.J. and FLETCHER, C. (1938) *Actuality in Schools*, London, Methuen.
10 CATTY, N. (Ed.) (1921) *Training in Appreciation: Art, Literature, Music*, London, Sidgwick and Jackson.
11 CATTY, N. (1921) *A Study of Modern Educational Theory and its Applications*,London, Sidgwick and Jackson (dedicated to the Goldsmiths' College Old Students' Association).
12 UNIVERSITY OF LONDON, GOLDSMITHS' COLLEGE (1979) *Postgraduate Prospectus 1980/81*, London, Goldsmiths' College, p. 2.
13 HOUSE OF COMMONS SELECT COMMITTEE ON EDUCATION AND SCIENCE, *Teacher Training, Minutes of Evidence*, PP 1969–70 (135-iv) xi, 213.
14 PP 1969–70 (135-iv) xi, 214–6.
15 UNIVERSITY OF LONDON, GOLDSMITHS' COLLEGE (1974) *Prospectus for 1975/76*, London, Goldsmiths' College, p. 56.
16 MARSH, L. (1970) *Alongside the Child in the Primary School*, London, A and C. Black, pp. 40–1.
17 PP 1969–70 (135-iv) xi, 269–70
18 UNIVERSITY OF LONDON, GOLDSMITHS' COLLEGE (n.d) [1974] *The Changing School: A Challenge to the Teacher: Report of a One-day Conference*, London, Goldsmiths' College.
19 BLENKIN, G.M. and KELLY, A.V. (1981) *The Primary Curriculum*, London, Harper and Row.
20 ROBINSON, P. (1971) 'Ideology in teacher education', unpublished MSc (Econ) thesis, University of London, Institute of Education.
21 BLISHEN, E. (1980) *A Nest of Teachers*, London, Hamish Hamilton, p. 43. A 'Dr.Moss' taught psychology, representing 'English empiricism at its most apoplectic, and belittling such theorists as Freud and Piaget. On Blishen's Emergency Training Course, philosophy and psychology were laid low. Essentially they were foreign products, and they were dealt with accordingly in many a lecture'.
22 *Times Educational Supplement*, 10 April 1959, p. 605.
23 NUT (1967) *Annual Report*, London, NUT, p. 45.
24 JARMAN, C. (1972) *Display and Presentation in School*, London, A. and C. Black, p. 19.
25 WALKERDINE, V. (1984) 'Developmental psychology and the child-centred pedagogy: The insertion of Piaget into early education' in HENRIQUES, J. and others (Eds) *Changing the Subject: Psychology, Social Regulation and Subjectivity*, London, Methuen, p. 190.
26 ISAACS, N. (n.d) (1965) *Piaget: Some Answers to Teachers' Questions*, London, National Froebel Foundation.
27 ISAACS, N. (1955) *Some Aspects of Piaget's Work*, London, National Froebel Foundation. A more straightforward text was ISAACS, N. (1961) *The Growth of Understanding in the Young Child: A Brief Introduction to Piaget's Work*, London, Educational Supply Association, which went through seven impressions to 1968.

28 Brearley, M. and Hitchfield, E. (1966) *A Teacher's Guide to Reading Piaget*, London, Routledge and Kegan Paul. Quotation from *Teachers' World* on dust-jacket. This book, and Isaacs, N. (1955) were recommended to students by Marsh, L. (1970).
29 Brearley, M. and Hitchfield, E. (1966) *op. cit.*, p. ix.
30 Beard, R. (1969) *An Outline of Piaget's Developmental Psychology for Students and Teachers* (Students Library of Education), London, Routledge and Kegan Paul.
31 Beard, R. (1969) *op. cit.*, p. xv.
32 Brearley, M. and Hitchfield, E. (1966) *op. cit.*, p. 2.
33 Donaldson, M. (1978) *Children's Minds*, London, Fontana.
34 Brearley, M., Goddard, N., Browse, B., and Kallet, T. (1972) *op. cit.*
35 Board of Education (1931) *Report of the Consultative Committee on the Primary School*, London, HMSO, p. xxvii.
36 *ibid.*, p. xiv.
37 Curtis, S.J. (1967) *History of Education in Great Britain*, London, University Tutorial Press, p. 604.
38 Ministry of Education (1950) *Challenge and Response* (Ministry of Education Pamphlet no. 17), London, HMSO.
39 Dent, H.C. (1977) *The Training of Teachers in England and Wales 1800–1975*, London, Hodder and Sroughton, p. 132.
40 DES (1967) *Children and Their Primary Schools*, London, HMSO, paras. 1017, 1018 and 1020.
41 DES (1967) *ibid*, App. 5 para. 15, tables E25 and E26.
42 Alexander, R., Craft, M. and Lynch, J. (Eds) (1984) *Change in Teacher Education*, London, Holt, Rinehart & Winston. See also Alexander, R. and Ellis J.W. (Eds) (1981) *Advanced Study for Teachers*, Guildford, SRHE.
43 Quoted in Thornbury, R.E. (Ed.) (1973) *Teachers' Centres*, London, Darton Longman Todd, p. 11.
44 DES (1967) *op. cit.*, Appendix 5, Table 20.
45 Dent, H.C. (1977) *op. cit.*, pp. 118–119.
46 DES (1967) *op. cit.*, para. 1018.
47 Blackie, J. (1963) *op. cit.*, p. 59.
48 WREC Papers, Brotherton Library, University of Leeds MS 731 Box 2 G1: Sub-Committee: Post-War Education 16 October 1945, Agendum 4, Memorandum.
49 Thornbury, R.E. (Ed.) (1973) *op. cit.*, p. 3.
50 Cook, A. and Mack, H. (1971b) *The Headteacher's Role* (British Primary Schools Today), London, Macmillan for the Schools Council, p. 7.
51 Alexander, R. and Ellis, J.W. (Eds) (1981) *op. cit.*, p. xi,
52 DES (1972) *Teacher Education and Training*, London, HMSO, paras. 2.2, 2.7, 2.11 and 2.16.
53 Taylor, P.H. *et al.* (1974) *Purpose, Power and Constraint in the Primary School Curriculum*, London, Macmillan/Schools Council, p. 13.
54 Ministry of Education (1959) *Primary Education*, London, HMSO, p. 114.
55 Taylor, P.H. *et al.*, (1974) *op. cit.*, p. 13.

5 *Professional Organizations and Media*

Closely related to the increasing professionalization of primary school teachers through their initial and in-service education and training was the growth of professional organizations as vehicles for the transmission of ideas and practices. Some, such as the National Union of Teachers (founded in 1870), and the National Froebel Union (founded in 1873), had existed from the later nineteenth century, but their role continued to change and develop in the post-war period. A newer society which contributed significantly to the diffusion of one aspect of progressive practice was the School Library Association (founded in 1937). A more formal organization supported by government funding, was the Schools Council (founded in 1964). All these are described below as examples, and not as a comprehensive survey; societies of much more recent origin, such as the National Association for Primary Education and the Undergraduate Primary Teacher Education Conference reflect continuing change in professional circumstances.

Also indicative of changing circumstances in the post-war era was the role of the professional press and other media, such as the work of the Schools Broadcasting Service, and the widespread use of film.

National Union of Teachers

At its annual conference in 1944, the Union adopted a programme of educational developments in line with its sense of stature as a professional body able to make contributions to educational thought and practice, and to its professed concern with the welfare of children in schools. Its Executive claimed a tradition of high idealism in education, helping to foster public opinion favourable to education, pressing for improved conditions and pioneering progress, so that by 1944 they considered it to hold a position of 'prestige and power in the life of the nation'. Resolutions had been passed at annual conferences before the war calling for the establishment of a research and educational bureau, and the question as the Executive saw it was:

> What modification can be made in the Union machinery to enable it to undertake educational work closely associated with the actual professional duties of the teacher?[1]

Implementation of this policy included the appointment of *ad hoc* consultative committees to which important questions of educational policy could be referred, the appointment of qualified research workers for research into educational problems, an information bureau to assemble and disseminate curriculum materials, audio-visual aids, and educational information, and refresher courses for members. In respect of professional development other important activities included sectional conferences, and the activities of the Education Committee together with its advisory committees.

Whilst the NUT was not explicitly committed to progressive ideals as part of its policy, its activities were important in increasing the sense of professionalism amongst teachers and allowing for the exchange of ideas and experience. Some who were young teachers in primary schools striving to develop their own practice along progressive lines have testified to the usefulness of Union activities in this respect. Documentary evidence is found in annual reports, in the pages of the *Schoolmaster and Woman Teacher* and in a variety of miscellaneous publications produced by the Union.

The circulation of information was important. In the case of primary school practice, two notable examples may be mentioned. In 1951 the Ministry's first *Building Bulletin* on primary schools was sent by the NUT to all county and local associations, drawing attention in particular to the arguments for teacher consultation contained therein, and on the basis of responses from some local associations, the Executive made representations to the Ministry of Education.[2] When the *Sunday Times Colour Magazine* published a feature on primary education in the autumn of 1963, the Union obtained extra copies and circulated them to local associations, offering up to a maximum of 250 copies per association if required for local publicity purposes, suggesting that copies should be passed on to

> local personalities who are concerned with education, officials of women's organizations and others likely to be interested in learning more about primary education.[3]

A programme of refresher courses began in 1948 when two national residential summer schools were held at Durham, with courses in infant, junior and secondary education, and at Exeter, where the topics offered were visual aids, drama and the teaching of backward children. No tuition fees were charged, the cost of tuition being met from central funds. Such was the success that in the following year five courses were planned at Ashridge, Herts., Brighton, Jersey, Leicester and Oxford. Some were to be concerned with particular subjects and some planned on broader lines and concerned with 'the general cultural education appropriate to teachers'. Thus a nine-day school at Brighton Training College dealt with 'The primary school', with two self-contained courses, one on 'Activity' and one on 'Backwardness', whilst that at Victoria College, Jersey, was to have sections for all stages of schooling. At Jesus College, Oxford, where eighty-nine people attended, the theme was 'Education and the individual child'; Sir Cyril Burt had a hand in the planning and lectures were given by leading educationists on topics such as 'Individual differences in children and their relation to school progress', 'The personality of the individual child' and 'The changing form of individualism'. In 1951, one of the summer schools was held abroad, setting a pattern that was to be followed in later years, although an exception was one at Brighton Training College which dealt with 'modern trends in the primary school' with special reference to the teaching of maths and science and to the development of school libraries.

A further opportunity for the dissemination of specialist views existed in the form of national sectional conferences, which were first held experimentally in the Christmas vacation of 1950/51. These concerned themselves partly with strategic issues. Arising out of the meeting in December 1953, for example, the Education Committee of the Union considered the overall question of 'the status of the primary school' in regard to class size, shortage of equipment, lack of teaching space and unsatisfactory school buildings, and it was proposed to run a series of articles in the *Schoolmaster* on these points. Status and resources are not to be entirely separated from the ideals of progressivism; whilst progressivists may have concentrated on questions of curriculum and teaching method, these could not be improved on a wide scale without better conditions and equipment, and in campaigning on these issues, as the Union did especially in the later 1950s and early 1960s, professional awareness of ideal practice was heightened and the potential of what the best primary education might offer was brought to the attention of a wider public.

In 1960 *The Schoolmaster* paid tribute to the sectional conferences as a firmly established 'educational workshop' in which teachers, having survived one of the most exhausting periods of the school year with its Nativity plays, parties and carol concerts, stirred themselves from their post-Christmas mental coma, to exert their professionalism:

> Those who talk lightheartedly about 'long holidays' in teaching might well reflect how many teachers give up their time to this sort of work, which, in our rapidly changing world, is an essential complement to the daily round of the classroom.[4]

In 1965 all sections were addressed at a joint open meeting by J.W.B. Douglas on the investigations of his medical research unit into the relationship between ability and educational opportunity.

The Primary Schools Advisory Committee reported to the Education Committee of the Union. It assisted in drafting the pamphlet *Fair Play for Primary Schools*, published in 1960. The Advisory Committee continued to make an important contribution to Union policy-making with regard to primary schools, as in 1964 when it assisted in collecting evidence for presentation to the Plowden Committee, published by the Union in pamphlet form under the title *First Things First*, or in pressing the Executive for a deputation to the Secretary of State which demanded *inter alia* that future primary school buildings should allow for improvements in staffing ratios and for the adoption of 'new teaching techniques'.

The Union's programme of educational development included the appointment of *ad hoc* Consultative committees to be comprised of members of the Union having the required knowledge and experience in regard to the topic under review. The first of these committees was appointed in June 1946 to examine the question of transference of children from the primary to the secondary stage, and its substantial report with extensive appendices, backed up with evidence or assistance from 118 local authorities and from most of the leading researchers of the day in educational psychology, was published in April 1949.[5]

Two particular concerns, highlighted amongst the recommendations, were that a child should have the kind of secondary education desired by his parents, and that the primary school teacher should be left free to serve the educational needs of pupils. The report recognized the danger that the school curriculum might become preoccupied with English and arithmetic to the detriment of other parts of the curriculum, and that these subjects themselves might be based on drill in for the examination paper or test. Concerning teaching methods in the primary school, it was noted:

> Whatever may be said in favour of adapting education at later stages to the after-career of the pupil, we are clear that the primary school should be left completely free to concentrate its attention on the immediate educational needs of its pupils. Especially during the last years in the primary school, the manner of learning is more important than the amount of factual knowledge acquired. Children learn by experience at the age suited to their capacity and not according to a time schedule prescribed by authority. They need time to learn to live, socially and joyfully, moving about among their fellows without embarrassment or restraint. They should learn also to trust themselves and their own ability to discover rather than to absorb

> passively what the teacher teaches. These things are possible only in circumstances of freedom — freedom of the child, and freedom of the teacher of serve the needs of his pupil. It is in these respects that the work of the primary school will suffer most from imposed haste and external constraint.[6]

In 1946 another Consultative Committee was established, to consider the 'aims, practices and achievements' of nursery-infant education, and this too reported in 1949.[7] Chaired by Lillian de Lissa, former Principal of Gipsy Hill Training College, a prominent advocate of the kindergarten movement and member of the New Ideals in Education conference, it was perhaps destined to produce a 'progressive' report and its twenty-one recommendations exhibit an approach to classroom practice which advocated team work 'in the interests of the children', the creation of a pleasant environment (good pictures to be available on loan from LEAs and wider choice of colours for interior decoration), as well as opportunity for serious professional development of teachers through refresher courses, visits to other schools and even sabbaticals. Professional opinion was widely drawn upon through 1000 questionnaires from infants' teachers distributed by advertising in the educational press and through the Union. The published document was in itself an instructive guide: it reproduced sixteen photographs from many submitted by teachers, a most important means of communication and inspiration where classroom practice and the classroom environment was concerned.

Ten years later, another NUT Consultative Committee reported on the curriculum of the junior school.[8] Charmingly acknowledged in the foreword was

> the help of an anonymous and composite little contributor who will probably never read the report, but whose evidence, unknown to him, we have tried to consult and respect throughout — the junior school child.

The declared aim of the Report was to stress two principles especially: the value of learning through direct experience, and the need to give children access to excellence 'in all the rich implications of the phrase', or, in another context, that learning should 'follow the growing maturity of the child' but should also be 'purposive'.[9]

The atmosphere of the school had radically changed:

> There is no part of junior school life that has changed more radically during the last thirty years than the relations of teacher and pupil. Parents often comment on the natural way children now approach their teachers, consulting them and feeling confident of their interest. This change is even sometimes misunderstood by the public, to whom the quasi-military regime of old

> times seems the only way to run a school and who do not realize that the discipline of the modern junior school is based on a respect for the staff so secure that a degree of informality and freedom is indeed desirable.

The proof of this change, the Report argued, lay in the absence of truancy as a social problem.[10] It was acknowledged that the freedom of the junior school had only latterly been learned from the good practice of the infant schools, but its philosophical basis was seen to lie in the individualism advocated by Percy Nunn, whose classic work of 1920 had been reprinted ten times in a decade, and whose values had been reflected in the Hadow Reports of 1931 and 1933 in their child-centredness and their reaction against conventional mass instruction. Some form of streaming, however, was thought to be advisable in the circumstances of restricted staffing and accommodation, although 'its channels should not be deeply or permanently dug' for it noted the recent psychological research casting doubt on the principle of classification on intellectual grounds.[11] The importance of a school's links with home and community were stressed. As far as teaching method was concerned, however, the report deplored a negative and wasteful divergence that seemed to range teachers and schools into two irreconcilable camps under the banners of 'formal' or 'subject-centred' teaching and 'activity' or 'child-centred' teaching (how modern this dichotomy sounds!). Certainly the process of maturing was a more acceptable notion than preparation for maturity, but the practice of skills was also necessary for 'mastery and subsequent economy of effort', so the answer lay in a judicious blend of drill and Dewey.[12]

Appointed in 1953, the Committee was chaired by Dorothy Dymond, a former lecturer in history at Goldsmiths' College and Principal of the City of Portsmouth Training College. Secretary to the Committee was E.S. Owen, MA, LLB, Head of a Worcestershire primary school and a man of high academic and professional standing, who may well have had contact with Schiller and Clegg.[13] Of the ten other Committee members, one only was from a training college, the others being all from primary schools, and none of the well-known 'progressive' authorities such as the West Riding or Oxfordshire was represented either amongst the Committee or in the list of forty-two individuals who submitted evidence.

The Union's weekly newspaper *Schoolmaster and Woman Teacher's Chronicle* (from 1964 renamed *The Teacher*), had wide readership in the 1960s (nearly 30 per cent of primary school teachers according to one market survey in 1969). It offered a spectrum of opinion within the Union, but of course the innovatory was more newsworthy, and Union activists were more likely to be on the side of progressivism. Reporting on the annual North of England conference in January 1960, an address on 'Trends in primary education' by Dr. A. Hay (Chief Inspector for the LCC) was given several column inches:

> Primary education ... is on the move'. The rate of movement was not uniform in all schools, ... but 'light is coming' and emphasis was changing from class teaching to active learning ... animated conversation and active participation was replacing formal teaching and passive reception. The project and other free methods created work which was both 'intense and first hand'. It spread to leisure time and the children became personally and closely involved. He had found primary schools using these new methods 'very happy places'. The children were at ease with strangers and possessed a natural and spontaneous confidence generated by the changed attitude of the teacher towards them and their mistakes.
>
> Such an approach gave scope to all children. The abler pupils were by no means overlooked.... There were ten-year-olds in Fulham using logarithms. Free writing had unlimited opportunities while the school was becoming more and more to be regarded as the base rather than the barracks. But he was well aware of the difficulties involved.[14]

Rather less space was devoted to the head of a Liverpool primary school who thought that 'the theory of play' did not match up to 'the theory of work':

> 'I think it is time that instead of laying so much emphasis on methods we should realize that different teachers have different methods provided they produce the results. I think some of us teaching old-fashioned methods have just as much courage as those who teach by the newer methods.' To judge from her reception many delegates had similar ideas.

The NUT's own sectional conferences were reported in the same issue. Points raised included parity of status and salary for primary teachers, and acknowledgement of the importance of the primary stage, especially in the shadow of the CACE Crowther Report on 15-18-year-olds, recently published. But R.E Wilkinson, a member of the National Executive and of the Primary School Advisory Committee, had told the meeting that:

> the primary schools had achieved a remarkable revolution in the last thirty years. There had been a colossal expansion of PE, swimming, dancing and athletics. Needlework had been transformed, and a whole range of crafts introduced. Visual aids, sound broadcasting, tape recorders, reference libraries, and 'centres of interest' had encouraged children to learn for themselves. New concepts of art teaching and musical education, school visits, open days and sports days had enabled the primary schools to send on children who were self reliant and independent.

J.S. Flavell (NUT member from Birmingham) had been invited by the Primary Schools Advisory Committee to prepare a paper on the teaching of mathematics in the primary school, a 'quite revolutionary and controversial document' which was to be printed for circulation to local and county associations for discussion; he had commended to the conference a realistic re-evaluation of the junior school curriculum;

> the aim in the primary school should be the stimulation of thought rather than the accumulation of facts. The junior school was crying out for a bold and imaginative lead.[15]

Within the same month appeared articles and news of practical application: a series on the organisation of small group work in primary PE, including use of apparatus, an account of a farming project for juniors, and the beginning of a series on 'Science in action', which incorporated the publication of work cards for children of different ages and abilities. Characteristic of later developments was the NUT publication of a new journal *Primary Education Review*, from 1976, which will be considered further in chapter 9.

National Froebel Foundation

The received wisdom in much progressivist discourse was that informality and child-centredness in the primary school filtered up from the infant school and the kindergarten. The National Froebel Foundation was a principal agent in this. The Froebel movement in England, though somewhat neglected in Selleck's account of early twentieth century progressivism, continued both before and after the Second World War to exert a powerful influence on the adoption of progressive ideals and practice in the primary sector. It did so in a variety of ways through initial training, through in-service activities, and through its publications.

W.H. Herford, one of his foremost English advocates, and author of *The School: An Essay Towards Humane Education* (1889), summed up Froebel's principles and method in two sentences: 'The end of education is harmonious development' and 'Learn by doing'. He added:

> Never, if you can help it, deprive the child of the sacred right of discovery.[16]

Froebel's principles, and the kindergarten movement which applied them, early gained respectability and official recognition, partly through the mediation of Alfred Bourne, Superintendent of the British and Foreign School Society's three metropolitan colleges, and through the sympathetic response of A.J. Mundella, Cabinet Minister with responsibility for education 1880–85. The Code of 1892 accepted the Froebel Certificate as a teaching qualification, and in 1904 the National Froebel Union was formed in accordance with a scheme drawn up by the Board of Education. By 1939 the governors of the NFU had assumed responsibility for training, in several recognized colleges, as well as for examining, and an increasing number of qualified teachers were seeking a Froebel teacher's certificate as a further qualification.[17]

There were acknowledged dangers in Froebel's approach. One, worthy of notice as it anticipates so closely the dangers remarked and too often realized in the adoption of 'progressivism' by primary schools since 1945, was the risk, noted by Charlotte Mason, that Froebel's 'gifts' and 'occupations' could easily become mechanical and might be adopted by teachers who lacked understanding of the spirit behind them. Others were that Froebelians were apt to ignore the distinction between work and play, and that the acquisition of reading and writing were postponed to an unnecessarily late period.

On the other hand a great strength of the movement lay in the adaptability of many of the English followers of Froebel. Eglantyne Mary Jebb, Principal of the Froebel Institute from 1932 to 1955, continuing as Chair of the National Froebel Foundation, pointed out in 1958 that modern Froebel colleges no longer subscribed to the teaching techniques of Friedrich Froebel, but followed his precept and example in insistence on close observation of children's growth and their natural ways of learning, and on making full use of modern psychology and research in child development.[18] This adaptability led to various fruitful associations with the Child Study Association, the School Nature Study Union, the New Education Fellowship and the Nursery Schools Association.

Reconstituted as the National Froebel Foundation in 1938, the organization found itself at the end of the war in a position of strength, with its associated training colleges, the Froebel certificate recognized in 1945 for qualified teacher status, a national bulletin, a network of local associations, and above all an openness to continuing scientific study of children and learning. Apart from the formal provision of initial and in-service qualifications, the National Froebel Foundation performed an important service for teachers, disseminating and reinforcing Froebelian ideals through its programme of meetings and activities. The task of advising on courses of lectures, summer schools, publications and public relations was delegated by the governing body to an Education Committee.[19]

To accompany the Festival of Britain, an exhibition was planned, to be held at King's College in the Strand. For twelve days at the end of August the large hall was to be divided into bays displaying material for use with backward readers, school libraries, a nature study corner, a music corner, and improvized play materials made from waste. In addition smaller rooms would be available in which the committee proposed to have; 'infant and junior classrooms showing furniture, material arrangements and children's work which might be found in a progressive school'. Stewards would be on hand to explain the exhibits, and an explanatory booklet would be available. It was also proposed to have some specialist lectures on different sections of the exhibition, but significantly a later Committee meeting decided that exhibitors themselves should lecture on their work; many schools were willing to contribute, but the names of exhibitors would not be shown.

'Tea discussion meetings' were held by the Foundation in the early 1950s, and on several occasions the College of Preceptors provided the location.[20] The topic for 1953 for example was handwriting, and Christian Schiller was consulted on possible speakers. Beginning with the celebration of the Froebel Centenary, the Foundation held an open meeting at the Conference of Educational Associations; in subsequent years a variety of guest speakers were invited, including James Hemming (the humanist, who gave evidence to the Plowden Committee) on 'Civilizing the comic' in 1955, and Marjorie Reeves of St. Anne's College, Oxford in 1957 on 'The concepts work and play in education'.

In 1958 Mr. Farnham of Goldsmiths' College agreed to speak on the scientific interests of children up to the age of 12. In planning the open meeting for 1962, the Committee considered four possibilities: Dr. Grey Walter had been approached to talk on his neurophysiological work but being ill was unable to accept, so a list of alternatives was drawn up to include: Dr. Jack Tizard of the Maudsley Hospital on his work with ESN children, Mr. C.E.G. Bailey on 'problems of space flight and the sort of understanding which the teacher must have to meet the needs of modern children', and Mr. J.M. Branson, an adviser in Essex, keenly interested in Piaget, to speak on science.[21] Progressivism was thus seen addressing itself both to the rapidly developing medical science of education and to the scientific needs of the modern world.

Three categories of Froebel publications appear to have played an important part in the dissemination of progressivism: the bulletin, bibliographies and pamphlets. The *National Froebel Foundation Bulletin*, a successor to the journal *Child Life*, which had appeared since the 1890s, was published six times a year in the 1950s. It offered short articles, book reviews, news of courses, practical hints and advertisements for posts vacant. A Committee discussion in 1950 referred to pressure on space in the Bulletin, which was described by implication as a journal of 'scientific standing'. Some years later, however, Miss Jebb reported the view that there was little of interest for students in its pages, and it was agreed to seek 'accounts of investigations or mild research' (sic) undertaken by individual students or student groups, tutors being asked to notify the Foundation of any such. Articles from former students should also be invited, the National Foundation of Parent-Teacher Associations might be asked for someone to write about parent-teacher cooperation, and a series of articles on handicapped children was suggested.[22] In the year of

Miss Jebb's comment, Bulletin no. 105 (April 1957) included Nancy Catty on 'The childhood of famous people: Dame Laura Knight', P. Woodham Smith on the history of the Foundation's premises in Manchester Square, and P.M. Pickard with 'Some personal observations' of an International Study Conference of the Association for Childhood in Washington, D.C. — anecdotal and not concerned with educational issues. However, a number of children's books and school books were reviewed. A summer holiday course was announced on 'Children and the world around them' at the Crescent School, Oxford; the study plan would be as for children, investigating, collecting and recording in infant and junior classrooms. Other weekend courses advertized included 'Creative art' in Bolton, 'Reading in the infant and junior schools' and 'Ragbag puppetry and masks' in London.[23] Thereafter, the standard of contents rose somewhat, with short articles on child psychology, Piaget, children and television, the primary school and the space age, children's books and school libraries.

In 1965, Alice Murton, Honorary Director of the National Froebel Foundation, became Editor of the retitled *Froebel Journal* (three issues per annum), and the contents became more substantial, with articles by Alec Clegg on 'Half our future', an account of the NFF evidence submitted to the Plowden Committee, and a report on an investigation into practical science activities in the primary school undertaken by the NFF with the support of the British Association for the Advancement of Science. A foreword by E.M. Jebb looked back at the work of the Foundation, its increasing recognition by the Ministry of Education and by the public; she noted that a social and educational revolution had taken place over the previous twenty years such that, for example, the pioneering three-year training course had now become standard, and the examining functions of the NFF had been taken over by the institutes of education. The Foundation's work now lay, she wrote, in conducting a dialogue between teachers on the curriculum and function of the primary school. Contributors to the journal in the 1960s included names such as Christian Schiller, John Blackie and Robin Tanner (all retired HMIs), the West Riding adviser I.R. Milne, Dorothy Gardner of the London Institute, and three Oxfordshire advisers, Edith Moorhouse, Christopher Jarman and Leslie Bennett.

The Froebel Foundation also published pamphlets, clearly written and well produced, which contributed to the dissemination of progressivism.[20] College tutors of the period have testified to their popularity, as indeed does the impressive printing history of many titles in the series. Harassed students and busy teachers welcomed the brevity of a pamphlet in contrast to the length of a book. The series covered theoretical (at least Piagetian!) as well as practical aspects of teaching; the majority of titles were aimed at immediate usefulness to the teacher in the classroom, but within the text a useful balance was maintained, relating practice to theoretical principles. *Scientific Interests in the Primary School*, for example, by Gwen Allen and others, contained a wealth of references to sources: a substantial list of books, visual aids and useful addresses. It dealt with the scientific interests of the under-8s, then with the junior stage, where five possible topics were described: magnets; the sea; air and flight; weather; and building a house, and materials for an investigation table were suggested. The authors then went on to describe some experiences in developing scientific interest in a Hertfordshire school, including visits to observe life beyond the classroom, not only workmen in the road and farm tractors, but the school cook and the caretaker too could be watched at work. But for all this intensely practical advice, the pamphlet ended with the necessity for reflection, and twelve questions to ask ourselves as teachers:

> Am I in touch with children's real interests? To what extent do we share, enjoy and explore together?

was the first question, whilst the last was whether we keep in mind the following statement from A.N. Whitehead?

> When you understand all about the sun and all about the atmosphere and all about the rotation of the earth, you may still miss the radiance of the sunset.

An indication of the way in which the Foundation kept up with new ideas, and helped to keep teachers abreast of them too, lies in the two pamphlets on number and on mathematics. In 1954 Molly Brearley wrote *Number in the Primary School* which expounded principles such as orderly development and acknowledging the rate of children's own learning. This pamphlet went through a number of editions until it was succeeded in 1965 by Margaret Ironside and Sheila Roberts' *Mathematics in the Primary School*. The text of the latter is significant as implying that 'theory' was now *leading* 'practice'. Since Miss Brearley's pamphlet had first been published, they argued, there had accumulated more knowledge and understanding of ways in which young children approach mathematics, though the application of such knowledge in the classroom had yet to be fully worked out; they aimed to consider 'the discoveries which are occupying the attention of teachers' and to point to some of the ways in which classroom procedure could be based on this knowledge. They felt that the shift from 'number' and 'arithmetic' to 'mathematics' reflected a growing awareness of the importance of mathematical ideas and relationships over computational skills. A suggested booklist included a dose of Piaget for teachers (including the recent *Child's Conception of Geometry*), and for children quite a number of titles on the *history* of mathematics.

It is perhaps evidence of the increasing professionalism of primary teachers, as well as of the expanding volume of research available, that good bibliographies were in demand. In March 1957 the Education

Committee agreed the publication of a book list 'arranged to cover definite fields of study and to include the most up-to-date textbooks in those fields'.

School Library Association

An important feature of progressivism was the attitude to books in the primary school. W.O. Lester Smith, professor of sociology of education at the London Institute, pointed out how archaic and obsolete attitudes persisted even when obviously wrong:

> One of the oddest prejudices about elementary schools was the belief that the children who attended them did not need books. Grammar schools were provided with libraries ... but it was usual to assume that all an elementary school needed in the way of books was a supply of readers appropriate to each 'standard'.[25]

This observation was made in Lester Smith's capacity as President of the School Library Association in 1958. In 1937 the Association had been founded with a largely public school and grammar school membership, but in the years after 1945 its journal reflected an increasing interest from the primary schools. In the *School Librarian* for 1948, Dorothy Davis wrote on school libraries for infants' and primary schools, and in 1951 M.V. Daniel, Principal of Hertford Training College, and author of the important progressive textbook *Activity in the Primary School* (1947), contributed an article on libraries in relation to education in the primary school.[26]

To some extent these developments followed changes in publishing generally; an expansion of cheaply available literature for adults, for example, occurred through the work of Penguin Books and the introduction of paperbacks in the 1930s. A growing interest in literature for young children was reflected in the work of the National Book League which published a recommended list of titles for children aged 4 to 14 in 1950, and of the public libraries, for instance their publication in 1952 of lists of books for children under 11.[27] The Ministry of Education maintained a collection of books for primary school libraries which could be consulted at the Ministry when not in use on courses, but whereas building regulations insisted on library rooms for all new secondary schools, no such requirement was laid down for primary schools. It had been a founding principle of the School Library Association that:

> children need an environment of attractive books from the beginning; and it is one of the first duties of the school to see that this environment is created.[24]

In November 1952 the Association held a small informal conference at its headquarters in Gordon House, London, at which the school representatives were mostly from London primary schools. From teacher training there was a substantial Froebel presence, with Barbara Rapaport speaking on the way modern teaching methods required a generous supply of books based on a recognition of the variety of individual needs and on the principle of giving children responsibility for their own work, and Elsa Walters describing the rapid development of children in the junior age range and their active approach to learning arising from natural curiosity and energy. Lilian Pierotti, Principal of Bedford Training College, was also to have been an delegate.[29]

Following the 1952 conference, a Sub-committee for Primary Schools was established, and two major reports followed, one on primary school libraries, in 1958, and another on using books in the primary school, in 1962. Sub-committee members at the time of the latter publication included Edith Moorhouse, County Senior Adviser for Primary Schools in Oxfordshire, and John Gagg, who had begun his advisory career in Oxfordshire, and proceeded to be County Adviser for Primary Education in Shropshire. The report was based on 'creative use of books' by more than seventy teachers, as it was concerned not to stand as simply 'theoretical prescription, or one person's experiences or opinions'; although these six dozen individual schools were widely spread about the country, it is perhaps not insignificant that an appendix giving an overall picture of four schools reflected some of the heartlands of progressivism: Hertfordshire, Sussex, Nottingham, and Oxfordshire.

Schools Council

Historical analysis of the Schools Council as an agency of curriculum development from 1964 to 1983 has yet to be made.[30] Here was a site in which the continuing contest for curriculum control was played out in institutional terms, and in a social and political context of rapid change. On the one hand teachers wrested from the Ministry's grasp an attempt by politicians and administrators to invade 'the secret garden of the curriculum' (as the Minister, David Eccles, had described it). On the other hand it may be said that the professional curriculum developers then squandered an opportunity to establish effective communication, not only with members of their own profession, but more crucially with the public at a time when the school curriculum became increasingly a subject for curriculum debate.

The Council aroused strong feelings both for and against its work. Progressivists in the Schiller mould seem to have disliked the large-scale bureaucratic enterprise which conflicted with their own ideal of more select informal networks and 'fostering chosen growing points'. But

Wragg took a broader view of a lost opportunity, describing the fate of the Schools Council as one of the saddest histories of any curriculum development agency.

> Alongside the Nuffield foundation in the 1960s it exerted enormous influence on the theory and practice of teaching and some of the country's most gifted teachers were seconded to a vast array of projects . . . by 1982 its obituary was being written. It was a shabby chapter in curriculum history which showed how aggressive politicians and civil servants and one or two silly Council members could obscure twenty years of largely good and imaginative work. In my view the Schools Council pioneered some of the best ideas ever adopted in Britain, or anywhere else for that matter.[31]

Publications by the Schools Council do not suggest a forum in which the tenets of progressivism were universally or unquestioningly accepted. On the one hand, Alec Clegg's contribution to the Third International Curriculum Conference, reported by Maclure in *Curriculum Innovation and Practice* (1968), stood out prominently for his faith in teachers and in communication between teachers, a process of 'fire-lighting' rather than of 'pot-filling'. He dismissed the high-powered thinkers who sought to contrive and foist curricula on the schools, preferring the teacher's judgment in assessing the individual child and its circumstances.[32] On the other hand, in working paper no. 22 (1969) on *The Middle Years of Schooling, 8–13* P.H. Taylor vented his less than enthusiastic response to some underlying principles of Plowden, including the alleged advantages of 'discovery' and 'exploration' methods of learning, although Alec Ross's summary to this paper tried to reconcile child-centredness with the demands of secondary school and 16+ exams.[33]

The Council itself was a great advocate of teacher-directed curriculum development through the medium of teachers' centres, one of its main objects being:

> to uphold and interpret the principle that each school should have the fullest possible measure of responsibility for its own work, with its own curriculum and teaching methods based on the needs of its own pupils and evolved by its own staff.[34]

The Birmingham teachers questioned by Taylor (1974) considered the Council marginally less influential on their classroom teaching than the national press. Preparation of a primary programme was deliberately deferred until the publication of Plowden, and its research and development projects in the first three years were largely concerned with maths, science and French. £2000 went to a project on parent-teacher cooperation, and £15,000 to the University of Birmingham for a study of the aims of primary education by Taylor and others already cited above, and this was against a total of £165,000 for primary school projects overall, although another £66,000 was spent by the Welsh Committee on a study of compensatory education for disadvantaged pupils aged 5–8.[35] Later came influential projects such as those on language by the Rosens and by Joan Tough.[36]

The Council exploited film as a medium of dissemination. One production, entitled *Mathematics and Living*, encouraged a change from the disembodied practice of computational skills to the exploration of real situations in which the skills might be applied. This was an account of the work pioneered by Edith Biggs, considered an important influence by many progressivists, as mathematics was a specific subject in which new approaches to learning were easily demonstrable and rationalized, and in-service courses on mathematics attracted large numbers of teachers.[37]

Propaganda in the dissemination of progressivism will be explored in chapter 7, but falling within this category, it may be argued, was a particular publishing enterprise of the Schools Council, effectively a new genre of literature employed in the propagation of progressive practice. This was a series of pamphlets published in 1971/72 under the general title: *British Primary Schools Today* prepared under the aegis of the Schools Council by the 'Anglo-American Primary Education Project', and supported by the Ford Foundation in America. The 'British Directorate' included Maurice Kogan, by then Professor at Brunel University, John Blackie, former Chief Inspector, and Molly Brearley, former Principal of the Froebel Institute in London, all of whom had been key figures on the Plowden Committee as Secretary, Chief Assessor and one of its most active members, respectively. The project thus provides one example of the extended influence of the Plowden Committee. A fourth member of the Directorate was Geoffrey Cockerill, Joint Secretary of the Schools Council (1970–72) on secondment from the DES. Prominent amongst the nine 'American participants' was Joseph Featherstone, Associate Editor of the *New Republic*, a Research Fellow of Harvard University, who had visited, been smitten by, and wrote widely on 'the British primary school'. Featherstone's experiences were based especially on Leicestershire. There was a journalistic tone in the presentation of these pamphlets, as well as propagandizing timbre to their content. Commercially published by Macmillan, there were twenty-three titles. Presented attractively in a small format with coloured covers, illustrated with photographs, and at the fairly cheap price of 40–50p each, they were explicitly aimed at American and British educators and teachers in training, as well as at the general public. Not surprisingly, some of the contributors, such as Molly Brearley, Richard Palmer, David and Elizabeth Grugeon and Christopher Jarman had been involved in broadcasting, and quite a number of the texts gave specific reference to relevant films from Eileen Molony's various BBC television series (*Discovery and Experience, Mother Tongue* and *The Expanding Classroom*) as well as to the film *Children are People* made at Stockwell College of Education. Other contributors included well-known progressivists Edith Biggs, Alice Murton and Henry Pluckrose.

According to Joseph Feathestone, the intention was mostly to document 'case examples', not to provide theoretical discussion and prescriptive manuals to informal education, but rather

> to present accounts from which deductions and generalizations can be made.[38]

The authors were described as 'either practitioners, or *expert observers*' [my emphasis], sustaining the emphasis to be found elsewhere in progressivist discourse on observing and describing; observing and describing was a key to the procedures of the Plowden Committee, and some of the chief promoters of progressivism amongst HMI, such as Schiller and Blackie, had learned about primary education by observing rather than by doing. Whilst some booklets in this Ford Foundation series were descriptions of practice based on experience, others gave accounts of small scale projects, visiting primary schools and describing aspects of their life.

Description of the process of innovation and change presented in these booklets closely reflected the state of progressivism in the later 1960s. The wide variation of quality to be found in schools was noted: Featherstone recognized that there were some informal classrooms and schools that were chaotic, though this was preferable to the dull routine of formal settings. There was no British model, no gospel, and British schools were marked by their eclecticism. Maurice Kogan, from his knowledge and experience of public administration, pointed out that a fundamental uncertainty about the processes of learning made education different from the prison service, defence or health, where the processes were relatively easier to define.[39] Thus Ann Cook and Herbert Mack, both from the City University, New York, pointed to the frustration of the many visitors who sought to establish 'models' or to clarify and document the fundamental ingredients of the English primary school for adoption elsewhere:

> The existence of an entire series of booklets (of which this is one) on the subject not only suggests a response to this growing interest, but also indicates the complexity of any replication.[40]

Featherstone, however, offered the optimisic vision of an essentially grassroots movement:

> Perhaps the most significant aspect of this whole series of British reforms is the way in which ordinary teachers in different parts of

> the country are coming to share a common approach and a similar vision of what good primary schools are aiming at, [even though the quality of teaching and children's work may vary greatly.] ... We are not here celebrating geniuses or saints, but the daily work of thousands of teachers.

Moreover the descriptions given in the series were seen by him as reports of work in progress — to be superseded as more was discovered about children, learning and teaching.[41]

There was implicit through many of these pamphlets a sense of teleology and a 'Whig interpretation' of change whereby a historical progress towards the present could be defined. The most explicit interpretation of change in this series was however that of J.M. Pullan, HMI since 1937, who had served in two areas with some reputation for informality: Nottingham and Bristol.[42] His four chapters described four schools: in 'Looking back' at the pre-war elementary school, whilst he recognized that many good teachers, mostly in infant classes, had been experimenting with new and improved methods, most teachers had adopted the traditional formal pattern. Meanwhile, many small village schools were following their own 'traditional informality' in which teachers and children joined together in a family atmosphere, and this he called, exercising perhaps an unconscious value judgment, 'natural informality'. Thence he proceeded to an account of the Connaught Junior Boys' School in Bristol, where boys from a city housing estate had responded badly to traditional methods, but which was transformed under the 'informal experiments' of its head, L.S. White, from 1953 to 1972. Finally, 'experiments out of necessity' explained how a 'chaotic' school in Battersea was changed in the 1960s by the 'thoughtful analysis' and 'bold and unorthodox methods' of its head, E.J. Norfield, securing trust and cooperation of the children and rising standards of behaviour, work and play. Probert and Jarman offered a hint of the differing shades of opinion on the nature of progressivism, and on internal processes of change.[43]

The implication of this series might have been that a considerable consensus had been achieved, yet there was a hint of foreboding beneath Featherstone's tentative boast that, despite their criticisms of the comprehensive schools:

> It is significant, perhaps, that so little in the 'Black Papers' debates concerns primary schools, where the most sweeping changes have been occurring. So far, however great the fears for secondary schools, conservative critics have not levelled persuasive charges of poor work or deteriorating standards at the primary schools.[44]

Perhaps he had an inkling that these were just around the corner?

Educational Press

Taylor's Birmingham teachers found the educational press only of little influence on their school, although it ranked more influential than HMI, colleges or universities.[45] What did the press have to offer concerning primary school methods, and how far was it a vehicle of progressive ideology? Market research of newspaper readership amongst primary school teachers produced the following results:

Percentage of all state primary school teachers reading:	*1969*	*1973*	*1978**	*1984*
The Teacher	47	45	45	42
Child Education	42	n/a	47	55
Teachers' World	25	30		
(from 1977: Junior Education)			17	31
Times Educational Supplement	23	33	39	43

(* teachers with purchasing responsibility)[46]

The Teacher, which had twice the readership of the Times Educational Supplement in the years after Plowden, has been considered above as one vehicle of the influence exerted by the National Union of Teachers. *Child Education* had a large and growing readership in the years covered by this market research, and was a long established periodical, having started publication in 1924. A journal of different character from *The Teacher*, it offered practical hints for classroom practice. This genre of literature, also available in book form, is largely ignored in this study, on the grounds that it omitted to communicate the essential principles of progressivism; it would not follow that teachers adopting such practical advice had thus assimilated, let alone applied, the ethos of child-centredness, informal organization or learning by discovery. On the other hand it could be claimed that these 'tips for teachers' may have encouraged more activity in the classroom, a more varied curriculum and the creation of a brighter classroom environment. Though they may have dealt in superficialities and appearances only, in some instances they might have provided the thin end of the wedge by which more progressive philosophies entered the classroom.

Progressive practices in the broadest sense were implicit in *Child Education's* text and presentation. Covers of this large quarto journal throughout the 1950s featured close-up photographs of children at play and at work. Coloured pictures and friezes for the classroom wall were included, especially in the seasonal quarterly issues. Even under wartime economy production, it appeared generous and attractive in these respects. In 1943, for example, was included a series of calendar pictures on the theme of 'Playtime', painted by Adrian Allinson, a well-known poster artist whose work adorned the London Underground. Also in this year *Child Education* launched a 'Children's League of Friendship', intended to be of value in teaching human geography and in fostering international understanding and goodwill; it featured stories of children in other countries and letters from children of different nationalities.

As well as plans and patterns for work in the classroom, stories, action songs, singing games and other materials, there were articles which discussed practical teaching based on reasoned approaches rooted in the facts of child development. The journal also ran an enquiry bureau answering readers' queries for which a coupon was included. Publishers' advertisements reminded teachers of classic books such as W. Viola's *Child Art*, Marion Richardson's *Writing and writing patterns*, and *The Practical Infant Teacher* edited by P.B. Ballard and published by 'New Era'. Correspondence colleges advertised too, offering help with Froebel examinations amongst other professional qualifications. Format and content remained very consistent throughout the 1950s, although advertisements by educational suppliers alerted readers to an ever increasing range of specialist classroom furniture and equipment.

Teacher's World was a professional journal of some considerable tradition.[47] Closer to the reality of the primary school world than the *Times Educational Supplement* in the 1950s, it contained mostly useful ideas and materials for lessons, with only the barest discussion of broader educational issues, and the latter in a fairly lightweight tone. Two of its regular contributors at different periods were John Gagg and Henry Pluckrose, who both also wrote many books of practical hints for the classroom. A front page article 'All play and no work' on activity methods provoked a great deal of controversy from teacher correspondents. John Gagg, Primary Adviser in Oxfordshire 1949–51, produced a rejoinder entitled 'Credo for human beings', and published a series entitled *These Modern Methods!* [exclamation mark in original]. This series set out to be a 'sensible' approach, discussing first the aims of education, or 'What are we trying to do?': to learn to live in a community, to acquire some basic knowledge, to live a full and enjoyable life now, and to be prepared for secondary education. These aims meant that you must give children activity, encourage initiative, keep control and teach some facts. In other words,

> There must be some BALANCE in your methods of teaching....
> There must not be fanaticism in either direction.[48]

A 'workable' syllabus, suggested Gagg, must be based on a common-sense blending of 'modern' and 'traditional' methods. His recipes for progressive practice (known affectionately to some teachers at the time as

'Gaggery'), were well illustrated in a series which appeared in *Teacher's World* during October and November 1950. Entitled 'Lively English for the primary child', it comprised a story about Philip and Joan to be read to the children, the highly artificial narrative interrupted from time to time to introduce

> plenty of extra work involving the other 'subjects' of the curriculum.[49]

The apostrophizing of 'subjects' in this context accurately captures the cautious and slightly equivocal welcome held out in the paper at this time to progressive practices. The Scottish Education Department's report on primary education was welcomed for its flexible and 'commonsense' approach to teaching methods.[50]

By the later 1960s, the paper displayed a much more sophisticated approach to pedagogical issues, with series, for example, by J.B. Mays on 'Homes and schools' and by Alfred Yates on 'Theory and practice'. At the same time it was more emphatic in its advocacy of progressivism. In the week before the publication of the Plowden Report, the cover photograph and comment introduced a pictorial article on Inglewood Infants' School, Carlisle; significantly, it felt that the term 'integrated day' needed to be explained to its readers, and qualifications about its application were painstakingly registered:

> This school employs 'the integrated day' system of teaching. This is a method in which each child may follow his or her own devices, although the teacher must, of course, ensure that each child does a certain amount of number work during the day. Also, the child's reading and writing skills must not suffer. This method recognizes that a child is an individual who has to learn in an individual way. The integrated day demands skilful and mature teachers.[51]

The Plowden Report was treated to extensive coverage from many angles: politicians, trades unionists, teacher trainers, advisers and others all contributing substantial articles. But no doubt the greatest impact in the environment of busy staffrooms would have been made by the picture features, — large photographic spreads of progressivism in action, now annotated by quotations from Plowden: illustrating a 'progressive view of primary education' as achieved through the work of Miss MacIver, Primary Organizer for Aberdeen, were photographs of infants in creative play, and the Plowden statement:

> prolonged periods of routine practice in, for example, computation or handwriting, reduce rather than improve accuracy. This is a lesson which is particularly relevant to schools working on traditional lines.[52]

Comment on the Plowden Report was also accompanied by the customary 'tips for teachers', such as Henry Pluckrose's series 'Have you tried this?', with suggestions for using coathangers and making chessmen from bottles.[53]

The *Times Educational Supplement* had traditionally aimed at the grammar school teacher, although when Harold Dent took over its editorship during the war he had worked hard to gain equal recognition for the public elementary system, and to persuade teachers to 'break away from this business of lecturing thirty or forty immobile children'. He spent much of his energy and time visiting exemplary classrooms, chosen from personal knowledge or recommendation, and reporting on the work there. From 1952 the paper had reverted to its former grammar school orientation. The editor, Walter James, saw himself more as a journalist than as an educationist; he recruited bright young writers direct from Oxbridge, many of whom specialized in arts criticism. According to Patricia Rowan, James saw the paper as

> a sort of poor man's *Spectator*, since he also believed it his duty to give the impoverished teacher the sort of arts coverage that he could not afford to seek out in the other weeklies and Sundays.[54]

He tended to antagonize figures of the educational establishment such as Sir John Newsom, Sir William Alexander and Sir Ronald Gould, but his one source of educational wisdom was Eric James, High Master of Manchester Grammar School; though the *Times Educational Supplement* consistently opposed selection by intelligence testing, it also resisted comprehensivization in the 1960s. Priorities in educational politics were such that the main debates concerned selection and organization of the secondary sector; and market forces as well as editorial policy may have been in operation, insofar as primary school teachers still had lower average salaries than secondary, and may have less commonly seen themselves as the career professionals likely to buy the *Times Educational Supplement*. Occasional special features, such as 'Pages for the primary school' were infrequent, and might be entirely taken up with advertisements for books and equipment.[55]

1960 may be taken as a sample year; there was little indeed on primary education, which appropriately reflected the view occasionally expressed in its pages that primary schools were the 'Cinderellas' of the system. A NUT publication in April entitled *Fair Play For Our Primary Schools* engendered some newsworthy debate by exposing the bad conditions of many primary school buildings. An ensuing Commons debate as reported in the pages of the *Times Educational Supplement* revolved largely around the question of resources, and the Labour MP Anthony Greenwood was quoted for his caustic observation that although the Russians had succeeded in landing a rocket on the moon, the Minister for Education had not yet managed to install electric lighting into a primary school in Somerset. Only a passing reference to the quality of teaching was made, by Mr Hornby (Conservative MP for Tonbridge) and endorsed by a leading article in the same issue, that there had been more invention and experiment in the primary school than in any other sector in recent years. However, the leader used these grounds to justify the continued attention to the resourcing of secondary schools since the most urgent need of the primary sector was for more and better teachers, and these were to found by improving secondary education: 'Teachers, not buildings, make for good education'.[56]

In the course of the year there were two special sections of primary pages, one exclusively reviewing school books, but the other featuring the latest achievements of school architecture, with larger classrooms to accommodate not only larger classes but also newer teaching methods, and conceived as self-contained home bases incorporating toilets etc. Also reported in May of that year was the Ministry of Education Development Group's Finmere School, Oxfordshire, in which, so the head was quoted: 'you couldn't teach in the old formal way even if you tried to'. On two occasions Dr. K. Laybourn, Chief Inspector at Bristol, was given generous space to describe the 'free and friendly' atmosphere and environmental exploration that were to be found in the best primary schools and to conjecture on developments of the next fifty years in a 'progressive' vein.[57] Mrs Hilda Pickles, under the title of 'The seamless robe', lambasted LEA officials for 'devouring one another over the organization of secondary education' when they could be engaging in more creative curricular experiments, and even chided the much respected BBC, 'our national nanny', for neglecting to integrate junior school subject studies in its schools broadcasts.[58]

Apart from the sudden switch in the balance of training from secondary to primary which the colleges were asked to accommodate in October, and which raised heated debate in correspondence and comment, the contemporary reader would have found no other matters of great significance touching primary education in the pages of the *Times Educational Supplement.* Only with benefit of hindsight can we see the first glimmering promise of Plowden on the horizon when Horace King, MP (a product of state schooling, a teacher and later Speaker of the House of Commons) called for a new enquiry into primary education echoed by a leader comment on the need for more guidance in the primary sector.[59] As if to reinforce this new interest, Fred Jarvis, then Head of Publicity at the NUT, announced a two-year touring exhibition of primary education to begin the following spring, intended 'to explain teaching methods and show the great progress made since the war'.[60]

Primary schooling inevitably received more attention in the pages of the *Times Educational Supplement* following publication of the Plowden Report in January 1967; the Report prompted many meetings and 'teach-ins' (a vogue term at this period), and these were reported, as also a great number of letters to the editor. Significantly a fair proportion of this correspondence concerned the implications for teacher training of Plowden's recommendations. In October 1968, Lady Plowden was reported addressing the Parents' National Education Union on 'the two revolutions'. The revolution already achieved was that of curricula:

> Two-thirds of the country's primary schools have changed completely since pupils' parents were there;

the revolution still to come was to establish the principle that parents really matter.[61] In January 1969, on the second anniversary of the Report's publication, Lady Plowden described it as 'not so much a report, more a way of life'. The *Times Educational Supplement* commented:

> Whether the Plowden report or the undoubted burgeoning of public interest in primary education came first is a meaningless chicken-or-egg question. What is certain is that the Central Advisory Council for Education charted a definite change towards the learning processes of small children.[62]

However, it was a commercial decision that led to a growth of primary coverage by the paper. In 1969 Lord Thomson took over The Times Publishing Company; market analysis showed a saturation of the secondary sector and a promising future development of the primary sector, and considered the paper currently too right of centre.[63] In 1960, the conscientious primary teacher would have learned little of progressivism from the professional weekly. Ten years on, a conscientious reading of the '*Times Ed*' would cost her a few more stolen minutes in the staffroom. The third anniversary of the Report's publication in January gave the cue for an assessment of 'Three years of progress' by Lady Plowden herself, who pointed out that the authors had instigated an unprecedented follow-up to any government report by meeting annually to consider developments that had been made. Her article hinged on the encouraging work of the Liverpool EPA Research Project and Lady Plowden's assessment was that

> the recommendations of the report have strengthened . . . trends in thinking in the primary schools and stimulated further thought. Now the spearheads of advance among teachers, colleges of education and administrators are moving firmly forward.

The best primary schools, she noted, had broken an age-long pattern of education, and these were still in a minority, but their thinking had coloured all primary practice.[64]

Obviously news items *reflect* events as much as they may subsequently promote change, and it was only to be expected that reports such as Southampton's reorganization of first and middle schools 'to be run on Plowden lines', or the new Labour leaders of ILEA first banning the cane in primary schools then planning to reduce primary class sizes to a maximum of thirty-five brought primary issues to the forefront. Moreover the General Election began to dominate the news with Tory promises to shift the emphasis of educational spending in favour of primary schools, followed by a similar statement of intent in the Queen's Speech. This was dubbed 'the Plowden opportunity' by the editor of the *Times Educational Supplement*, who exhorted Mrs Thatcher as Secretary of State to take the series of practical suggestions in Plowden as her starting point.[65] Curriculum and teaching methods did not, however, receive particularly dominant attention in this year.

1971 opened with coverage of the NUT Primary Teachers' Sectional Conference, at which the Union's Primary Schools Advisory Committee called for increased capitation allowances. In the ensuing year, a great deal of attention was paid to old school buildings, beginning with an investigation by reporters into working conditions in five deprived, very old, primary schools. A DES Report on class sizes in primary schools was covered in April.[66] In July, a 'Plain Man's Guide to Primaries' (sic) appeared. This was a double-page spread by Caroline Moorhead, with photographs of a primary classroom and of children's work; more children's work was illustrated the following week.[67] Ted Wragg has pointed to the importance of stimulating accounts of the work of gifted teachers in primary classrooms, which appeared in the *Times Educational Supplement*:

> So far as teachers' professional development is concerned there is still nothing more effective than reading about or seeing a successful model.[68]

That autumn, the paper also announced publication of the Schools Council/Ford Foundation Series *British Primary Schools Today.*

Occasionally, the professional press could provoke comment from the national dailies. An article by Sybil Marshall in July 1971 gave rise to fulminations by Bruce Kemble, education correspondent of the *Daily Express*: 'End playtime and get the children learning'.[69]

School Broadcasting

In the report of a conference discussion on 'The integrated day' at the University of Exeter Institute of Education in 1971, it was recorded that

> radio and television programmes do not seem to have a place in the integrated day.[70]

There was a sense shared by many progressivists that educational broadcasting was inimical to child-centredness, as it clearly could not cater for individual needs, and (before the arrival of audio and video-recording) was available only at a fixed point in the timetable. It may well be that the media also suffered in some eyes from association with popular culture which the school's mission was to counter.

However, in one of the key areas of the progressive curriculum, that of music and movement, schools broadcasting made an important contribution to dissemination of particular approaches, a hidden form of in-service training, and despite its inadequacies offered a better facility than many teachers could produce from their own resources. Though the programmes of music and movement may not have lived up to the ideals of some who felt that descriptive work was suggested, to the neglect of the *elements* of movement, and that interpretation was given precedence over self-expression, yet the approach adopted by the broadcasters was more progressive than many established practices, and a Froebel pamphlet on music in the junior school included advice on using radio programmes. The educational use of radio was widespread and increasing; the number of 'listening schools' (primary and secondary) grew from 15,000 in 1945 to 28,000 a decade later. Though independent of the Ministry of Education, closer liaison and official approval was reflected in the publication of a tribute to the BBC's record, and encouragement to headteachers to make use of broadcasts.[71]

Briggs (1979) identified a number of currents in the BBC's approach to education: the Reithian philosophy which had linked education and religion in public broadcasting; the vision of Mary Somerville (appointed by Reith as Director of School Broadcasts from 1931) of creating a richer culture through broadcasting; and a tradition of

> wise delegation by the Corporation of responsibility . . . to a body broadly representative of the best educational opinion in the country.[72]

The Beveridge Report of 1951 on the future of broadcasting, revealed pride in the achievements of the BBC's educational services and the tributes to its quality made by the Association of Education Committees. Papers in the BBC Written Archives show that a firm relationship had been built up from the earliest years of schools broadcasting in the 1920s and 1930s, with the New Education Fellowship.

In 1947 the former Central Council for School Broadcasting was reorganized. The new School Broadcasting Council had a number of sub-committees for programme planning, which met twice a year. The shift from a discipline-based to a developmental approach to education was reflected in the terms of reference of sub-committees, which were no longer to deal with different 'school subjects' as before, but with different 'age-groups' among schoolgoers. These sub-committees were to start from the presupposition that school broadcasting was

> much less a medium of instruction than a means of extending and enriching the child's environment.[73]

Primary I Programme Sub-Committee dealt with the age range 5–7, and Primary II with programmes for 7–11 years. The composition of these sub-committees was complex since they sought to represent accredited outside interests in the educational world as well as institutional ones within the BBC.

Long service, experience and status in the educational world were evidently major considerations in making senior appointments. Miss D.M. Hammonds, for example, was Chief HMI for Educational Developments and Staff Inspector for School Broadcasts and Drama, retiring from the Ministry in 1949, and had been a member of the Central Council for Schools Broadcasting from 1935 to 1946. A Ministry representative on the Schools Broadcasting Council, she chaired the Primary II Sub-committee from 1947 to 1954, and according to Harman Grisewood, Director of the Spoken Word, she made a 'contribution of outstanding value to the Council's work'.[74] She was succeeded in the chair by Miss F. Tann, who had been Chief Inspector for Primary Education until her retirement in 1952. However, a significant indication of the values espoused by the Council is found in an annotated list considering the qualities of individual teachers who might be invited to a conference on broadcasting for infants. Age appears to have been a factor, as various candidates were described:

> young, broad-minded, level-headed, intelligent
>
> young and progressive
>
> about 45, progressive and keen
>
> middle-aged but intelligent and progressive
>
> elderly but energetic and keen
>
> elderly but very sound judgment
>
> old but very keen and progressive.

Youth was clearly not everything:

> youngish — a bit opinionated
>
> youngish — a broadminded but very voluble lady
>
> young in spirit and broadminded, age about 60.[75]

In the early post-war years the core of the Primary I Sub-Committee, chaired by Dr. Elsa Walters, lecturer at the Froebel Institute and author of two Froebel pamphlets on *Activity and Experience*, seems to have been composed almost exclusively of women. By contrast Primary II had a majority of men. Sitting together on this Committee in the early 1950s were two characters who feature elsewhere in the dissemination of progressivism, Christian Schiller and Edith Moorhouse. The influence of their philosophies may be seen in some of the minutes and notes of discussion. At a meeting in October 1952, the programme for 1953/54 was approved, and gives some idea of the range of curriculum covered by the Schools Broadcasts:

Title	*Age range*
Music and Movement II	6-8
Stories and Rhymes	about 8
Time and Tune	about 8
For Country Schools	8–11
Adventures in English	about 10
Nature Study	about 10
Rhythm and Melody	9–11
*World History**	about 10
Singing Together	9–12
Travel Talks	9–12
Health Talks	10–15

* Title altered at the next meeting to *Stories from World History*.

Various considerations raised by the Committee reveal the concerns that must have been particularly felt by progressivists in relation to radio broadcasts, for example that the purpose of the nature study series should be to act as a supplement to school studies, and the desirability of encouraging practical follow-up by suggestions to teachers.[76] In 1953 it was decided to replace a series entitled 'Living in the country' by one 'For country schools'. It was recognized that as there were many small primary schools catering for an age range of 8–11 (senior classes disappearing as the 1944 Education Act reorganization took effect), the mean target age of 10 adopted by the former series should now be reconsidered. At a meeting in February 1953 attended by Schiller and Moorhouse, the initial proposals for revision were criticized as containing too much geographical content, and the sub-committee suggested that broadcasts in the series should as far as possible be planned to start with what the child has seen and experienced and lead out from this to the unfamiliar. They considered however that while the environment of the primary school was one of the teacher's resources, its use should be a spontaneous one and not simply in response to broadcasts. On the other hand, these rural children tended to be isolated and broadcasting could help to extend and enrich their experience. 'A broadcast series which took them outside the environment was needed, rather than one which was based on it', and the aims of the programme should include an appeal to the children's imaginations and draw some of its material from stories of life in other places and at other times.[77]

Music was an aspect of the primary school curriculum dear to the hearts of those concerned with the personality of the child, and with its creative and expressive potential (Froebel's singing rhymes, for example, were an important legacy) and 1953 saw a major review by the Schools Broadcasting Council on music in the junior school. A survey was made including reports from, and meetings with teachers and from six education officers who went into school to listen alongside the children, as well as discussion with HMI, music lecturers in training colleges and LEA music organizers. In addition, a national conference of music specialists was held in London in June 1953, and great weight was attached in the Report to its opinions. The Report also lamented that junior school music teaching should be the job of the general practitioner because

> the view is still strongly held in some quarters that, as a matter of educational principle, the junior school child should not have different teachers for different subjects.

Most training colleges were trying to cater for the situation by providing basic or background courses, and in some these were compulsory for prospective junior school teachers, but the musical calibre of students was such that the colleges had an uphill task.

This was a problem not only for junior school music in general, but also for the broadcasters themselves.

> Over all other problems ... looms that major one which derives from the widely varying capacity of teachers using the broadcasts....

But the review also identified the 'problem' of a widely varying capacity amongst the children, thus acknowledging individual differences and the difficulty of broadcasts in catering for these.[78] Indeed, the most common criticisms levelled at the two series *Time and Tune* and *Rhythm and Melody*, seem to have arisen from a child-centred perspective. In rhythm and notation training *Time and Tune* had been 'inclined to attempt what has been beyond the power of many children to grasp', and in *Rhythm and Melody* there had been a tendency to divorce 'theory' from other work. For orchestral instruments, more listening and less explanation was desirable, especially in *Time and Tune*, and 'listening music' had suffered in both series from lack of time and from insufficiently attractive presentation. One education officer observed that

> It is a well known and regrettable fact that musical theory which is only justifiable as a means to an end, has so often in the past been taught as an end in itself and neither teacher nor pupils have given much thought to the reasons for mastering this study. It would be a great pity if Rhythm and Melody were to perpetuate this pointless and unbalanced approach,

whilst another commented after hearing *Time and Tune*:

> My impression is that verbal descriptions of instruments are unnecessary at this stage. The picture is there in the pamphlet.

> What we want listeners to get used to is the tone of the instrument, not so much the principles of mechanism. I believe the best way to teach instrumental tone and compass is by contrast.[79]

Most striking is the relative formality of the prescriptions which emerged from the specialists' conference. Yet a written summary of the discussion at this conference reveals that although a more progressive approach failed to predominate, it had been strongly expressed by some participants. Amongst those present were Christian Schiller, HMI, Staff Inspector for Primary Schools; Ruth Foster, HMI, Staff Inspector for Physical Education (responsible for the new Ministry of Education handbooks encouraging a developmental and creative approach to movement); B.A.R. Shore, Staff Inspector for Music; Mrs P. Goldesgeyme (formerly Misss Anne Mendoza), lecturer in music at the Froebel Educational Institute, and a member of the Schools Broadcasting Council and of the Primary II Sub-Committee; and Miss E. Barnard, Senior Lecturer in Music at Goldsmiths and a member of the Primary I Sub-Committee.

Miss Barnard defended the teaching of notation as one aspect of an integrated approach to music teaching. She

> thought it deceptive to put things under different headings. Surely what we're trying to do is to get children to experience music. Everything arises out of this. You try to get children to understand the symbols and then apply them to music, so singing, activity, cooperation and reading all come out of listening and have to be balanced.

The Staff Inspector for Music agreed with the inclusion of notation, and acknowledged the necessity and realism of compromise in broadcast programmes. Schiller, however, was not wholly in agreement:

> the conference had spent a long time considering music but hadn't considered these young, growing persons. What evidence is there that growth in musical development is different from that in other arts?

He developed the analogy with the creative activity of painting and said that he had heard in *Woman's Hour* the previous week recordings of tunes made up by children of 5, 6 and 7. Ruth Foster took a stance which seemed by implication to question the value of broadcasting at all; she said that the conference was talking of children

> as if they were homogeneous. She would have thought there was a great range of musical ability in the Junior School; but as all children seemed to do the same thing at the same time, she wondered if the best children are being kept back and the others being bored.

Miss Mendoza hoped that it was not always necessary to link listening with doing; most children, she thought, would listen to suitable music for its own sake.[80]

Film

Production of film for teaching purposes was developed in the 1930s by a variety of agencies, including, for example, the Dartington Hall Film Unit, but by 1939 only 857 out of 30,000 schools had a projector. War brought an increase in the use of film for general information and for propaganda, as well as a means of instruction in the armed forces. Recognition of the need for government finance to develop educational use of film, together with a concern that curriculum control and teaching methods were to remain the province of the teaching profession, resulted in the establishment in 1948 of a National Committee for Visual (later Audio-Visual) Aids in Education, whose task was to determine films to be made and to provide professional advice. At the same time an Educational Foundation for Visual Aids was set up to provide a means for supply to LEAs, later taking over responsibility for film production.[81]

In the later 1940s prospects were bright: from 1949 to 1951, 125 films were completed, but government finance dried up with the severe economies of 1952, so that in the years 1951–54 only forty films were made. Recovery began thereafter; in 1957 LEAs increased their subscriptions to the National Committee to include finance for film production; the National Committee's name was to be a hallmark of good educational content and high technical and artistic quality. The mid-1960s were boom years for film in schools, 15,000 of which now had film projectors. *The Schoolmaster* reported in 1960 that many secondary schools were beginning to make their own films for curriculum purposes, and in the same year the NUT and the Society for Education in Film and Television joined together to offer Young Film-Maker Awards for films made in school.[82] The use of audio-visual aids in school was encouraged by the Plowden Committee.

Some attempt must be made to assess the influence of this medium in the professional training of teachers and in the dissemination of progressivism. Films could be shown time and time again, as for example the Oxfordshire film *Village School* which was still being shown on in-service courses in the late 1970s, more than twenty years after its original production. It was a medium particularly adaptable for use in in-service training, as it was highly mobile and could be used to disseminate ideas and practices amongst a large audience. Its appropriateness to the dissemination of progressivism is evident in two characteristic features of the medium: the vividness and impact of the visual image is especially apt for portraying the arrangement and decor of classrooms, the creation of a classroom environment and the display of children's work by which many progressives set such store, and the moving image aptly captures the children engaged in activity. By comparison with video, much used for similar purposes in more recent years, film was expensive to make, so that decisions about what was to be filmed, and how, were more crucial; and to justify the cost, an extensive audience and reasonably prolonged use would have to have been envisaged.

A particularly striking example was that produced under the title of *The Creative Spirit* by Mary Ellison, Primary Adviser for Shropshire County Council who gave evidence to the Plowden enquiry. It dealt with the integration of the expressive arts. The location was Attingham Park, a country house adapted for use as an educational centre after the Second World War, similar in some respects to the West Riding's Woolley Hall.

In the film, children from three different junior schools were shown on educational visits to Attingham Park. In one sequence the topic of 'water' was taken, and different groups of children selected the media of dance, drama, prose, poetry, painting, modelling, collage and music in which to express their responses. Performances and displays for parents were presented on their return to school, the commentary stressing the importance of parental support. A second sequence portrayed other groups of children exploring the theme of 'pattern'. A number of important points were made. Firstly, nature is taken as the source, the environment being searched for pattern in nature. Secondly, the children's work was self-directed; they made their own choices and acquired the tools to express themselves with a stress on experiment in different media, techniques being taught to individuals or small groups as required. Boys were shown preparing a drama based on space, inspired by a ring of tree trunks, whilst girls were seen doing needlework — sex stereo-typing was yet to be identified as one obstacle to child-centredness. Thirdly, the children's total absorption, and thus their happiness, was underlined by the commentator; the children were working 'happily and sensibly', and by this means they readily accepted discipline and high standards. This feature of their work was advocated as inculcating an attitude to life and providing an answer to the increasing modern problem of boredom. Again the end result is shown through classroom displays, creating a meaningful environment and encouraging good standards. For every individual, the film concluded,

> involvement in the creative arts is not something added on, it is at the core of the curriculum.

Although a larger-scale production of this kind was quite a costly exercise, the medium did offer opportunities for recording 'good practice' on a less ostentatious scale. Tutors at Sidney Webb College in London, made films for teaching purposes, using Oxfordshire primary schools amongst others, and two notable films were produced by Stockwell College (a college with historic Froebelian connections): *Children Are People* (1970) was directed by Lorna Ridgway, followed by *The Task of the Teacher* (1973) under the same direction.

Good examples of the genre, and ones which were used extensively in his later career as a teacher-educator, were the two short films made by Christopher Jarman as a young teacher in Hampshire. *Weeke at Work* was filmed in 1962 in his probationary year at Weeke County Primary School, for the benefit of the parents on open-day in an area where there were strong academic pressures for 11+ successes. The second film *What Shall We Do With Freedom?*, was made two years later at Hamble School in 1964, and significant developments are seen between the two. Brought together in a later video version entitled *Pre-Plowden Primaries*, the linking commentary told how Jarman had been invited by Robin Tanner, following a general inspection at Weeke, to visit Oxfordshire schools. 'That day', he said, 'was a Damascus road experience for me'.

> This was a revelation to us; we'd never seen schools able to work in such freedom till then, and I had never seen such high standards of work and behaviour from children.

With him on the same visit was Howard Probert, a young head at Hamble, who encouraged Jarman to join his staff; together, they later wrote a book in the Schools Council series *British Primary Schools Today*.[83]

Edited and produced to a very high standard, great use of close-ups was made to show children quite engrossed in their learning activity working individually or in small groups, and also to reinforce the close observation of nature which was one of the leitmotifs of the film, and of the children's curriculum. The commentary's explanations were Piagetian, from an emphasis on practical work or concrete operations with money and weight in the first film, to a key scene in the second, in which children were shown working together on a great collage: experience of as many materials as possible, it was explained, was essential to growth, and the children were provided with anything which can be used as a concrete aid to abstract thinking. Experimental science played an important part in the film, but the arts and crafts were also central, and their roles in the curriculum were described in a highly significant way, for technique and creativity were subtly balanced. The use of tools and materials is carefully and individually taught but the activities which follow are unlimited. From William Morris, doubtless via Robin Tanner, came a romantic analogy with the middle ages, for in working clay the children, having played a little, were given some adult guidelines but then they pass on the techniques, like a medieval guild. A child packing the kiln for firing provided a final symbolic sequence: 'We put our pots into the kiln and trust they'll turn out to be good ones'.

Notes

1 NUT (1944) *Educational Developments of the National Union of Teachers: Statement by the Executive for Presentation to the Easter Conference 1944.*
2 NUT (1951) *Annual Report* p. lvi.
3 NUT Archive, Circular C.219/63, 4 September 1963.
4 *Schoolmaster*, 8 January 1960.
5 NUT (1949a) *Transfer from Primary to Secondary Schools: Report of a Consultative Committee*, London, Evans/NUT. The NUT was also a publisher of books on the curriculum such as J.S. Flavell *Mathematics in the Junior School.*
6 NUT (1949a) *op. cit.*, para. 130.
7 NUT (1949b) *Nursery-Infant Education: Report of a Consultative Committee Appointed by the Executive of the National Union of Teachers*, London, Evans/NUT.
8 NUT (n.d) (1959) *The curriculum of the Junior School; Report of a Consultative Committee*, London, Schoolmaster Publishing Co. Ltd.
9 *ibid.*, pp. 11 and 154.
10 *ibid.*, pp. 35–6.
11 *ibid.*, pp. 32 and 40.
12 *ibid.*, pp. 29–31.
13 Evan Owen also sat on the earlier Consultative Committee on Transfer, and was later President of the NUT from 1958/59. His experience included a senior lectureship at Shenstone Emergency Training College, Kidderminster, and membership of a UNESCO Seminar in Brussels on the teaching of history. A philosopher and a linguist, tribute was paid to his love of learning, his work for freedom of the teaching profession from political and religious discrimination, and his care for backward children (*The Schoolmaster*, 26 April 1957, and biographical note in NUT Library). As a senior and long-standing leading member of the Worcestershire County Teachers' Association, it is likely he would have had contact with Alec Clegg and Christian Schiller, HMI.
14 *Schoolmaster*, 8 January 1960, p. 78.
15 *ibid.*, pp. 50–1.
16 Lawrence, E. (Ed.) (1952) *Friedrich Froebel and English Education*, London, Routledge and Kegan Paul, p. 42.
17 Lawrence, E. (Ed.) (1952) *op. cit.*, pp. 56, 67 and 71.
18 Jebb, E.M. (1958) 'Froebel opinion', *Times Educational Supplement*, 2 May.
19 This Education Committee also had responsibility for advising on the conduct of examinations. In 1951 it became known as the Standing Committee, and a Standing Sub-Committee for the London Colleges dealt with proposals for examinations and courses of study at constituent colleges of the London Institute preparing students for the teachers' certificate of the National Froebel Foundation. For convenience it is referred to here throughout as the 'Education Committee'.
20 An historic connection between the Foundation and the College of Preceptors lay in the figure of Joseph Payne, first Professor of Education appointed by the College in 1873, who was a founder member of the London Froebel Society in 1874.
21 NFF Education Committee, Mins, 11 May 1961.
22 NFF Education Committee, Mins, 24 February 1950 and 3 May 1957.
23 *NFF Bulletin* no. 105, April 1957.
24 A select list of titles in date order of first publication: Walters, E.H. (1951a) *Activity and Experience in the Infant School*, 7th revised edn, 1968, repr. 1970; Walters, E.H. (1951b) *Activity and Experience in the Junior School*, 6th rev. edn, 1965; Brearley, M. (1954) *Number in the Primary School*, 3rd edn, 1960; Theakston, T.R., Isaacs, N. and others (1955) *Some Aspects of Piaget's Work*, 8th edn, 1965; Allen, G. and others (1958) *Scientific Interests in the Primary School*, 4th edn, 1965; Parr, D.M. (1959) *Music in the Primary School*; Hutchinson, M.M. (1960) *A Simple Gardening Project with Young*

Children: From Seed to Seed, rev. edn; BOARDER, S.F.K. and others (1960) *Aspects of Language in the Primary School*; HUTCHINSON, M.M. (1961) *Practical Nature Study in Town Schools*; MANN, B.F. (1962) *Learning Through Creative Work (the under-8s in School)* 5th rev. edn, 1971; IRONSIDE, M. and ROBERTS, S. (1965) *Mathematics in the Primary School*, 2nd edn. 1965; ISAACS, N. (n.d) (1965) *Piaget: Some Answers to Teachers' Questions*; ISAACS, N. (1967) *What is Required of the Nursery-infant Teacher in this Country Today?*.

25 SLA (1958) *The Library in the Primary School: Report of the Primary Schools Sub-Committee*, London, SLA, pp. 3–4.

26 DAVIS, D. (1948) 'The school library in the infants' and primary school', *School Librarian*, 4, 2, July pp. 67–9; DANIEL, M.V. (1951) 'The library in relation to education in the primary school', *School Librarian*, 5, 6, December pp. 378–84. Daniel's books, *Activity in the Primary School* (1947) included an account of the formation of a library in a Manchester junior school.

27 LINES, K. (comp.) (1950) *Four to Fourteen: A Library of Books for Children*, London, National Book League, 2nd edn. 1956; MCGILL, H.M. (comp.) (1952) *Books for Young People: Group 1, Under Eleven*, London, Library Association, 2nd edn. 1955.

28 SLA (1953) *Suggestions for Primary School Libraries.*

29 Walters and Rapaport were Lecturers at the Froebel Institute. Lilian Pierotti's regime at Bedford is documented in SMART, R. (1982) *Bedford Training College 1882–1982: A History of a Froebel College and its Schools*, Bedford, Bedford College of Higher Education.

30 A beginning has been made with PLASKOW, M. (Ed.) (1985) *Life and Death of the Schools Council*, Lewes, Falmer Press.

31 WRAGG, E. (1985) 'Flowers from a secret garden', *Times Educational Supplement 1910–1985*, (Supplement to *TES*, September, p.4).

32 MACLURE, J.S. (1968) *Curriculum Innovation in Practice*, London, Schools Council/HMSO, p. 28.

33 SCHOOLS COUNCIL (1969) *The Middle Years of Schooling 8–13 (Working Paper no. 22)*, p. 86.

34 SCHOOLS COUNCIL (1967) *Curriculum Development, Teachers' Groups and Centres (Working Paper no. 10)*; SCHOOLS COUNCIL (1968) *The First Three Years 1964/67*, p. 3.

35 SCHOOLS COUNCIL (1968) *op. cit.*

36 ROSEN, C. and ROSEN, H. (1973) *The Language of Primary School Children*, Harmondsworth, Penguin; SCHOOLS COUNCIL (1977) *Talking and Learning, Schools Council Communication Skills in Early Childhood Project*, London, Ward Lock Educational.

37 Reported in the *Times Educational Supplement*, 28 May 1965; SCHOOLS COUNCIL (1965) *Maths in Primary Schools, Curriculum Bulletin no. 1.* A later film was *Free to Move* on primary PE — so heavily booked was the copy in the NUT library that a waiting list of twelve months built up (NUT *Annual Report 1967*, p. 107).

38 FEATHERSTONE, J. (1971) *An Introduction: British Primary Schools Today*, London, Macmillan for the Schools Council, p. 3.

39 KOGAN, M. (1971) *The Government of Education: British Primary Schools Today*, London, Macmillan for the Schools Council, p. 11.

40 COOK, A. and MACK, H. (1971) *The Headteacher's Role: British Primary Schools Today*, London, Macmillan for the Schools Council, p. 7.

41 FEATHERSTONE, J. (1971) *op. cit.*, pp. 9 and 13.

42 PULLAN, J.M. (1971) *Towards Informality; British Primary Schools Today*, London, Macmillan for the Schools Council.

43 PROBERT, H. and JARMAN, C. (1971) *A Junior School: British Primary Schools Today*, London, Macmillan for the Schools Council.

44 FEATHERSTONE, J. (1971) p. 17.

45 TAYLOR, P.H. and others (1974) *Purpose, Power and Constraint in the Primary School Curriculum*, London Macmillan/Schools Council.

46 Research by NOP Market Research Ltd., quoted by permission of the *Times Educational Supplement.*
47 *Teacher's World and Schoolmistress* (incorporating *Secondary Education*) had been founded in 1911 as *Woman Teacher's World*, and absorbed *Schoolmistress* and *The Teacher*. Renamed *Teacher's World* in 1913, from 1957 to 1966 it was issued in two parts: primary and secondary. In 1977 it was absorbed into a new journal *Junior Education.*
48 *Teacher's World*, 9 November 1949; Gagg moved on from Oxfordshire to Shropshire, and wrote widely, including *Commonsense in the primary school.*
49 *Teacher's World*, 11 October 1950.
50 *Teacher's World*, 22 November 1950.
51 *Teacher's World*, 6 January 1967.
52 *Teacher's World*, 20 January 1967.
53 *Teacher's World*, 13 January 1967.
54 Rowan, P. (1985) 'Out of the shade', *Times Educational Supplement 1910–1985*, (Supplement to *TES*, September) pp. 5–6.
55 *Times Educational Supplement* 9 May 1958, pp. 732–7.
56 *Times Educational Supplement* 13 May 1960, pp. 975 and 981.
57 *Times Educational Supplement* 4 March 1960, pp. 430–1.
58 *Times Educational Supplement* 11 November 1960, p. 635.
59 *Times Educational Supplement* 11 November 1960, p. 531.
60 *Times Educational Supplement* 25 November 1960, p.722.
61 *Times Educational Supplement* 25 October 1968.
62 *Times Educational Supplement* 10 January 1969.
63 Rowan, P. (1985) *op. cit.*, pp. 5–6.
64 *Times Educational Supplement* 16 January 1970, p. 2.
65 *Times Educational Supplement* 24 July 1970, p. 2.
66 *Times Educational Supplement* 1 January 1971, 29 January 1971, 30 April 1971 (*DES Reports on Education* no. 70).
67 *Times Educational Supplement* 2 and 9 July 1971.
68 Wragg, T. (1985) *op. cit.*, pp. 3–4.
69 *Time Educational Supplement* 2 July, 12 and 17 September 1971; *Daily Express* 6, 7 and 8 September 1971.
70 Walton, J. (1971) *The Integrated Day in Theory and Practice*, London, Ward Lock Educational , p. 77.
71 Ministry of Education (1952) *School Broadcasts* (Ministry of Education Pamphlet no. 20), London, HMSO.
72 Briggs. A. (1979) *Sound and Vision: The History of Broadcasting in the United Kingdom*, vol. 4, Oxford, Oxford University Press, p. 805.
73 'Notes on School Broadcasting in 1947', 20 May 1947, quoted in Briggs, A. (1979) *op. cit.*, p. 828.
74 BBC Written Archive R16/310/6 Note by H. Grisewood (DSW) 7 September 1954.
75 BBC Written Archive R16/371 Letter from D.M. Hammonds to R.C. Steele 26 April 1944.
76 BBC Written Archive R16/318 Minutes 2–3 October 1952, Min. 117, 118 and Minutes 10 February 1953, Min. 124.
77 BBC Written Archive R16/318, Minutes 10 February 1953 and Paper for meeting 5–6 October 1953.
78 BBC Written Archive R16/318 Draft Report on Music in the Junior School, no date [1953] paras. 27 and 28.
79 BBC Written Archive R16/318 Draft Report on Music in the Junior School, no date [1953] paras. 34 and 37.
80 BBC Written Archive R16/318 Music and Broadcasting in Junior Schools 19 June 1953, Summary of Discussion.
81 NCAVAE/EFVA (1966) *Educational Films 1946–66.* The National Committee ceased to exist in 1981 when funding of its activities by the LEAs ended, after which, some its functions were absorbed by the EFVA, which continued in existence.

82 *Schoolmaster* 1 January 1960; NUT *Annual Report 1965*, p. 76.

83 PROBERT, H. and JARMAN, C. (1971) *op. cit.*; Hamble was one of the schools chosen for a visit by the Plowden Committee. I am grateful to Christopher Jarman for the loan of his film.

6 *Architectural Form and Educational Idea*

Since the beginnings of architectural criticism, good buildings have been deemed to require three main qualities: 'commodity, firmness and delight'.[1] 'Delight' is the aesthetic criterion which requires the buildings which we use to be pleasing to the senses. Some aspects of aesthetics are affected by structural elements, and aesthetic requirements certainly overlap in many respects with the function of the building.

A particular aesthetic aspect is the symbolic role of a school building in its locality. Frequently neglected by educational, and indeed architectural historians, the strong visual symbolism of the school building tends to convey both pedagogical ideals and the representation of state authority in a period of compulsory schooling. A fine analysis with regard to the school board period has been made by the architectural historian Mark Girouard.[2] Girouard shows how the choice for the board schools of 'Queen Anne', an early eighteenth century style based on essentially classical and renaissance details, not only helped to provide a better environment in respect of the light and air which children required, but also contrasted sharply with its Gothic precursors in symbolizing a non-denominational and a more enlightened and more 'rational' approach to education. Symbolism of a particular educational philosophy was manifest in the open-plan primary schools of the post-war period. 'Open-plan' itself became a common, if inaccurate, term for representing a method of primary schooling, often used interchangeably with terms such as 'progressive', 'informal', 'child-centred' and so on. Much of the publicity given to supposedly 'new methods' in primary education in the 1950s and 1960s created associations in the public and the professional mind, with recognisable images of an almost revolutionary new kind of building.

'Firmness', in its narrowest sense the stability of the structure, is an engineering consideration which requires no separate treatment as concerns school buildings, although engineering factors such as environmental control, the maintenance of warmth and light for example, will be seen to impinge on function and appearance. 'Commodity' comprises the functional requirements which are very specific in providing for the education of young children. They have, indeed, become increasingly specific as the profession and practice of both architecture and education have become ever more specialized. In 1847 one of the earliest English treatises specifically on school architecture was published, and in 1871 E.R. Robson was the first consultant architect to be appointed by a local school board.[3] In the century since then, specialist building types have evolved,[4] and at the same time pedagogical theory has gradually developed, to a fine degree, distinctions between appropriate types of schooling for different age-ranges.

This chapter seeks to examine the diffusion of educational ideals through the medium of architectural development.

Architects and Building Branch

A significant feature of the post-war situation was the growing public awareness of architecture and town-planning. For example, the impact in Britain of refugees from the German Bauhaus with ideas of architecture based on social needs, such as Walter Gropius who built the famous Impington Village College for Cambridgeshire in 1939, together with other architects and academics such as Nikolaus Pevsner, contributed significantly to stimulating popular interest in the built environment in the post-war years. The Festival of Britain on the South Bank of the Thames in 1951 was one feature of this development. It included a display on 'The new schools', which incorporated a fully furnished classroom in which children's 'project work' was displayed and explained. The exhibition catalogue referred to 'the kind of tools and the sort of environment that are now being devised for the schoolboy and schoolgirl' to get the best out of contemporary education; in the primary school not only desks and chairs, but also libraries and 'the whole paraphernalia that will enable him to take part in physical education and art and drama'. Infants were depicted working at trapezoid desks (with the tapering legs so characteristic of the 'Festival of Britain style').[5]

The mood of post-war reconstruction lent an impetus and status to public sector building in general. Five thousand, or more than one in six schools had suffered war damage. The ideals embodied in the 1944 Education Act provided a new framework which the buildings had to serve, of which the clear demarcation of primary education as a stage of schooling from 5–11 was an important feature, and with the envisaged abolition of all-through elementary schools, planning could concentrate on the specific needs of the younger age group. The total number of children in grant-aided schools was 5.1 million in 1946, rising to 5.7 million in 1949 and to 6.8 million in 1956. Although the initial leap was accounted for partly by the raising of the school leaving age to 15 in 1947, there was also the rise in birth rate between 1942 and 1948, and this so-called 'bulge' was to pass through primary schools between 1947 and 1960. By 1956 over 1.77 million new school places had been provided, of which 60 per cent were in new schools, and more than 1,000,000 of the places were in the primary sector.[6] New building regulations were introduced in 1944, the earlier regulations having been suspended and replaced by 'Suggestions' in 1926 during the financial crisis. The new regulations represented a considerable advance over the standards reflected in the 1936 suggestions, for example playground space increased by 7 per cent, classrooms by 54 per cent, and daylighting — the minimum daylight factor being raised from 0.5 per cent to 2 per cent with a recommendation of 5 per cent.

Interest in school design within the architectural profession was encouraged by the Royal Institute of British Architects which set up a School Design and Construction Committee in 1945, chaired by C.G. Stillman, the County Architect of West Sussex and a leading expert on school design. In the same year a pamphlet was published jointly by the RIBA and the NUT entitled *Planning Our New Schools*, and in October 1947 a two-day conference organized by the Institute and the Ministry of Education on school planning and construction was attended by 400 architects. This was followed by an exhibition entitled 'New schools'. The exhibition booklet[7] provided a thumbnail sketch of the educational background, laying emphasis on the 'broader aspects' of cultivating 'good citizenship and development of character', 'good neighbourliness' and 'civic responsibility', referring also to a report debated by the London Education Committee in 1943 which had proposed 'bringing the school into greater touch with life'. The exhibition included a section on 'The school and the community' concerned with the involvement of parents and more general educational use of school premises. Other sections dealt with 'creating the environment', in particular opening up the shcool to its surroundings, and with 'School equipment and furniture' where the emphasis was on flexibility and lightness. An advertisement placed by the Educational Supply Association was for chairs and desks in light alloy and plywood 'combining strength, lightness and beauty of appearance', 'fabricated by new and revolutionary processes', and 'in keeping with all that is modern in architecture'. These were considerations prophetic of developments over the next two decades.

But in publicizing developments in primary school architecture and heightening professional awareness, a leading role was taken by the Ministry of Education itself. Christian Schiller wrote of a group of new young architects coming 'as a scarcely believable surprise':

> Their appearance changed the whole pattern of thinking and doing, as when a new piece enters the kaleidoscope; instead of

> trying to assess the needs of young children in terms of square feet of floor space, we began to talk of ... an environment in which children could explore and live and learn.
>
> And here were gifted young men and women ... waiting to work out such thoughts on their drawing boards and bring them to life in the materials of a real building.[8]

He was addressing the question 'How comes change?' and expressed his preference for 'living experience' over historical analysis. Historians, however, may see the work of architectural development groups in the Ministry as something more than a happy coincidence. An Architects and Building Branch was formed in 1948 and within it a Development Group consisting of architects, quantity surveyors, HMI and administrators was established. Maclure (1984) gives a detailed account of the formation of the Development Group and the personalities involved.[9]

Stirrat Johnson-Marshall was appointed Chief Architect in 1948. Eric Pearson was one of the HMI appointed early on (1951) who for many years undertook the role of providing a formal channel of advice on 'leading educational practice and thinking' to the architects. However, David Medd and Mary Crowley (later Medd) whom Johnson-Marshall had brought with him from Hertfordshire County Council, and who long exerted considerable influence also had their own valued network of informal contacts among progressive teachers, Mary having the main interest in primary schools. Their function was to pioneer new forms of design to meet new educational requirements, working with manufacturers to develop new building components and techniques, and applying the results of research. Through prototype projects a team would undertake a commission for a local education authority, working like a firm of private architects by paying especially detailed attention to educational requirements.[10] David and Mary Medd later described how they saw the informality of their personal relationships as architects with their clients, adapting the language of progressive pedagogy to their own researches:

> ... it became possible for both education and its environment to unfold and develop as interdependent parts of a single enterprise of first hand exploration and discovery.[11]

At the same time, Leonard White, an architect for the ILEA, had some doubts about this relationship in practice, seeing the environment of Eveline Lowe School (one of the Development Group's projects) as 'architecturally superimposed'; he thought it better to make a more neutral background and to encourage teachers to create their own backcloth.

> I sometimes wonder whether architects are the right people to choose what kind of environment is required in a school and

> whether teachers are not themselves more capable of assessing background colours and surfaces which they can change at will.[12]

Architectural Literature

The resultant buildings became showpieces and were much visited, but results of the Development Group's work were also disseminated by means of publications. In giving school architecture a high profile within educational debate, a strategic role was played by the Ministry's publicity, far more elaborate and sophisticated than that of the old Board of Education. A new relationship between the Ministry and the local education authorities gave the former the role of disseminating information and advice drawn from an overview of national developments, but the *Building Bulletins* were far more than mere administrative devices. The first Bulletin was published in 1949, and declared its intention to give informal advice and 'to reach a wider audience than official letters'. By 1957 fifteen titles had been published, six of these running to second editions, and 120,000 had been sold, not only nationally but abroad. A later criticism that the Development Group had produced insufficient publicity, and had failed to communicate effectively educational philosophies and trends to architects generally, seems hardly justified by their activity.[13]

The Bulletins were attractively presented in a neat octavo format with striking photographic covers and lively typographic and graphic layout.

> We hope that architects will find the bulletin useful. But it will not serve its purpose unless it evokes the interest of all those whom architects regard as their clients.[14]

In the very first issue interest was expressed in the views of readers who were encouraged to correspond with the editor. However, although some editions did publicize LEA initiatives, this promise of a dialogue was not really fulfilled in the content of subsequent issues.

The very first of the Bulletins was entitled 'New primary schools' and enouraged a more compact approach to school design, and a more varied approach to classroom design, scaled to the child, more intimate, more domestic and equipped for small group work. The purpose of the Bulletin was stated as an

> attempt to review the requirements of the primary school as a whole, what is needed *educationally* in terms of space, fittings and furniture; and in terms of physical conditions such as heating, lighting and general amenity.

> The basis of school design is not only a schedule of area and building regulations, but the *needs and activities of growing children and of their teachers.*
>
> The school needs to provide ... uncrowded space and opportunities for making and for doing.
>
> ... a sense of security, protection and unity which is the same kind as that of a good home ... fresh air, sunshine, light, warmth and good food. (my emphasis)[15]

A second edition appeared in 1955.

Bulletin no.6 illustrated primary school plans from twenty LEAs representing a wide geographical spread accompanied by a commentary and in some cases constructive criticism. The foreword proclaimed its purpose as

> concerned solely with the educational function of the buildings. Its intention can be summarized by quotation from the Rules published by the Education Department in 1885. 'School planning is the science of thoroughly adapting every part of a building, even the minutest detail, to the work of school teaching'.
>
> If the bulletin serves to bring administrators, teachers and architects together to discuss and advance the science of school planning, its purpose will have been fulfilled.

This Bulletin also carried advertisements for the Hadow Report of 1931 (still in print), and for the Ministry of Education Pamphlets *Story of a School* and *Seven to Eleven*, discussed in chapter 7 as propaganda for progressivism.

A good example of the way in which educational philosophy was embedded in the Building Bulletins may be illustrated by tracing their advice on the decoration of schools. Children of primary school age are

> intensely interested in the material objects around them, and should be surrounded with good colours, shapes, forms and textures, and will thus grow to understand and appreciate beauty and simplicity.[16]

The Development Group noted that use of colour in British buildings tended to remain conservative, the current fashion for pastel shades being unobjectionable, but that colour could make a positive contribution rather than remaining simply a neutral element in the environment. It could have an important effect on the happiness of children while they are at school, and on their taste and feeling for colour and form in later years. Colour was regarded as 'a most effective medium for arousing feelings and emotional response'. What might appeal to adults will often prove too sophisticated or too dull to make a direct impression on children.

> Children are, on the whole, gay and energetic. They react spontaneously to bright, cheerful colours. Large numbers of children with their quick movements and varied clothing, make a sparkling pattern which can be reflected in the colour scheme, particularly in the scale and disposition of strong accents and patterns.[17]

Colour should be varied through the school, appropriate to different levels of stimulus required in different parts, such as classroom, hall and circulating spaces. Sculpture and mural decorations were also encouraged, as long as close collaboration with the architect was maintained.

> A 'professional' mural must not make children feel that their own paintings are crude, nor should it play down to them, but rather encourage them to try for themselves.[18]

Indeed space could be made for the children's own murals.

'Child-centredness' was the philosophy expressed throughout so that the school building should be conceived as the children's rather than an adult's space, though there is no evidence in the Bulletins that children themselves were consulted on their preferences. Thus colour had an important role to play in

> making the classroom spaces really belong to the children, comfortable and cheerful; for it must be remembered that they will spend a lot of time in these spaces, and will look upon them as their own particular homes.
>
> The wall surfaces up to 2'0" can have the brightest and most stimulating colours and pattern treatment, and this will merge with and reflect the stimulating pattern of the children and the furniture. Thus by emphasising the scale and exciting pattern at *low level only*, the room will become a children's room and not just an adult's room into which the children are allowed to come.[19]

These considerations applied not only to the classrooms but even to the school hall, which was

> above all the place where the children carry out their own activities.[20]

As so often in child-centredness, judgments or assumptions are made by adults about what motivates or stimulates children. Often these were based on such observations as were possible, yet there is little evidence in the Bulletins that children themselves were consulted. Consultation of the children's tastes does not seem to have been undertaken by the Development Group themselves, though it became a marked feature of research elsewhere in the early 1970s.[21]

In their discussion of decoration, a particular aesthetic dominated which relates closely to the arts and crafts ideals discussed in earlier chapters. *Building Bulletin* no. 1 suggested that paint was not the only surface material; natural finishes could also be encouraged, such as fairface brickwork, tiles, wallboarding and fabric. Concepts such as naturalness, unity, simplicity, are found reflected, for example, in advice such as that the decor of the classroom should

> express the inherent quality of materials within the physical environment of the classroom: the woodiness of wood, the whiteness of white, and the softness of a carpet.[22]

Building Bulletins would not have reached an audience beyond those with professional interests, but a publication aimed at a wider public was Pamphlet no. 33 (1957) entitled *The Story of Post-war School Building*. Its attractive cover design, a line drawing of a spacious informally planned classroom with large windows, Venetian blinds, trapezoid tables, displays of artwork, nature specimens and potted plants, provided a graphic advertisement of what was considered best in school architectural practice, and the volume was generously illustrated with double page spreads of photographs representing developments in 1900, 1930, early post-war and mid-fifties designs. Coloured diagrams identified a three stage development of post-war primary plan-forms (and parallel developments in secondary schools). Its address to the lay person and its intention to improve public understanding was explicitly stated in the text, which surmised that although most people recognized change in fashions and in the style of motor cars which had taken place between the later 1930s and mid-fifties few people realized that similar changes had taken place in the ideas, practice and organization of education. In justifying primary schools of a more open-plan character, it appealed to the analogy in post-war housing and the need to live more compactly; dual use of space such as assembly halls used for dining may involve some inconveniences, but represented

> the common sense compromise which, as householders, we are prepared to make in our own homes in order to ensure value for money.[23]

Value for money was indeed the leitmotif of the pamphlet which devoted much space to the economies which had been made in the period 1951–56, the total area per child in primary and secondary schools together had been cut by 40 per cent, and cost savings of £1 per square foot (aggregating to £12m per annum) had been achieved, despite the steep rise in building costs.[24] In its description of developments in design, the pamphlet continually returned to this theme, so that where the merits of the 'cluster' plan were considered, five advantages were put forward: two of these concern economies and efficiency of administration, and one concerns upholding the standard of the physical environment such as daylight and ventilation; only two strictly pedagogical considerations, flexibility and informality, were given:

> (1) it is not wedded to any one particular concept of how a primary school should be organized, or of how a primary school should be taught. On the contrary it aims at providing large simple spaces, which can be adapted by the teacher to his particular needs, rather than a number of small specialized ones which will prove inflexible. . . .
>
> (5) it results in buildings that are informal in character and lends the school a domestic rather than an institutional atmosphere.[25]

Various DES Reports on Education also helped to publicize architectural activity: no. 27 'School design through development' (December 1965), no. 66 'Trends in school design' (October 1970), and no. 71 'School building' (August 1971).

The literature of primary school architecture was also enhanced by the imaginative publication in 1969 of an *Educational Brief* drawn up for the architects of St Thomas of Canterbury RC Primary School, Manchester. Published as a 50-page pamphlet, with illustrations, plans and details, it described in plain language the educational requirements of the school and the architects' provisions to meet these.[26] Chairman of the Joint Advisory Panel which prepared the brief was Dr. K. Laybourn, Deputy Education Officer of Manchester, and formerly Chief Inspector in Bristol, which had been well known for its progressive infant schools.[27] The school had been selected as an experimental project, in the knowledge of rapid developments in primary education and radical changes in school design. The Plowden Report was newly published as the Panel began its work. Its contents had 'made a profound impression upon members', and its findings were accepted as 'an authoritative basis for our thinking':

> In its final form the Educational Brief deliberately incorporates many of the findings of the Plowden Committee and looks forward to the time when they can be put into general practice.

The National Union of Teachers helped to encourage an awareness of school architecture amongst the profession. The Ministry of Education's *Building Bulletin* no. 1 was circulated on publication in 1949 to all local associations of the Union for discussion, attention being drawn to the promises of teacher consultation in planning.[28] Although this principle of teacher consultation in planning had been acknowledged by two House of Commons Select Committees on Estimates in 1952/53 and 1961/62 the Union still found cause to reiterate their demand fifteen years later.[29]

As part of its policy of educational development in the post-war period the Union set up consultative committees. The first of these, on the nursery-infant school, made strong recommendations concerning the value of the environment, drawing attention to the colour of walls, the desirability of pictures, and also commented on the condition of school buildings.[30] A later consultative committee was appointed in 1953 to consider the curriculum of the junior school. Its report in 1959 included a chapter on school buildings; some of the newer developments were welcomed, and 'as a consequence of cooperation between architects and teachers' many built especially between 1945 and 1952 'offer encouraging facilities for modern methods of teaching', though economy measures had subsequently restricted the programme.[31] Flexibility in classroom layout with light, moveable and well-made furniture was welcomed, and plugged power points and piped water in every class was considered necessary. A telling parallel with contemporary developments in domestic architecture was made;

> In recent years much research and creative design have gone to the equipment ... of domestic kitchens, so that every activity taking place there may be performed in the easiest and most effective way. We should like to see an equal amount of attention given to the built-in fittings of classrooms.[32]

But reservations were also expressed about overlarge windows, the reduction of circulation space, and the incorporation of toilets in self-contained classroom units which made them too isolated for the rest of the school community, all three being perceived defects which receive corroboration from other sources.[33] The Union also drew attention to the poor condition of older school buildings in two pamphlets, in 1960 and 1963.

In 1974 the Union again raised the voice of teachers on architectural matters through its enquiry into open-plan schools. Explicitly, the Union committed itself to no opinion on the organizational and curricular merits of open planning. Implicitly, the tone of the published report was favourable to many aspects, although in resisting the imposition on its members of a particular educational method, it noted that this was one still untested and whose effects were not yet known. The report reproduced the plan of six schools, including Finmere, Oxfordshire (opened in 1959), St Thomas of Canterbury, Manchester (opened in 1970) and Chaucer Nursery and Infant School, Ilkeston, Derbyshire (opened in 1974), all of which had also been publicized elsewhere.[35] In evaluating open-plan schools, the report referred to the difficulty of defining the term, and to a variety of arguments for and against which made it impossible to reach firm conclusions. Team teaching was recognized to require careful structuring and harmonious relationships between individual teachers. The need for a good staff-pupil ratio and the importance of careful record keeping were stressed. Amongst the disadvantages for children were the possibility of visual and aural distraction, and the liability of individuals feeling lost if unable to immerse themselves readily in groups.

For the purposes of its report, the NUT conducted a survey of teacher opinion through local associations of the Union. Seventy replies were received, amongst which a minority could give no information as they lacked direct experience of open-plan schools. The replies understandably came from a higher proportion of those who had experienced open planning, and expressed a generally positive response. When compared with traditionally built schools, most associations considered that as far as teaching methods were concerned, more flexibly designed buildings helped to achieve educational benefits in terms of children's gain in independence, in social maturity, initiative and self-discipline, and in variety of work; children were observed to develop at their own rate, show an increased interest in their work, and become more relaxed. Most respondents, however, did not consider that open planning helped children to improve their standard or presentation of work, or depth of study.[36]

Critical thinking about architectural practices espoused by the progressives was disseminated through two important research projects. In 1967 the Pilkington Research Unit at the University of Liverpool Department of Building Science conducted an enquiry into the environmental qualities of new primary schools. It was noted that the high reputation of the British primary school had been earned by a small proportion of new buildings, the majority being mediocre, and criticism was levelled at the Development Group for failing to produce an adequate definition of the purpose and function of primary education in a form usable by designers. There had also been a lack of appraisal of buildings in use, owing perhaps to the absence of any objective criteria.[37] The first large-scale educational research into open-plan schooling as such was the Schools Council project from 1975 to 1978 conducted by Neville Bennett and others. Its report, fully published in 1980,[38] estimated that about 10 per cent of all primary schools were now of open-plan design, and that this proportion was likely to increase.[39] An important criticism which emerged was the lack of effective communication between the designers and the users of open-plan buildings. The aims of teachers were similar to those in conventional schools, but their working experience included high demands of organization and cooperation, and physical exertion; their view of the curriculum was wider, with more sense of continuity and more involvement with parents and community. Surprisingly, however, in the light of the ideals which an open architectural form was evolved to foster and facilitate, the research found, as had an earlier survey by Evans (1979),[40] a considerable degree of curriculum timetabling and ability grouping.

Model Buildings

Some remarkable school buildings themselves became vehicles for the diffusion of 'progressive' ideals. Well publicized and often visually striking, certain notable architectural structures came to stand as visual images of a 'new' approach to teaching young children, just as about the same time, stylistically emphatic university campuses such as the Colchester tower blocks of Essex or the Norwich ziggurats of the University of East Anglia became visual symbols of the new higher education. The close attention paid by some LEAs to particular new primary school projects also resulted in the appointment of several enthusiastic and dynamic head teachers who gave publicity to their schools, which often became centres of attraction for visits from other teachers within the authority and beyond. It has been argued elsewhere that the growth of private transport and development of film and television greatly facilitated this process of publicity for new model schools.[41]

A key school building, because so amply documented in the Bulletins, was Eveline Lowe Primary School. Commissioned by the London County Council and intended as a cooperative project between the Ministry of Education Development Group and the local authority, it was hoped to apply the lessons drawn from rural schools, exemplified at Finmere, Oxfordshire, in 1959, to a deliberately chosen urban location which contained few play facilities for children, few social facilities for adults and which appeared to need support of nursery school facilities.

> Village schools have a distinctive character. The combination of small numbers, a wide range and a diversity of interests and abilities, produces a more subtle relationship between teachers and children than occurs in most large schools, and encourages the sharing of skills, experience, facilities and space. There are many who believe that this is the right way of working in primary schools generally, and that it should not necessarily be confined to village schools where it has emerged so strongly.[42]

The ideal of the village school was a powerful element in progressivism.

The internal arrangment at Eveline Lowe, and technical considerations concerning effects on pupil-teacher interaction, teaching methods and curriculum will not be dealt with in detail here; some discussion may be found elsewhere.[43] What is to be considered is the overall impression of the school, an educational ethos expressed in the language of architecture. The building was described in two Building Bulletins[44] and became something of a show school, much visited. Its first head, Mrs Aggett, travelled far and wide talking of the school and its work. Its historical importance lies also in its relation to the Plowden Committee which had been established in the same year as the planning of Eveline Lowe was begun, and Nora Goddard, an ILEA Inspector seconded to the secretariat of the Plowden Committee joined the planning team. Moreover, by 1963, as the planners of Eveline Lowe perceived it, rapid changes in teaching methods had been taking place since 1958 owing to a deeper understanding of the ways in which children learn and the ever increasing pace at which knowledge, skills and ideas were communicated.[45] This acute self-consciousness of rapid change is characteristic of professional developments at the period, and refers in part to the popularization of Piagetian ideas during these years. The headteacher was appointed a year in advance, to

> travel throughout the country to *meet others in her profession whose work has been influential in primary school practice*, appoint her staff and develop a team spirit among them. In this way she *made valuable links with schools in other authorities* and achieved a keen understanding of the *derivations* and opportunities of her own school. [my emphasis][46]

Eveline Lowe was described by a later headteacher, Wendla Kernig (1975–85), as designed to look like a row of country cottages amidst the surrounding high-rise flats and urban through-routes.[47] Certainly, viewed from within it has the character of a verdant clearing in a concrete jungle. An informal group of variegated red brick single storey buildings with pitched roofs surround green lawns, a landscaped adventure playground, low-walled flower beds, tubs, shrubs and trees. It conveys by its scale and asymmetry a relaxed and safe haven from the tower blocks which rise above it. The new school was planned for an age-range of $3\frac{1}{2}$–9 years, and in stark contrast the upper juniors remain housed in an former special school dating from earlier this century, a somewhat forbidding two-storey block in smoke-blackened London stock brick surrounded by a tarmac playground.[48] The contrast of two school buildings so close by symbolizes the contrast between two philosophies of education expressed in bricks and mortar. A forbidding ten foot high wall surrounding the earlier school is penetrated only by a solid wooden gate, which gives onto the asphalt playground, while the open fences and articulated recesses of the modern school buildings reveal a variety of entrances, the main one marked by its flanking flowerbeds, proceeding by way of an awning, a gradual transition between interior and exterior, and thence by a welcoming hall decorated with children's work.

Internally, the later building radiates a cosiness and security equivalent to that expressed by the external elevations. Spaces leading off from the entrance hall where stripped pine lines the ceilings and walls, provide an ample circulation space divided into bays to give a sequence of window seats and display areas with storage space below. This is a space, light and warm, used appropriately for dining at midday, but also at other times, inviting one to linger, rest and study the displays. Original wicker lampshades contribute to the warmth, still hanging and still as appropriate to their environment as they appear in early photographs illustrating the Building Bulletins. It was a particularly photogenic feature and conveyed something of the then new 'Habitat look', applying domestic decorative values in an institutional context.

Variety of space and surface texture, as with facilities for display, was one way in which the building was to play an active role as a stimulus to learning. As the planners recognized in the schools which they had observed, activities which appeared at first sight unplanned generally proceeded within a carefully conceived framework:

> Undoubtedly, one of the most important elements in this framework was the character of the environment and the challenge to imagination and invention which it provided.
>
> Fenestration, furniture and proportions, will all be deployed to encourage different use by children and teachers. . . .
>
> They need encouragement to go their own way under the influence of things they can see, touch and feel, rather than in a plain, characterless space. . . .[49]

Another striking feature is the so-called 'Kiva', a den or quiet room furnished with a stepped and carpeted floor and with bunk beds; rather dark with its walls wood-panelled and windows relatively small by comparison with the rest of the school, it forms an intimate space. In other school plans, such as Hampton Station Infants School (completed in 1969) the equivalent space is described as a 'snug', a charmingly evocative term which recalls, not inappropriately, some of the cosiness of a village pub!

A key to the creation of this warm, domestic environment was the use of carpet. Carpeted floors served a dual purpose, both physically deadening noise and helping to designate a 'quiet area' by producing the appropriate character and associations. New developments in carpet technology assisted in this application of carpets to schools. For example, a special hardening of the fibres, noticeable only to the touch but not to sight,

> may just have the effect of removing an excessive sense of softness and luxury which may, in some circumstances, seem inappropriate.[50]

The new technology was thus apparently welcome not only for its hardwearing properties, but also for retaining a vestigial hint of the puritanism which traditionally informed school design!

The evaluation of Eveline Lowe by a team of HMI, ILEA inspectors and architects six years after its opening made observations about the building in use. Not all teachers had worked as cooperatively as might have been liked. Careful maintenance of home and shared areas had been identified as essential, and elements noted as lacking included a central area for reference and story books, and a parents' room. However, tension had noticeably relaxed with the friendliness and freedom encouraged by the building, and children's oral skills had improved with more things to talk about. Criticisms were made elsewhere, however, about the structure itself, for example by Leonard White, an architect for ILEA, who considered that the number of load-bearing walls and built-in changes of level made the building inflexible and incapable of change by the teachers to meet changing needs.[51]

Another well-publicized London school was Prior Weston in the Barbican, built in 1968. Although softened by curtains, carpets and cushions, the open spaces were quite large, so that here team teaching was almost unavoidable. One observation was that problems were encountered through the impossibility of acoustically isolating areas, which limited the flexibility of the building in practice.[52] Its first head, Henry Pluckrose, who had also served as a deputy head at Eveline Lowe, considered that of all the schools he had worked in, Prior Weston was nearest his ideal.[53] A very striking post-Plowden architectural statement at Thurmaston in Leicestershire highlights the complex relationship between aesthetics and function in the context of 'child-centredness'. The architects Ahrends, Burton and Koralek, gave it a very exciting look from outside, rather high-tech, with its canted glass surfaces. Inside, the textures were varied and humane: plenty of white sandlime brick, and wood panelling. Moreover, as Colin Ward observed:

> In an almost Victorian way, it is full of odd corners and surprises, changes of level and view that are calculated to stimulate the imagination of the young.[54]

Yet several classic problems afflicted this building in use — poorly modulated natural lighting, poor sound insulation, and maintenance and heating costs. As in many schools, a shortage of wall display space arose from the combination of three factors: openness of plan, over-articulation of surfaces and extensive glazing. A highly contrasting example, also built by a prestigious architectural firm, was Maguire and Murray's St Paul with St Luke Primary School, Bow Common, in London's East End. Its external structure was a large unmodulated 'agricultural shed' giving none of the variety of broken contours, nooks and crannies which surround Eveline Lowe. Most of the visual embellishment was lavished on the inside of this building.[55] Bow Common embodied a response to better cost information available since the design of Eveline Lowe, for external enclosure turned out to be a highly expensive element. The ratio of external wall to enclosed space had therefore to be kept as low as possible.

Cost became an increasingly important factor as far as the DES was concerned in the 1960s, as also the speed of construction so that timetables for educational building could be adhered to. Thus, system building was encouraged along the lines that had earlier been developed by a number of local authority consortia and by 1970 41 per cent of school building was executed according to such methods. Although flexibility and design qualities were not necessarily impaired by system building, a number of disadvantages followed in practice:

> The use of building systems in a regime of rigorous cost control is rather like the introduction of the potato as a staple diet in a peasant economy.... Introduced to cope with particular situations — the urgent need for school accommodation in Hertfordshire after the war, or the problem of subsoil maintenance in Nottinghamshire — inevitably they became the norm against which the initial cost of alternatives was judged.[56]

The 'thin end of the wedge' in terms of cost criteria, system building also carried the prospect of dull uniformity; according to one architectural critic, it reflected a well-intentioned Utopian enthusiasm for good quality and high technical performance through high spending. Schools could be designed and completed very rapidly, but

> they provided an unacceptable architectural image — a uniform, box-like standard which suspended individual taste, wit and humanity — ubiquitous but nowhere in particular.[57]

A number of factors in the early 1970s began to affect attitudes to public building in general and schools in particular. The 1973 oil crisis began to curb investment available for schools, and the downturn in population projections began to indicate a declining demand. Some public disquiet about system building arose from incidents such as Ronan Point, and the collapse of high alumina beams. Consumerism was a growing movement so that popular opinion increasingly wanted its voice heard and the public were less likely than architects to be excited by the technical details, however wonderful, of system building. More importantly, conservationist attitudes were waxing and a new appreciation of the architectural merit of old schools, particularly in their contribution to the character of the local environment, opposed a policy of demolition and replacement (which was in any case becoming less viable on economic grounds). Practical considerations also applied; old schools properly adapted could provide more generous space and better energy conservation. By 1973 consortia construction of schools had fallen to 35 per cent and was declining rapidly. The adaptation of old schools had already drawn some interest through the 'Plowden competition' of 1968, intended to encourage the opening up and making more flexible of interior spaces in old school buildings,[58] and newer primary schools featured more often the solid brick walls and pitched roofs of 'post-modernism'.

School and Community

In the relationship of scale between the school building and its built environment, Eveline Lowe School represented an interesting reversal of the late Victorian arrangement in which three-decker board schools dominated the smaller working class housing which often surrounded them. Now it was the school which seemed better atuned to children, and the habitations which loomed over it in an inhuman scale. An important aspect of school architecture is in symbolizing visually the relationship of the school to its community.

Elementary schools had traditionally been closely involved with the life of their community, but in the period since 1945 the nature of the relationship has changed in many respects. It is risky to generalize when regional and local circumstances differ so widely and when so much is dependent in fact upon personalities. Changing roles of managerial and governing bodies are not simply a product of adjustments to the legal or administrative structure, nor of political policies, but are also heavily coloured by social and cultural factors. A charming illustration of changing relationships in a rural area has been illustrated with regard to the furnishing and facilities in schools. Edith Moorhouse, newly-appointed primary adviser in Oxfordshire following the Second World War, noted that the furniture of rural primary schools had been augmented by 'gifts from the "big house"'. Not only pianos and bookcases, but trophies from colonial administration and the like were 'gathering dust and gloom' in the classrooms, and great tact was required in the removal of such objects since 'the feudal influence in some rural schools was very real'. In addition, schoolrooms were cluttered by other impedimenta such as Women's Institute chairs and tables, polling booths and Oddfellows boxes, signifying the use of the local school for other community purposes.[59] By 1967 the Plowden Committee recommended a rather different view of this relationship between community and school, in which the school's role included initiation of community involvement.

A deliberately experimental architectural brief drawn up in the wake of Plowden for St Thomas of Canterbury RC School, Cheetham, Manchester, expressed this changed relationship in terms of design and furnishings. 'St Thomas of Canterbury School should become an integral part of the community beyond its walls'. It followed Plowden in the intention to entice parents in through the strategy of developing a community school, and took up the economic argument that a capital investment of such proportions provided by the community should not be regarded as a private enclave. Thus the entrance hall must be designed and furnished to make parents feel welcome, and furniture, especially chairs, must be provided and stored for adult use, and appropriate and cloakroom and toilet facilities were to be provided.[60]

In a broadsheet produced by the Architects and Building Branch of the DES in 1983, the relationship as revealed by Edith Moorhouse's experience in the 1940s was conceived quite differently.[61] Referring to a DES survey of 1978/79 it pointed out that 64 per cent of primary schools were regularly used and 89 per cent occasionally used outside school hours in term time. In the school holidays 15 per cent were regularly used. But the gist of the advice is that the school might become the leading partner in this relationship. With some additional district funding, the Chaucer Infant and Nursery School at Ilkeston, Derbyshire, had incorporated and furnished for adult use a meeting place where parents, staff and other adults connected with the school could make personal contacts in a relaxed and informal atmosphere, a valuable facility in developing closer links between school, parents and community. At Guillemont Junior School in Farnborough, Hants, despite the unavailability of any additional local finance, the LEA decided to build a PE hall just large enough for adult badminton, and to group a craft workshop with kiln, a music/drama room and a darkroom as a complex which could be isolated from the rest of the school and thus used outside school hours with no fear of disturbance to children's work or displays in the other teaching areas. Moreover this complex centred around a cookery bay which could double as a snack-bar, refreshment facilities being regarded as an essential feature to attract community use.

In the planning process, it was stressed, educational decisions must come first, but the value of provision for the community was underlined in the possibilities for developing close links between school, parents and the local population. A fundamental change in relationships is reflected in this advice and in the examples given. In the first *Building Bulletin* community use of the premises outside school hours had been acknowledged, but it was argued that adult requirements should not overshadow the needs of the children;[62] in the years between 1949 and 1983 the school had acquired a more predominant role. Where once the school facility had been used for convenience, now the school was initiating activity. As an ideal the educators had come to see their role not in narrow terms related to a particular age-group amongst local children, but as an influential force in the community. From the point of view of local people, the school's role as an agent of the welfare state had extended with the provision of ancillary services (such as health and dental care), school meals, and professional advice to parents. Education was increasingly portrayed as a cooperative task between home and school.

With parents entering schools more freely as a consequence, so the school building, inside as well as out, becomes its public face. Before the advent of compulsory published curriculum statements, most visitors would have formed their impression of its ethos from what they saw in the material environment, and 'progressive' teachers, conscious of this fact, use the environment to convey their aims and achievements. It is the fruit of the children's labours that provides the concrete evidence of achievement. It provides also a means of communication between teachers and children. Before term, teachers carefully choose and display material designed to motivate and inform, and as term progresses so the best work, or that most preferred by the teachers, is chosen for display less conspicuously as a means of reward for its authors, than as a continuing reinforcement of the learning process. These displays of children's work confirm to visitors the aims and achievements of the school. A Froebel pamphlet on primary school design stressed the importance of display in creating a stimulating atmosphere. Christopher Jarman, an Oxfordshire adviser and author of a book on display and presentation in primary schools, referred particularly to the use by the headteacher of foyer, hall and corridors, in order to present a lead to the rest of the staff in showing children that their work is valued.[63] This was a significant feature of Oxfordshire primary schools, and one that we shall return to in chapter 8.

Architecture and decor has always served to convey meanings in this way. The high walls, asphalt playgrounds and tiled corridors of Victorian board schools promulgated a particular educational philosophy. Bricks and mortar expressed the founding aims, classroom decoration the more temporary concerns of the teachers. Faded prints of class photographs at the turn of the century show framed portraits of Queen Victoria or General Gordon, popular engravings such as Millet's *Angelus* or teaching aids like maps and charts. By the mid-twentieth century it seems that these means were very consciously exploited by progressive schools and teachers to promote their educational philosophy.[64]

Notes

1 Wotton, Sir Henry (1568–1639) in *Elements of Architecture* (1624).
2 Girouard, M. (1977) *Sweetness and Light*, Yale, Yale University Press, pp. 64–70.
3 Robson, E.R. (1874) *School Architecture* reprinted Leicester University Press in 1972.
4 Pevsner, N. (1976) *History of Building Types*, London, Thames and Hudson.
5 Cox, I. (1951) *The South Bank Exhibition: A Guide to the Story It Tells*, London, HMSO.
6 Ministry of Education (1957) *The Story of Post-war School Building; Pamphlet no. 33*, London, HMSO, pp. 6–8. The birth of the British movement for a 'social architecture', and school building as a contribution to the ideal of sharing technical and cultural development justly among all, has recently been explored by Saint, A. (1987) *Towards A Social Architecture: The Role of School Building in Post-war England*, London, Yale University Press.
7 RIBA (n.d.) (1948) *New Schools: The Book of the Exhibition by the Royal Institute of British Architects*, London, RIBA.
8 Schiller, C. (1972) 'Introduction' in National Froebel Foundation *Designing Primary Schools*, London, National Froebel Foundation.
9 Maclure, S. (1984) *Educational Development and School Building: Aspects of Public Policy 1945–1973*, London, Longman, pp. 61–7.
10 DES (1965) *Reports on Education* 27, 'School design through development'; Pile, Sir W. (1979) *The Department of Education and Science*, London, George Allen and Unwin, p. 79.

11 MEDD, D. and MEDD, M. (1972) 'Designing primary schools' in NATIONAL FROEBEL FOUNDATION *Designing Primary Schools* London, National Froebel Foundation, pp. 7–8.

12 WHITE, L.G. (1972) 'Designing schools for young children' in NATIONAL FROEBEL FOUNDATION *Designing Primary Schools*, London, National Froebel Foundation, p. 25.

13 MANNING, P. (Ed.) (1967) *The Primary School: An Environment for Education*, Liverpool University of Liverpool Department of Building Science, p. 64. In the eighteen years before Manning's research (1949–66), the Development Group published thirty-three Bulletins, and in the next eighteen years (1967–84) twenty-seven Bulletins, thirty-six Design Notes, six A & B Branch Papers, and more than thirteen A & B Branch Broadsheets. The following are particularly relevant to primary education:

Building Bulletins

no. 1 (1949) New primary schools (2nd edn 1955)
no. 6 (1951) Primary school plans
no. 16 (1958) Development Project, Junior School, Amersham
no. 3 Village schools (2nd edn 1961)
no. 21 (1963) Remodelling old schools
no. 23 (1964) Primary school plans: A second selection
no. 35 (1966) New problems in school design: Middle schools
no. 36 (1967) Eveline Lowe Primary School, London
no. 47 (1972) Eveline Lowe School appraisal
no. 53 (1976) Guillemont Junior School, Farnborough, Hants
no. 57 (1980) The renewal of primary schools: Planning for the eighties

Design Notes

no. 11 (1973) Chaucer Infant and Nursery School, Ilkeston, Derbyshire
no. 19 (1979) Building user manuals: Guillemont Junior School
no. 32 (1983) Designing 8–12 middle schools

Buildings such as Amersham Junior School, Bucks (opened in 1957), Finmere Village School, Oxon (opened in 1959) and Eveline Lowe Primary School, Southwark (opened in 1966), all projects designed by the Development Group, became well-known classics partly because of the accessible documentation available in the Bulletins.

14 MINISTRY OF EDUCATION (1949) *BB* no. 1, 1st edn.

15 *ibid*, p. 2.

16 *ibid*.

17 MINISTRY OF EDUCATION (1953) *BB* no. 9, 1st edn p. 5.

18 MINISTRY OF EDUCATION (1949) *op. cit.*, p. 42.

19 *ibid.*, p. 29.

20 *ibid.*, p. 14.

21 Two projects seeking children's opinions were: BLISHEN, E. (1969) *The School That I'd Like*, Harmonds worth, Penguin, and Manchester Playspace Project (1975) *Ask The Kids*.

22 MEDD, D. and MEDD, M. (1972) *op. cit.*, p. 11.

23 MINISTRY OF EDUCATION (1957) pp. 10, 32 and 38.

24 *ibid.*, pp. 4–5. Value for money was also a consistent theme of the *Building Bulletins*.

25 *ibid.*, pp. 39–40.

26 SALFORD DIOCESAN SCHOOLS COMMISSION and MANCHESTER EDUCATION COMMITTEE (n.d.) (1969) *St. Thomas of Canterbury R.C. Primary School: An Educational Brief*. The completed school was described by PEARSON, E. (1972) *Trends in School Design: British Primary Schools Today*, London, Macmillan for the Schools Council.

27 Laybourn was the author of articles on progressive primary developments in the *Times Educational Supplement*, 4 March and 2 December 1960. In 1967 he travelled to Sweden with David and Mary Medd and Eric Pearson to study the architecture of comprehensive schools: DES ARCHITECTS AND BUILDING BRANCH (1970) *Design Note* no. 4, 'A visit to some Swedish schools.'

28 NUT (1951) *Annual Report* and PSAC Mins 27 April 1950.
29 NUT (1977) *Annual Report*, p. 82.
30 NUT (1949) *Nursery-Infant Education: Report of a Consultative Committee*, London, NUT/Evans.
31 NUT (1959) pp. 47–8.
32 *ibid.*, p. 51.
33 As early as 1952 the House of Commons Select Committee on Estimates expressed its concern about the proportion of glass in school buildings. Although a cheap building material, too much glass created heating problems and sometimes glare, both of which required further expense to overcome. (H.C. 1952–53 (186) v para. 41 and recommendation 10). In the context of his concern for the psychological and sociological consequences of architecture, Manning (1967) identified the impact of certain plan-forms in the isolation as well as the integration of groups; plan forms could have effects which might require careful administrative procedures to overcome. A later Development Group design, that of Guillemont School in Farnborough, Hants., attempted to solve circulation problems by the introduction of short, corridor-like spaces (DES (1976) *BB* no. 53).
34 NUT (1960) *Fair Play for Our Primary Schools* London, NUT; NUT (1963) *State of Our Schools*, London, NUT.
35 NUT (1974) *Open Planning: A Report with Special Reference to Primary Schools*, London, NUT, para. 21; MINISTRY OF EDUCATION (1961) *BB* no. 3 (2nd edn); SALFORD DIOCESAN SCHOOLS COMMISSION AND MANCHESTER EDUCATION COMMITTEE (1959) *op. cit*; DES A & B Branch (1973), *Design Note* no. 11.
36 NUT (1974) *op. cit.*, p. 27.
37 MANNING, P. (Ed.) (1967) *op. cit.*, p. 15.
38 BENNETT, N. and others (1980) *Open Plan Schools, Teaching, Curriculum, Design*, Slough, NFER for the Schools Council.
39 This proportion corresponds with the findings of HMI in their sample of schools for the Primary School Survey of 1975, in which they found about one tenth of classrooms of open or semi-open plan.
40 EVANS, K. (1979) 'The physical form of the school', *British Journal of Educational Studies*, 27, 1, pp. 29–42.
41 See chapters 4 and 8.
42 DES (1967) *BB* no. no. 36 *Eveline Lowe Primary School*, London, HMSO, p. 3.
43 MACLURE, J.S. (1984) *op. cit.*, pp. 133–5, and 166–7; SEABORNE, M. and LOWE, R.A. (1977) *The English School: Its Architecture and Organization*, London, Routledge and Kegan Paul, pp. 176–7; and especially DES (1974) *BB* no. 47.
44 DES (1967) *BB* no. 36 *Eveline Lowe Primary School*, London, HMSO; and DES (1972) *BB* no. 47 *Eveline Lowe School Appraisal*, London, HMSO. It was visited by the Primary Advisory Committee of the NUT and was noted as having attracted enormous attention, NUT (1974) *op. cit.*, para. 14.
45 DES (1967) *BB* no. 36 p. 3.
46 *ibid.*, para. 33 (my emphasis).
47 Wendla Kernig in conversation with the author, May 1986.
48 However, the interior of this older building had been made bright and casual, the former classroom spaces having been adapted in a variety of informal ways, and some adjacent waste ground has been acquired by the school and grown wild for nature study.
49 DES (1967) *BB* no. 36 paras. 10 and 83.
50 *ibid.*, para. 98.
51 DES (1974) *BB* no. 47; WHITE, L. (1972) *op. cit.*
52 RINGSHALL, R. (1983) *The Urban School*, London, GLC/Architectural Press, p. 77.
53 PLUCKROSE, H. (1977) 'Open plan schools, — An environment for learning' in NATIONAL FROEBEL FOUNDATION *Designing Primary Schools*, London, National Froebel Foundation.

54 Ward, C. (1976) *British School Buildings: Designs and Appraisals, 1969–1974*, London, Architectural Press, pp. 29–38.
55 *ibid.*, pp. 73–86.
56 *ibid.*, p. x.
57 Ringshall, R. (1983) *op. cit.*, p. 62. Also: 'generally architects were critical of this system'.
58 Kay, J. (A & B Branch, DES) (1969) *RIBA Journal* (December) 'Report on Plowden competition and remodelling of old schools'.
59 Moorhouse, E. (1985) A Personal Story of Oxfordshire Primary Schools, 1946–1956, Oxford, privately printed, pp. 45–6.
60 Salford Diocesan Schools Commission and Manchester Education Committee, (1969) *op. cit*, p. 23.
61 DES, A & B Branch (1983) *Broadsheet* no. 15, 'Community use of primary schools', London, HMSO.
62 DES (1949) *BB* no. 1, p. 14.
63 Lancaster, J. (1972) 'The artist looks at the school environment' in National Froebel foundation, *Designing Primary Schools* London, National Froebel Foundation; Jarman, C. (1976) *Display and Presentation in Schools*, (2nd edn) London, A. and C. Black, p. 5.
64 Cunningham, P. (1987) 'Open plan schooling: Last stand of the progressives?' in Lowe, R. (Ed.) *The Changing Primary School*, Lewes, Falmer Press.

7 *Propaganda and the Public Image*

The progress of progressivism in the years after 1945 had to do not only with professional reorientation, but also with a broader acceptance of progressivist principles by a wider public. Aspects of social and economic change which contributed to this acceptance (but which also led eventually to a challenging of professional authority on the curriculum) are described in chapters 2 and 9. In the propagation of the progressive educational ideal amongst the public, a number of agencies had a role, including the Ministry, teacher unions, and the mass media.

Ministry of Education

With the experience of war-time information and propaganda behind it, the government devoted considerable energy to promoting the new education settlement through the printed word and through film. From 1945 a new role in dissemination devolved upon HMI, compiling pamphlets for publication by the Ministry, described by Edmonds as

> a new anthology of the ideas and practices which teachers are successfully developing in their schools.

and by 1979 Sheila Browne, Chief Inspector, was proposing that HMI needed to use its voice publicly through television, radio, film and the printed word, for its knowledge and opinions to reach those who influence education or consume its product.[1]

As far as primary education was concerned, the underlying themes were progressivist. In the new series of Ministry pamphlets, numbers 14 and 15 were devoted to primary education. Both published in 1949, *Story of a School* was directed more at professionals, whilst *Seven to Eleven* was written with parents in mind.[2] *Story of a School* was written by A.L. Stone, the Birmingham headteacher whom both Clegg and Schiller had met during their work in Worcestershire, and whom Clegg attracted to the West Riding to work as an adviser. Schiller reputedly persuaded him to write this thoughtful account of his work at Steward Street Junior School, Birmingham. Publicizing the work of a 'good school' in this way was a new departure, and characteristic of Schiller; visiting selected schools was the principal activity for students on his later in-service course, and the identification and description of 'good practice' became a basic approach by which the Plowden Committee later worked. *Story of a School* met with objections in the National Union of Teachers precisely because of its fostering publicity for a particular school.[3] The pamphlet specifically requested teachers not to embarrass this school with visits.

A pamphlet of thirty-six pages, its cover reproduced a painting by children of the school and inside were eight pages of photographs, four of movement and drama, and four of modelling and painting. Thus an arts-based curriculum was portrayed, its priorities reflected in the chapter headings of the text:

Movement	Music and arithmetic
Drama (mime, costume, speech)	Arts and the growing child
Art	Teaching
Art and composition	

Stone gave a carefully argued, but distinctly behaviourist, rationale for turning to the arts as the basis of education which should pervade his school; the 'three Rs' he thought, should become a secondary consideration, not undervaluing their importance, but believing that the development of a child's personality demanded greater attention. Interest and concentration which could be developed through the arts, would lead to greater self-discipline. Art was also conceived of as a form of social therapy; freedom (not licence) would allow these children to find an inner beauty to counter the lack of beauty in their environment, resulting in less antagonistic social conduct. Art rather than craft was encouraged to begin with, as craft imposed rules which the children could not handle. Children 'finding themselves' was a leitmotif of the text. 'All the arts have a common beginning in movement' was the caption to one picture, whilst another showed children 'Responding easily and fearlessly to the thoughts within'. In music, Stone felt he had failed to find an approach which ensured full 'absorption' by the children, perhaps because it had been dealt with as interpretation rather than as a creative act. Freedom in the use of space was also important; children painted on the floor, on the teacher's desk, in corridors, ignoring the dreary premises and old furniture.

> Painting went on all over the three-storey building. We found it necessary, before we went home, to make sure that we locked no children in the school.

Seven to Eleven published in the same year, was 'written for mothers and fathers'. It was a glossy pamphlet with many photographs, mostly from schools in the Nottingham LEA which became noted as a centre of progressivism. In simple, if not condescending language, it set out to explain the new structure of school provision, child development and the contribution of the school to this, and a description of junior schools in their present state, as well as 'the sort of school which it is our task to create'.

In several respects, the pamphlet's themes anticipated those of the Plowden Report almost twenty years on. Children learning through play, the tradition of English infants schools, was 'this country's greatest gift to education'. Children's physical development was of the utmost importance, and observing this was a job for the expert — a trained teacher; the teacher had to understand how each girl and boy in the class was growing, and help to make their bodies grow to the full. Natural instincts of children to explore the world about them, to read, to count and measure, to express themselves through art, were all described. In the 'school of tomorrow', in a typical class of forty-two boys and girls (classes were currently often nearer fifty), an arithmetic class would see some children measuring the playground, some working an improvised shop, others doing written sums, and others learning their tables and being tested by the teacher:

> The children are all busy, and through the activity they are learning how to use their powers and their powers are growing with use. They are learning also through experience.[4]

In another class, painting and telling stories continued simultaneously — different aspects of the same activity. Finally, it was observed that a good school was a community of teachers and parents; interest and understanding of a child's life at school would be something every school would need.

> The junior school is at the beginning of its history. Its tradition has yet to be made . . . It is our task to create in our time a junior school not only with fair buildings, not only with small classes, but giving a happy and healthy growth to all children from seven to eleven.[5]

Parents with children of all ages were addressed in a pamphlet published by the Central Office of Information for the Ministry of Education in 1950, *Our Changing Schools: A Picture for Parents.* As propaganda for the new educational order, the publication had a specific but broader target than the title implied:

> In this huge national task of educational development are engaged not only local education authorities and the Ministry of Education, not only teachers, parents and pupils and the staffs of

> training colleges and universities, but also experts in many branches of professional work, and in many trades: lawyers, surveyors, architects, administrators, clerical workers, artists, craftsmen and builders. It is surely important to the success of the work that all concerned in it should have some general picture of what it all means in human terms.[6]

Its author, Roger Armfelt, was well suited to writing such a publicity pamphlet, having worked for the BBC as Secretary of the Schools Broadcasting Council; he had also enjoyed a varied career as (public school) teacher, HMI, Chief Education Officer, and latterly Professor of Education.[7] To modern ears the text sounds rather like the stilted documentary style of radio interviews of the period. Dialogues between fictitious characters were presented. The scene was set in a Victorian three-decker building (the accompanying photograph was of the Hugh Myddleton School). Mr Green, the young teacher, was conversing with Mr Jones, septuagenarian school manager:

> 'You see the three Rs don't loom so large nowadays'
>
> Mr Jones was shocked — deeply shocked, and Mr Green had to explain:
>
> 'Well I shouldn't have put it quite like that. We do care, of course, about the three Rs. We're bound to. There's not much we can do without them. We say that if we set about educating in the right way, they will come in due time of their own accord.'

Concern was not for curriculum only, but for school buildings which would be more child-centred:

> Miss Jenkinson was following the inspector's eyes round the room.
>
> 'Look at that door', she said. 'When one of my little ones wants to open that he has to reach up and almost hang on the handle to turn it. Usually, of course, we open it for him, which is just what we don't want to do. Or suppose he wants to pin something on the wall — well he can't. Or to look out of the window — well, he can't do that either ... We talk about fitting education to the children — I don't see how we can ever do that unless we make a start with the buildings.'

Superiority of the country over the city as a setting for primary education has already been discussed as a theme of progressivism; in *Our Changing Schools* it was clearly expressed:

> 'My second wish would be simple enough. It would be for grass — grass for my little ones to roll on.'

> 'And that', replied the inspector, 'is about the one thing which this site will never provide.'
>
> 'Well, there are about 900 children in this building. What's to be done about it?'
>
> 'H'm.' The inspector thought for a moment. 'Move the school somewhere else I should say.'

After a passing reference to suburban schools, the best of the new in primary schools was described in rural terms; chapter 2 was about the village school, and only the secondary sector enjoyed separate chapters on town schools and country schools.

David Eccles, Minister of Education, announced publication of a Primary Education Handbook in November 1959 as the first in a series of important documents and reports due to appear in the ensuing months, and the *Times Educational Supplement* thought that he ought to be well satisfied with the ample publicity given to it by the daily newspapers.

> When crowded journals find it prudent or profitable to notice reports from Curzon Street, it looks as if there really is some truth in the suggestion that the nation is at last stirring from its apathy and beginning to take an interest in its schools. [8]

That it may have been perceived as 'propaganda' is suggested by the various journalistic reactions, one newspaper seeing it as 'mere subjective impression instead of the fruits of fundamental research', and others seizing upon it for its criticisms of selective exams. The '*Times Ed*' was somewhat pompous about the latter reaction, noting the qualified nature of the Handbook's views on 11+, and stressing that this was only one of many topics dealt with:

> Teachers will know this. Many of the public will not. The nation may indeed be stirring from its apathy. Evidently, however, it still has a long way to go before it can be trusted not to concentrate its interest on too narrow a front.[9]

But David Eccles was clearly thinking in terms of its propaganda value for the primary sector of the profession, when he hoped that

> primary school teachers feel that they have a friend in Curzon Street who is always ready to help them and see that their work has a fair share of the growing recognition which the public is giving to education in general.[10]

During the war, the government had made considerable use of film as propaganda, a use continued in promoting the educational settlement of the post-war years. Film had been used as early as 1925 by Newcastle Education Committee during its Education Week, to inform the public about its activities in schooling, and amongst the notable documentary film-makers of the 1930s, Basil Wright had turned his attention to education in *Children at Schools* (1937) which revealed the insanitary and overcrowded conditions in some school buildings. Following such initiatives, war-time productions for the Ministry of Information had included *Tomorrow is Theirs* (1940) on secondary education, and *Our School* (1941) on curriculum and teaching methods at Bampton Senior School, Devon. The British Council film *Learning to live* (1943) portrayed the various levels of schooling in Britain, *Near Home* (1946) advocated the value of local studies, *The Three 'As'* (1948) ('age, ability and aptitude') promoted the new secondary modern school, whilst *Emergency Trained Teacher* (1948) (an amateur production sponsored by the Ministry of Education) and *Teaching Young Children* (1949) (professionally made for the Ministry by the Realist Production Company) advertised one-year and two-year training respectively, the latter aimed at recruiting much needed infant teachers. *Charley Junior's Schooldays* (1949), a cartoon film by the leading animation firm of Halas and Batchelor, featured 'Charley' explaining the different types of school in Britain.

As regards primary education, a distinctly progressive ideology and practice was portrayed by the film *Village School* (1941) produced for the Ministry of Education. Here at 'Ashley Green' with a shortage of teachers for a school roll swollen by evacuation, the children were of necessity working much of the time as independent learners, and were making practical use of the environment, such as the school garden for growing vegetables.[11] Film was subsequently used to portray the benefits of the 1944 Act, and to accompany Ministry of Education pamphlets.[12]

'Plowdenitis'

To view the Plowden Report as propaganda is not to ignore other aspects of its wide-ranging significance as a policy study and a work of empirical research, but to focus particularly on the unusual publicity (almost 'razzmatazz') with which an official report was propagated and received. Wilkinson (1987) has noted specifically with regard to this Report that:

> the socio-linguistic 'meaning' of a text is not confined to the surface meaning of the words. It is a question also of status, power, previous and subsequent texts, historical context, timing, the frame of reference and the response of the reader, particularly in this case the teacher, and so on. Public documents in particular can bear a wealth of such meanings.[13]

Plowden surveyed an aspect of British education of which many already felt proud:

> If one part of our system is known and respected abroad it is the primary school, with its art, activities and successful learning,

boasted the *Times Educational Supplement* in January 1967, announcing publication of the Report.[14] It sold 68,000 copies in its first year. In 1969, Lady Plowden thought that:

> The effect of the Report has been to accelerate the pace of change — to endorse the revolution in primary education which has been taking place since the war.[15]

After three years the sales had reached 117,000.

How many teachers must have been in the position of one who, speaking at a National Association for Primary Education (NAPE) conference to celebrate its twentieth anniversary, pointed out that he did not read the Report when originally published as he could afford neither the money to buy it, nor the time required, but knew its contents through digests.[16] The Report and extensive publicity surrounding it, 'created a mood' through which its message was doubtless communicated to most teachers. To some extent, these diffuse forms of dissemination applied to subsequent reports such as Bullock, Cockcroft, Warnock and Swann, which were better known through press commentary, summaries, in-service evenings and word-of-mouth than through the original texts, and the effects of these diverse forms of dissemination have to be considered; certainly they must serve to generalize and perhaps distort the contents, and Plowden apologists have argued that one feature of subsequent events was a misunderstanding and misapplication of the teaching methods proposed by the report. But none of these later reports could match the publicity given to Plowden.

The Plowden Report was the last to be produced by the Central Advisory Council for Education (England), which had been established under the 1944 Education Act (and was only formally dismantled in 1986). Though Herbert Andrew, Permanent Secretary at the DES, when questioned by a House of Commons Select Committee in 1970, put technical reasons for the failure to reappoint the CACE, Christopher Price, MP, later proposed the view that the Plowden Report marked the end of an era which relied on an anti-democratic consensus among the elite of educational policy-makers.[17] Halsey (1987) has referred to

> the amiable reflections of an essentially amateur Establishment of the 'great and good',

as being no longer appropriate for the formation of educational policy.[18] The CACE (England) had been chaired by professional educationists and amateurs alike, sir Fred Clarke (1945–48) and Sir John Newsom (1960–63) amongst the former, Sir Samuel Gurney Dixon (1948–56), trained in medicine though with long experience in local government of education, and Sir Geoffrey Crowther (1956–60), economist and journalist, amongst the latter. Bridget Plowden was also one of the latter, and unequivocally an Establishment figure; a Director of Trusthouses Forte (Crowther was chair of the same board of directors), a magistrate and governor of two secondary schools, she was the daughter of an admiral and married to the former Chairman of the Atomic Energy Authority, who had himself chaired a Committee of Enquiry on Public Expenditure from 1959 to 1961. Other lay members of Plowden's Committee came from a similarly Establishment background, such as the two designated 'housewife and parent': Mrs M. Bannister, whose father, Per Jacobsson, chaired the International Monetary Fund, and the Hon. Mrs. J. Campbell, daughter of Lord Adrian, Master of Trinity College, Cambridge.

Another feature of the Committee was the prominent group of professionals representing sociology and social policy, such as Professor David Donnison of the London School of Economics, Timothy Raison, editor of *New Society*, and Michael Young, Chairman of the Social Science Research Council and Director of the Institute of Community Studies. From the world of primary education Molly Brearley of the Froebel Institute represented teacher education, whilst the notably progressive LEAs, West Riding, Oxfordshire, Nottingham and Bristol were also represented.

The tenor of the Report regarding curriculum and teaching method seemed predetermined by the organization of the enquiry, for, as Lady Plowden reflected:

> We were guided in our enquiries by HMIs who directed us to those parts of the country where what they considered the best practice was taking place.[19]

The institutions visited were mostly primary, infant and nursery schools, but included some play groups and a few secondary schools. Twenty-three in Bristol were visited, but only five in Birmingham, twenty-nine in Oxfordshire but only one in Buckinghamshire (that being Eton College!), nineteen in Nottingham city and two in Nottingham county, twenty-one in the West Riding and two in Sheffield. Durham, Essex, Hampshire and London were all well represented in the sample. This geographical bias corresponds to some extent with that of subscribers to the posthumous volume of Christian Schiller's writings.[20]

The Report was published in a period which was still (just) one of steady economic growth. Unlike later official reports it carried no opening disclaimer on public expenditure implications, and Anthony Crosland, then Secretary of State, managed to secure £16 m. additional funding for designated Educational Priority Areas proposed by the Report.[21] The success of the Report as propaganda for primary education in general (if only because of previous neglect of the sector), is to be measured by the high political priority which the education of young children was accorded in the 1970 General Election. The Conservative Manifesto made promises which Mrs Thatcher as Secretary of State then met in the Queen's Speech with £38.5 m. to replace 600 of at least 3000 Victorian primary school buildings still in use.

The format of the Report is of interest as it was published in two large books weighing together nearly two kilos, by comparison with which the Hadow Report of 1931 had been a very slim volume. The second part of the Plowden Report carried a wealth of research evidence based largely on the findings of the 1964 *National Survey of Parental Attitudes and Circumstances Related to School and Pupil Characteristics* which stands as one of the more substantial monuments to large-scale sociological research commissioned to inform policy-making in this decade. For size, Plowden could not compete with the Robbins Report of 1963 which ran to six volumes, but a feature denied to Robbins was the insert of forty-six photographs of children at work and play, four of which were in colour. These illustrations offered not only an extensive iconography of progressive curriculum and teaching method, but also the representation of school as a haven from the urban and suburban environment.

The importance of digests has already been implied. The '*Times Ed*' provided a four-page synopsis on 13 January, *The Teacher* summarized the report on the same day, and the National Union of Teachers soon produced a digest in pamphlet form. More important for the general reader perhaps, the Advisory Centre for Education published a thirty-one page summary (the full report ran to nearly 1200 pages) entitled *Plowden for Parents*, in March 1967. Here the National Survey was welcomed as the most important piece of research in the Report, one of many significant findings being the correlation of parental interest to the child's educational performance. Recommendations about school buildings and staffing were also prominently identified by ACE and it is of interest that immediate discussion of the report mostly concerned issues such as home and school, educational disadvantage, and nursery education, namely the social aspects, — which also dominated debates in the House of Lords (14 March) and the House of Commons (16 March), along with resource implications. Teaching methods and curriculum were less in evidence in all this clamour, although the question of corporal punishment caught the public imagination. An unprecedented feature was the extent to which an official report on education was promoted and personified in the figure of its chairperson. On 22 January 1967, soon after its publication, Lady Plowden spoke to a crowded public meeting at the Friends' Centre, organized by the Council for Educational Advance, the first of many public appearances in the following years. The eulogy of a *Times Education Supplement* leader offers a graphic reflection of the excitement and enthusiasm engendered:

> The report's proposal is imaginative, even romantic. It strikes a nobler note than is often heard today. Earlier names spring to mind — Lord Shaftesbury's and even young Disraeli's[22]

Amongst the accolades may be counted honorary degrees from five universities granted to Lady Plowden in the years followng the Report.

From 1967 onward the Advisory Centre for Education held an annual conference entitled 'The Plowden Conference', again, an unprecedented tribute to an official Report on education, and again personalized by the close involvement of Lady Plowden herself. The Council for Educational Advance published a report entitled *Plowden Two Years On* in May 1969, based on a survey of implementation by LEAs of recommendations concerning pre-school provision, flexibility of entry and parental involvement. From the evidence of the forty-nine LEAs which replied, it was concluded that limits on progress were due to financial stringency; willingness to act in the spirit of the Report was not wanting. In a foreword, Lady Plowden identified also advance in the emphasis on children learning as individuals and in organization of schools to that end (though there was in fact hardly any evidence for this presented in the returns from LEAs):

> The Report has been and still is a talking point for teachers. But perhaps its greatest achievement was to bring primary education for a time into the forefront of educational thinking, both in this country and abroad. It must not be allowed to slip back into obscurity, nor must the progress which has been made be checked, because of ill-informed criticism by those with little first-hand knowledge of the best primary schools.[23]

At Goldsmiths' College Leonard Marsh mounted a 'Plowden Course' with Lady Plowden chairing the Board of Examiners, and the new 'primary base' for teacher education was christened 'the Plowden wing'.

The Plowden Report embraced elements of the 'liberal romantic' and of the 'social democratic' approaches to primary education. Its wide publicity was perhaps due more to the social recommendations of the Report, though these included tenets characteristic of progressive pedagogy, such as more parental involvement and the abolition of corporal punishment. Curricular recommendations, on the other hand, aroused criticism fairly early. Indeed Christian Schiller himself, soon after its publication, noted its neglect of what actually happened in the classroom; he found it was not cohesive, much of its seemed the work of sociologists rather than of those concerned with the teaching of children, and perhaps its greatest mistake lay in dealing with 'subjects'.[24] Other critics observed inconsistent and sometimes contradictory approaches to different areas of the curriculum.

The contest over curriculum engendered by the Report arose not only from external attacks, but eventually from internal dissension amongst supporters of a progressive approach. The promotion of Plowden, the nature of the movement to which it gave rise, created difficulties for the progressivists in response to attacks from other ideological viewpoints in the *Black Papers* or the popular press, for example as provoked by the 'William Tyndale affair', and in respouse to questions raised by research such as that of ORACLE or Bennett. In 1972, the sixth annual Plowden Conference, still being run in association with ACE in Cambridge, was beginning to moot the formation of a 'Plowden Club' with a core membership of about 100 of the regular attenders, together with teachers who had attended the 'Plowden Course' at Goldsmiths' College. Lady Plowden herself appealed against polarization and in-fighting and talked of muddled thinking on both the right and the left wings of the curriculum debate. Eric Midwinter thought that Plowden-orientated teachers had done a fine job in terms of method and attitude, but had been less clear about objectives and less resolute about content; the curriculum had to engage with the social environment, and school had to show more response to society's demands.[25] A rift began to appear as ACE abandoned the annual Plowden Conference in 1974 and the informal group who ran it moved their base to Bishop Grosseteste College, where Leonard Marsh had been appointed Principal in the same year. Marsh acclaimed the conference as a unique meeting point which had helped to produce a cadre of headteachers, inspectors and advisers who could spread an understanding of what 'good progressive schooling' was about. By 1976 criticisms were being made of the 'Plowden club' as

> an exclusive self-congratulatory group enjoying a false cosy consensus about primary education.

These were the words of a former Director of the Plowden Conferences, who also reflected:

> Many of us now realize that all was *not* wonderful in the late 1960s and early 1970s and during the 'Plowdenitis' epidemic (a virus that was mainly caught by those in teacher training and the inspectorate).[26]

It may have been the predictable fate of a report that had in effect become a totem for curriculum ideologues, that external challenges were inadequately understood. As a *Times Educational Supplement* leader put it:

> A visit to the [Plowden] conference is, no doubt, a wonderful resuscitation for flagging kindred spirits. But if the movement — if a movement it really is — is to fight its corner . . . it needs to do more than sustain the converted . . .
>
> Lady Plowden says politics must be kept out of education but, . . . education is politics in the broad sense: the onus rests on the supporters of progressive and informal methods to demonstrate the value of what they are doing and to defend the gains they have made.[27]

National Union of Teachers

The NUT was considered in chapter 5 for its role as a disseminator of progressive practice amongst primary teachers. Here it is studied as an originator of wider publicity. A number of its various publications were aimed not only at its own members, but were also intended for a wider audience, for politicians in particular and for the public at large. *The Nation's Schools* [1934], a large format book of photographs had described educational activities in the state sector with a marked emphasis, reflecting the influence of Percy Nunn amongst others, on practical craft.

An early example, as the campaign for a more equitable distribution of resources in education gained momentum in the later 1950s which eventually saw fruition in the appointment of the Plowden Committee, was the pamphlet published in 1960, *Fair Play for the Primary Schools*. In a foreword, the General Secretary, Ronald Gould, noted that the work of the primary schools was not widely understood, and therefore the conditions which hampered its development were little appreciated:

> Most people would agree that primary schools are happy places; few understand that within them, happiness is not achieved by 'messing around', but by capturing the children's interest in purposeful activities of all kinds.[28]

The booklet was mostly concerned with deficiencies of buildings, staffing and equipment, but was prefaced with an account of the change in primary education since the Hadow Report of 1931 and the Union's approbation of this change in its Consultative Committee Report on the junior school curriculum.[29]

> The changes involved ... have generally been made without abandoning the practices which have stood the test of time. The cult of 'free discipline', which in its early days occasionally got out of hand, has given way to a cultivation of self-discipline arising from a carefully nurtured acceptance of responsibility. 'Projects' that once tended to be ends in themselves unrelated to the main purposes of the school are now judiciously integrated into carefully prepared syllabuses and have become, as they should, the handmaiden and not the master of the curriculum or, to be more prosaic, means rather than ends. Again, there was an almost fanatical preoccupation with intelligence and attainment testing with their concomitants, elaborate records, which were in danger of becoming ends in themselves. These have now been replaced by such testing and recording as will assist in fostering the child's mental and emotional development. The interest of children has been captured through the use of new techniques and through purposeful activity, with the consequence that

> children show a more lively interest in all that is attempted. Work in the basic subjects is no less thorough because it is made more interesting than it was in the old days.[30]

The last of these claims was backed by reference to the Ministry of Education's observation of a marked increase in reading ability between 1948 and 1956, especially in the primary schools. Also published in 1960 *The Education Story*, 'a book which captures the spirit of education', was designed to communicate

> an impression of life in schools today. It describes the kind of thing that is done, and suggests why it is done.

Its forty-four pages were profusely illustrated, including centre pages in full colour. In 1963 appeared *The State of Our Schools*, an exposé of deficient school buildings, especially primary schools; in 1965 and 1967 pamphlets, well produced and illustrated, laying out the Union's memorandum of evidence to the Plowden Committee, *First Things First*, and its comments on the eventual Report.[31]

In the mid-1960s the NUT had a flourishing Publicity and Public Relations Department, the senior official of which was Fred Jarvis, later to be General Secretary. Evidence of how this was put to the service of propagating enlightened approaches to primary education is contained in documentary films produced by the Union which received considerable television and media coverage: *I Want To Go To School*, released in 1960, was produced by the 'Free Cinema' director Karel Reisz, premiered before politicians and journalists at the National Film Theatre, taken up by BBC TV, given peak-hour transmission in a Friday evening prime slot between *The Third Man* and *The News* and two repeats within the year. The *Radio Times* announced it as an

> outstanding documentary film ... in many respects a sequel to the award-winning *We Are the Lambeth Boys* ... Brilliant and incisive observation of children at work and play ... A film recording some reasons why children today are singing a variation on the old theme 'I don't want to go to school'.

Whilst the school featured, Beechwood County Primary, Luton, was not a model progressive school, the film's

> panorama of work and play at the junior stage and its sense of the zest and family atmosphere of a good primary school,

were designed to reach a mass audience through a new medium. It aimed to communicate 'the essence of a creative teacher-child relationship' and the message that, at the junior stage, a basic attitude to learning as joyful discovery was to be established, so that parents and the general public might gain

> a fuller understanding of current teaching methods and of the more informal approach to the child which has revolutionized the atmosphere of the schools.

The television screening was greeted with acclaim by the national press. Hilary Corke, TV critic of *The Listener*, however, was in no doubt as to its propagandist nature, and was not impressed:

> 'I want to Go to School' was rapturously announced as the *premiere* of an 'outstanding documentary'. Oh dear no. This was just the old stuff, radiant children's faces ... The noises of the playground all sweetness and socialized light. This was 'relying on subject' with a vengeance.
>
> As this programme rolled on, I began to think that I must have strayed into the wrong channel. Is *everything* in the modern school world really so *utterly* rosy? Surely this was a commercial for the Ministry of Education? And then, sure enough, in a flash at the end, so hastily suppressed as to become almost subliminal, was the information that this film was 'produced for the National Union of Teachers'![32]

The Happy Adventure, depicting life in Gossops Green Infants' School, Crawley, was completed in 1965 and was again taken up for television by the BBC, and received a second national showing on BBC1 in September 1966.[33] As a means of stimulating high standards of educational journalism, the Publicity and Public Relations Committee proposed in 1965 the presentation of annual awards for the best examples of radio, TV and press reporting of education.

Informal receptions were held at Hamilton House, the Union's headquarters, for representatives of the media and for politicians; at Christmas 1964, no less than three Secretaries of State for Education were present — Michael Stewart the current incumbent, and later successors Reg Prentice and Ted Short. A reception was also held for Lady Plowden and her Committee members in the course of their labours.[34] In 1966 the annual conference called for a campaign to raise the prestige of primary education to a level comparable to that enjoyed by other sectors of education, and to call for more funds for primary schools. Astutely, the Publicity Committee decided to await publication of the Plowden Report, preparing itself to be in a strong position to respond to requests from the media for facilities and to help journalists seeking to follow up the Report. Regional public meetings were held to focus attention on the needs of the primary schools and on 'the injustice of the primary differential', and a large public meeting addressed by Lady Plowden, was held in London.[35] In this the Union worked closely within the Council for Educational Advance, a federation of education consumer and pressure groups which had been established following the Campaign for Education in 1963;[36] the Council's offices had been accommodated at Hamilton House, and Fred Jarvis had acted as its Secretary.

Radio

In disseminating progressive educational ideals amongst a wider public, the mass media had a considerable part to play, and in the period under discussion radio and television were increasingly important as networks for public information. For the mass media in general, innovation is attractive and newsworthy, so that progressive practices might be expected to be given a higher profile than reporting of traditional practices.

On 29 June 1951 the latest annual report of the Ministry of Education was greeted on the Home Service with a special *News Commentary*. The report itself had included a retrospect of the previous half-century and the news coverage included an account of progress made in education since 1900. Presumably also by way of celebrating the event, a programme was broadcast on the same day entitled: *Looking At Things — A New School.* In the later 1940s there had been a noticeable increase in the output of radio broadcast material relating to education.

Some were addressed to parents as educational 'consumers', reflecting the new hopes, and new ideas and methods in the air engendered by post-war reconstruction (although a questioner on *Brains' Trust* was sufficiently sceptical to ask: 'Has the advance of education in the last fifty years added to human happiness?')[37]

5.6.46	West	*Our Children's Future — The New Junior School*: Prof. B.A. Fletcher
23.10.49	Scotland	*New Education Methods*
7.11.49	Home Service	*The Rising Generation*: children are people — how should they be taught?
22.4.48	North, N. Ireland	*Public Enquiry — Our Schools*: do they teach the wrong things?
27.9.49	West	*Parents' Questions About Education*
26.11.49	Light Programme	*Now's Your Chance — Your Schools:* including Toby Weaver and John Newsom

Obviously the building of new schools was frequently a matter worthy of record, especially by regional stations:

19.1.49	West	Opening of a new County Primary School at Welland, N. Devon.
9.3.49	West	First prefabricated aluminium school at Bristol (incl. recording by George Tomlinson).

11.3.49	West	Opening of four new aluminium schools in Bristol.
1.12.50	North, N. Ireland	Going up — the West Riding's new Schools.
10.1.51	Midlands	Coventry's new aluminium school.
12.1.51	Midlands	*Around and About*: opening of Whitmore Park Primary School by George Tomlinson.

Teachers were the focus of some programmes, beginning of course with the post-war recruitment drive:

12.2.46	Light Programme	*Job In Hand — Schoolteaching*: Mary Sturt
4.11.46	Home Service	*Teachers in the Witness Box*: is education too bookish?
20.1.48	Midlands	*We Want To Teach*: emergency training scheme for teachers
21.2.48	Home Service	*In Town Tonight*: School Teacher — Phyllis Taylor

And some programmes appealed to parental interest in their children, especially in the context of developments in psychological study of child development:

4.9.45	N. Ireland	*Teaching For Pleasure — Self Expression and the Ordinary Child*: R.L. Russell
25.7.47	Midlands	*Your Children — Children and Their Teachers*
7.6.48	Light Programme	*When Your Child Starts School*: by a child psychologist (anon. — Dr. M. Fordham)

Schonell featured prominently as a contributor to such programmes:

15.3.49	Midlands	*Midlands Miscellany*: The intelligent child who fails — the work of the University of Birmingham remedial centre: F.J. Schonell

and in a more highbrow vein:

19.9.49	Third Programme	*New Concepts in Education*: three talks by Prof. F.J. Schonell: 1 Present theories in teaching
24.9.49		2 Social and economic factors that may influence ability
28.9.49		3 Attitudes to learning and their effect on the pupil

Woman's Hour often provided a forum for educational discussion:

10.9.47	Light Programme	*Woman's Hour*: The schools of today and tomorrow — primary schools

16.8.49	*Woman's Hour*: Helping children to succeed — learning to read: Dr. F.J. Schonell
6.9.49	*Woman's Hour*: Helping children to succeed — making work a pleasure: Dr. F.J. Schonell

Other titles of *Woman's Hour* features reflected the growing interest in relationships between home and school:

27.6.–18.7.50	Light Programme	*Home Life Comes to School* (4-part series produced by Isabel Laird)
2.–16.1.51	Light Programme	*For Your Information — Parents and Schoolchildren* (3 part series produced by Roland Earl)

and two features dealt with two 'pioneers of progressivism':

10.10.49	Light Programme	*Woman's Hour*: Susan Isaacs by D.E.M. Gardner
1.11.50	Light Programme	*Woman's Hour*: guest of the week — a talk on Margaret McMillan, pioneer in child welfare and nursery schools by Mrs C.R. Attlee

An exchange of correspondence between Joseph Trenaman, Further Education Liaison Officer at the BBC, and Lady Simon of Wythenshawe offers an insight into the making of such programmes. Lord Simon of Wythenshawe, the Manchester industrialist and Labour peer, as chair of the BBC Governors from 1947–52 involved himself far more actively in the Corporation's affairs than had his predecessors, and senior administrators were sometimes subjected to 'double interrogation' by Lord and Lady Simon in their flat at Marsham Court. On 26 September 1952 Trenaman wrote to Shena Simon about a proposed Light Programme series on parent-child problems. The producer, Miss Eileen Molony, was already consulting a number of people, including Ruth Thomas, for psychological advice. They were also arranging for one or two PTA meetings to be addressed by Miss Thomas on phases of normal child development, followed by questions from the floor; the purpose was to ascertain what questions most worried parents, although this ulterior object would not be revealed to the audience. Lady Simon replied:

> With regard to the series on parents and children, I feel that what is often overlooked in these discussions is the importance of the children's toys, that is to say, hints to parents as to the right kinds of toys to give their children. In my opinion, bricks are far and away the best for they can play with them from the time when they are quite small until they are ten or eleven, if they have the

> necessary imagination and the Mother or Father has been able to guide them in their earlier efforts.
>
> I wonder if you know a book now out of print by H.G. Wells, called *Floor Games*? It is very difficult to get hold of nowadays, but there may be a copy in your library. It is most suggestive in this respect and bricks we had made for our children thirty-five years ago are still in use with the grandchildren.[38]

Trenaman wrote back hoping she would not mind that he had passed her letter on to the Director of the series, and compared his own experience of bricks made by a local carpenter for his two girls:

> both children played with them for years, and the edges are now worn quite smooth from the various knocking down games that went on. Thank goodness there were building-up games, too!

The audience research, and the reference to 'authorities' as part of the process of production are thus well illustrated.

By 1960 the annual radio output on educational matters had increased enormously. The Crowther Report was topical and attracted quite a lot of coverage, as did 11+ selection exams, the opening of new secondary schools and private education. One edition of *Voice of the People* included interviews on the 11+ at Thornsby, — and on the question of whether Prince Charles should go to Eton! *Ten O'Clock*, on the Home Service on 16 December, interviewed Philip Vernon about his new book and the controversy as to whether intelligence tests were 'a true guide to brain power'.[39] 1960 was also the centenary of Margaret McMillan, marked by several commemorative programmes, one of which included recollections by her friends and fellow workers and another featuring Mary Davies, Principal of Rachel McMillan College at Deptford. Certainly the work of the McMillans seems to have had a higher public profile then, than it has enjoyed in later years.[40] The scientific basis of education was underlined in a *Woman's Hour* series entitled 'Science and children'. The first programme, on mothering, featured James Robertson of the Tavistock Clinic, and the second, on reading, Dr. Wall, Director of the NFER.[41] On the Third Network, a ten-part series entitled *Parents and Children — About Learning* was psychologically based, presented anonymously by W.J. Israelsohn, lecturer in the Department of Growth and Development at the Institute of Child Health.

Primary schooling enjoyed relatively little separate attention at this time. A curiously skewed series entitled *A Day at School*, compiled and produced for the Home Service by Owen Leeming, featured (in this order): 1. 'An independent school', 2. 'A public school', 3. 'A secondary modern school', 4. 'A convent school', each programme described as 'an attempt to portray a school through the events of its daily life'.[42] However, Molly

Brearley, Principal of the Froebel Educational Institute, and Elizabeth Hitchfield, an educational psychologist and lecturer at the same College, presented a programme entitled *Teachers and Children*; they joined in a discussion with four students on the topic of teaching methods in the junior classroom and 'characteristic remarks made by teachers (and parents)' were considered. Originally broadcast on the Home Service in January, it was repeated on the Third Network three months later with the promise that 'this programme may interest parents who wonder about activity methods'.[43]

Progress in radio treatment of education may be illustrated by contrasting a series entitled *Teachers in the Witness Box* broadcast in 1946, with the presentation by Molly Brearley and some of her students in 1960. A series of ten programmes on the Home Service, the 1946 broadcasts shared a format in which educationists were 'cross-questioned' by parents.[44] The quotations are here used advisedly for these dialogues were carefully scripted and rehearsed, and the parents sometimes sound like stooges. One such parent indeed was Barry Bucknell (later impresario of Do-It-Yourself on television) and the climax of the series was Bucknell questioning Michael Stewart, MP, on the topic: 'Can you be taught what to think?' — a consideration of bias and conviction in education. Programmes included several on secondary education for all and its segregation, in which Jack Longland, CEO for Derbyshire, took the witness stand, and the question 'Is education too bookish?' was parried by two grammar school masters. Schools and community, and education for industry were also topics introduced. Of particular interest for primary education, however, were some of the earlier programmes in the series. In the first 'a Tyneside parent' confronted Professor B. Starkey with the question 'What should be taught and why?'. The parent had been overwhelmed with suggestions from her children, and she asked the professor if he was open to criticisms from children. 'Certainly', he replied, 'there's too little of what one might call "consumer research" in education. Teachers need to know the child's point of view', and he countered that parents were not entirely blameless in creating pressure all round for results, success, and a place in class. The third broadcast, entitled 'Learning to grow', was primarily an argument for nursery schools, during which the questioning parent obligingly pointed out that he had started school at the age of three; Dorothy Gardner, Head of the Department of Child Development at the Institute of Education, replied that this would be an appropriate starting age for modern children so long as appropriate nursery education was provided. On the question of 'Learning about your neighbourhood', Mr. J.J.B. Dempster was introduced as an expert (later Dr. Jack Dempster, CEO for Southampton and author of texts on education),[45] and a parent put to him the point that:

> The poor, oppressed taxpayer sees daily . . . wandering about up

> and down the various towns and cities, boys and girls who seem to be a pack of sheep ... in the attendance one or two school teachers. Is this the new educational craze 'local study'? Why are you spending money on this kind of thing?

Mr. Dempster, in reply, asked his questioner what he knew of *his* neighbourhood, and ably argued the benefits of environmental education.

Molly Brearley and Elizabeth Hitchfield were already known for their broadcasts on *Parents and Children* to which many teachers listened. On one occasion they gave the children themselves a platform in the studio, and it was this venture that gave rise to the idea of bringing in four student teachers just returned from teaching practice. The consequent discussion was broadcast on the Home Service in January 1960 under the title *Teachers and Children.*[46]

'Students', Miss Brearley said

> are just as concerned as parents are that children shall learn to read and write and do arithmetic as and when they become ready for it, but we share the belief that this readiness is an individual matter and is best achieved by individual methods, however big the class.

The students had all been teaching for a term and 'struggling with greater or lesser success' to put these ideas into practice. This discussion, though doubtless carefully prepared, sounded more spontaneous than the programmes of fourteen years earlier. Points that emerged from the students' experience included the need to regard children as people — 'no use thinking you're talking to a lot of puppets', a rejection of 'Victorian conformity to social etiquette', the self-confidence that grew from informal methods, and the possibilities of effective learning through play. Professional issues included the need for flexible furniture in the classroom, and the recognition that such an approach was bound to be hard work at the beginning, though more rewarding in the end.

> I should imagine the interest stays. I can't think of anything worse than imposing the same things on a set of children day after day.

Also accepted was the teacher's responsibility of explaining her methods to the parents, and of showing 'that learning does arise in this way'.

Parents and children were being accorded increasing attention as 'consumers' of education. Though 'consumption' in the technical economic sense was a long-established concept, and the consumer of goods can be identified in an 1897 Sears Roebuck Catalogue published as a 'Consumer's Guide', the *Oxford English Dictionary* increasing currency in the later 1950s of terms such as 'consumer durables' and 'consumer guidance'. Even more important perhaps, the use of 'consumer*ism*' became frequent in the 1960s, the *Times* noting in 1969 that

> Academics have muttered darkly about 'consumerism' meaning an exaggerated respect for the real or supposed requirements of the consumer;

and the *Sunday Times* in 1970 identified consumerism as 'the outgrowth of the consumer-protection movement of the 1960s'.[47] (Consumerism also developed another significant meaning as a doctrine advocating continual increase in the consumption of goods as the basis for a sound economy, a definition advanced by Vance Packard (1960) in *The Waste Makers*). Radio and the consumer movement joined hands in a series produced for Network Three in 1963. Entitled *Education Today: The Existing Opportunities* the broadcast scripts were written by Edward Blishen and Brian Groombridge, and published in book form.[48] The former had taught for ten years in secondary modern schools and was well known as a broadcaster on educational issues, and as author of the book *Roaring Boys*, whilst the latter, after involvement with adult education, was now Director of the Research Institute for Consumer Affairs. The series was aimed at 'parents with some immediate practical problem' such as, significantly, 'how to choose a good primary school', but it was also concerned with the longer-term question of improving the educational system.

1963 saw a 'Campaign for Education' launched by the Archbishop of Canterbury at a mass meeting in London, its manifesto calling on the government to commit itself to a plan for the advancement of state education based on the implementation of the 1944 Act and a massive increase in higher education. Brian Jackson's Advisory Centre for Education had been founded a few years previously and more recently the first of the local Associations for the Advancement of State Education which by now had formed themselves into a national confederation of more than fifty associations. As the foreword to the published scripts pointed out:

> interest in our educational system, concern for the way it works and desire for information about it have never been more widely or intensely felt.[49]

The description given of infant education was distinctly Froebelian in tone, and one of the experts invited to comment was Margaret Brearley of the Froebel Educational Institute, shortly to join the Plowden Committee. Another commentator was Nora Goddard, Inspector for Infants Schools with the London County Council and a coopted adviser to the Plowden Committee which was convened that year. A compensatory view of the infants school was given, describing it as potentially a much richer environment, with all its stimuli for language and learning, than the home. Reassurances were given on the value of play:

> A child may seem to be bringing home reports only of what looks suspiciously like 'playing about' — but behind the play (which is much more than play) lies the teacher's knowledge that only by such preparation can a child be made ready for formal teaching.[50]

Reinforcing this view of the teacher's professional expertise was the advice that parents should give help in writing or reading only with the closest cooperation of the school, and the recent innovation of some schools inviting parents for an evening to explain their methods was applauded as sensible and helpful.

As for the 20,000 junior schools in England and Wales, the presenters pointed out that aims and achievements naturally varied. Behind the outlook of 'the best of them' lay a definition of their work suggested by the Hadow Report of 1931, the curriculum thought of in terms of 'activity and experience'; the importance of 'involvement' of the child was explained by comparison with the passivity of a traditional formal lesson. In good junior schools throughout most parts of Britain, it was claimed, teachers were beginning to intersperse lessons of a formal kind with 'projects' in which 'each child has something to contribute and there can be no sleepiness or inattention'; this definition of 'good schools' was a presentiment of the Plowden Report. The published book included a short bibliography of 'Further reading' on which Margaret McMillan, Lillian de Lissa, Susan Isaacs, Dorothy Gardner and Nancy Catty are all represented.

On the question of streaming, Professor P.E. Vernon and Mr. Edward Harvey, head of a primary school, were introduced effectively to outweigh a rather tentative account of its possible benefits given by Professor H.C. Dent. In the fifth programme on selection for secondary education, Dr. Wall of the NFER was allowed to cast some doubts on Professor Vernon's scepticism concerning intelligence testing, but was followed by J.W.B. Douglas and Dennis Marsden on the influence of social class, the argument rounded off by Dr. Cook, Deputy Education Officer for Devon, appealing for comprehensive schools as a way out of the problem.

Television

Television in the early 1950s was still a relatively new phenomenon, and reached only a proportion of the population, but was of growing importance as a public medium: fewer than 10 per cent of homes received television broadcasts in 1951, with an estimated five million viewers in the early 1950s. By 1978 more than 90 per cent of homes had TV.

Much of its programming on education and child care during the early 1950s was directed in daytime broadcasts at women (those women who were not at work) and who could afford television. *Leisure and Pleasure*, scheduled at 3.15 p.m. on a weekday afternoon was, as its subtitle made explicit, 'For women'; on Thursday 12 January 1954, in the 'I'd like you to meet . . .' slot, was presented Lady Norman, President of the Nursery Schools Association. Facing the announcement in *Radio Times* were advertisements for Royal lemon meringue pie filling, a free trial tube of Euthymol toothpaste, and the offer of a free pamphlet on leather soles: 'This important leaflet should be read by everyone, especially parents'. Thus caring parenthood and domestic comfort were associated with an interest in education, education that was particularly child-centred in its approach.[51]

About the Home was another such regular feature, and in October 1954, under the heading of 'Family affairs', a headmistress was to discuss some new ways of teaching young children. Along with Slumberland divans and Mangers' sugar soap, Mr. Therm shared the page:

> Hot-water babies grow up healthy . . . grow up to bless their wise mothers who saw to it they had a daily dip.
>
> Most infants up to one year old are bathed daily. By four years of age only four out of ten get a daily bath and after that age bathing becomes something of a spasmodic affair. Don't take chances with your child's health; teach him the value of hot water by persevering with regular baths.

After this it comes as little surprise to find John Newsom billed to report on the opening of the hundredth new school in Hertfordshire, accompanied by soft Andrex and a big towel bargain.[52]

John Newsom, Chief Education Officer for Hertfordshire, was a frequent guest commentator and no doubt his engaging personality, as well as his talent for publicity, was the reason for this. Maclure (1984) has described him as 'a man of infectious enthusiasm and drive . . .', 'a complex character not without his share of egotism, ambition and a taste for power'.[53] As well as the more domestic programmes already referred to, he appeared on what seems to be the first treatment of education by *Panorama* in February 1954. A list of early television broadcasts on education illustrates the frequency of Newsom's appearances:

28.10.48 Film: *Child Learning by Experience* — this film was designed primarily for teachers in training.

10.3.53 *Leisure and Pleasure*: Interview with John Newsom, CEO, Herts.

14.4.53 *Leisure and Pleasure*: Talk on education by John Newsom.

26.5.53 *Leisure and Pleasure*: Children's education.
28.7.53 *Leisure and Pleasure*: Schooling: John Newsom.
12.1.54 *Leisure and Pleasure*: Lady Norman, President of the Nursery Schools Association interviewed.
17.2.54 *Panorama*: Discussion on the system of school exams between Mrs Morrison and John Newsom.
20.4.54 *Leisure and Pleasure*: Margaret Mann shows a film made while she was a student at a teacher training college and tells how her training worked in practice.
26.8.54 *About the Home*: a mother sending her child to a primary school for the first time discusses her problems with an experienced headmistress.
31.8.54 *Leisure and Pleasure*: Mary Hill gives advice on buying clothes for school.
21.10.54 *About the Home*: Family affairs — living and learning: a headmistress discusses some new ways of teaching young children.
18.1.55 *Leisure and Pleasure*: New schools: John Newsom.
12.2.55 Film: *Learning to Live*: How children from 4 to 15 are taught and taken care of in a typical school.

Panorama looked at experiments with the Initial Teaching Alphabet in 1960, filming at Aylward Infant School, Stanmore, and interviewing Isaac Pitman, but otherwise primary education featured negligibly on television that year. The 11+ exam and 'cramming' was a prominent issue: *Tonight* dealt with it on 30 December 1960, repeating a film on the topic, presented by Antony Jay and first shown in May 1959, and on 9 January following, *Panorama* also publicized 'the dangers of cramming'. Oxford and Cambridge Universities appear more often than primary schools in the programme index for 1960, and a lot of questions to *The Brains Trust* were concerned with the stratified system of secondary schools. However, the NUT film on primaries *I Want To Go To School — Children at Work and Play*, co-produced by Karel Reisz, was screened in January and repeated twice, in April and October.

It is hardly surprising that with the publication of the Plowden Report on 10 January, the year 1967 got off to a good start with media coverage of primary education. In fact the work of the Plowden Committee from its inauguration in 1963 was well publicized, and could be said to have stimulated popular attention to primary education throughout the mid-sixties, as discussion below of the work of Eileen Molony will help to illustrate. The evening before publication *Panorama* featured an open meeting on education in Britain, with Anthony Crosland, MP, Secretary of State for Education and Science. Most of the regional magazine programmes paid attention to the Report on its publication: Dr. Jack Dempster, CEO for Southampton, and Dr. Daniel

Cook, Deputy CEO for Devon, were interviewed for their respective regions, in Birmingham and Manchester local headteachers, and in Wales student teachers were invited to comment. On *24 Hours* Sir Edward Boyle, Sir Ronald Gould and Moira McKenzie were joined in debate. Two days later, the same programme featured 'Teaching machines'. The following day *Tomorrow's World* also looked at Plowden. Through the months that followed, frequent references to primary education were found amongst the schedules of regional programmes: *South Today* interviewed Molly Brearley for her views on the NUT Pamphlet *Classroom Revolution, Midlands Today* talked to John Milward about his new method of teaching children to read, and *Look North* included a film and interview with Keith Matsuff, headteacher of a 'do as you like' school — Crosby County Primary in the East Riding.[54]

Later in the year the teachers' pay dispute and their action became the main focus of attention as far as education was concerned; in July a discussion between teachers and parents was held on *24 Hours* concerning the refusal to supervise school meals and to work with unqualified people, and in August the same programme featured 'a teacher who left the profession to become a dustman for more money'. In the autumn, debates on education in relation to the Liberal and Labour party conferences were also televised. On the anniversary of the Plowden Report, however, Timothy Raison, a Plowden Committee member, appeared on the question of whether the report's recommendations were being carried out, and the programme included a video recording of Anthony Crosland's open meeting with parents exactly a year previously.

In the aftermath of Plowden, primary education received a great deal more television time. Notable was the work of Fyfe Robertson on *24 Hours* who seems to have taken the subject of education to his heart in the early months of 1968. A report on Airdale Junior School and the work of Mrs Pyrah's 'new advanced teaching techniques which involve encouraging the not so bright children to communicate better', was followed by one on Abbey Grange School near Leeds where 'children are taught to work on their own and obtain practical experience of the subjects they study'. His coverage extended also to teacher training at All Saints' College.[55]

It was no doubt the atmosphere engendered by Plowden that gave so many opportunities to one outstanding producer in this field, but her interest in the education of young children went back much further in her career. Eileen Molony had been editor of *Woman's Hour* and later a producer in the Talks Department in the years after the war. A writer of children's stories, many of which were broadcast in the early 1950s, she also worked on *Children's Hour*. For the Light Programme she had been employed to produce a series on parents and children.[56] She later moved to the Western Region, where her husband was Chief Inspector for the LEA in Bristol.

Growth and Play was a ten-part series first broadcast on Channel 1 in 1964 and repeated on Channel 2 the following year. The series began with a programme on *The Importance of Play* by Molly Brearley, who was also involved on later items in the series, which included *The Nursery School, The Infant School, Working Together, Play with Words* and *Playing with Numbers.* Following this Eileen Molony was engaged in the production of other series such as *Discovery and Experience* in 1966, repeated in 1967, *The Spring of Learning* (1967) *Mother Tongue* (1967) and *School and Home* (1968). Most notable as regards diffusion of progressive ideas and practices through the medium of TV, was a ten-part series *The Expanding Classroom* first screened in the spring and summer of 1969 and repeated in the autumn, six of the programmes being given a third showing in August and September 1970. The entire series began with a progamme entitled *Elizabethan Village,* and continued with studies of Eveline Lowe School (see chapter 6), and Bucklesbury Farm. The next three programmes looked at processes of learning: *Children's Concepts, Enterprising Infants* and *Metrication and Decimalization,* whilst numbers 7 and 8 contrasted a school on a new estate in Swindon with the village primary school at Eynsham in Oxfordshire (see chapter 8). Programme 9 dealt with French in the primary school, and the final episode of the series *Does it Work?* consisted of a debate between G.H. Bantock and Molly Brearley.

1976 was a year in which television turned its attention to the education of young children. January saw the launch of a ten-part series on nursery education on BBC2, repeated in April and May on BBC1. Experts associated with this extensive and thorough series included Willem van der Eyken who edited a programme on the history of nursery education, Eric Midwinter who spoke on the Home Link project in Liverpool, Joan Tough on language, and Geoffrey Matthews on mathematics. Regional transmissions such as *Home Ground* on 20 February dealt with 'The education row' and featured Professor Alec Ross, Margaret Higginson and Ray Johnson, whilst the following month *Peninsula* addressed itself to the question 'Are our children learning?' discussing methods of grouping children in primary schools.[57] By now, however, the mass media were publicizing the challenges to progressivism implied by Neville Bennett's research and by the outcry over events at the William Tyndale Junior School in London, events which will be more fully considered in chapter 9. No doubt it was the publicity given to Bennett with the implication that perhaps older styles of teaching were more reliable than 'modern methods' which inspired Pebble Mill to film an interview with Brian Tolley on 'education in schools over a century ago and how it has changed today'.[58] Hard on the heels of Bennett, Robin Auld's lengthy enquiry into the William Tyndale affair was published and *Panorama* covered this with a dramatized reconstruction and debate.[59]

Press

It was not new for the popular press to take an interest in schools, but as education became more prominent on the political agenda in the 1960s, so the newspapers informed and reflected public interest. The *Daily Mail*, in 1925 had run a prize competition to produce a curriculum for girls, and in 1937 the *News Chronicle* organized an architectural competition for the design of an ideal school.[60] A press innovation symbolic of the prosperity and consumerism of the 1960s was the Sunday Colour Supplement, first appearing as the *Sunday Times Colour Section* (later *Magazine*) in February 1962. One or two of its issues over subsequent years depicted progressive primary education for the leisurely consumption of its weekend readership. Sandwiched between a range of typical Colour Supplement fare, articles on Benedictine monks, Italian vineyeards, cookery and music, was a full-page colour picture of a wide-eyed infant beating a drum, and the bold headline: 'HOW DO I KNOW WHAT I FEEL TILL I SEE WHAT I SAY?' (This text from *Alice in Wonderland* was a favourite progressive slogan).[61] Lena Jeger, journalist and former Labour MP, described in this article 'one of the best primary school systems in the world'. 'Completely unheralded, our primary schools have been undergoing a quiet revolution'. She referred to the official survey being undertaken by Lady Plowden, and thought it safe to predict that the gap between educational research and teaching would be found to be less in the primary schools than elsewhere, for 'the best teachers have long been doing what theoreticians later tell them to'.

The schools visited, described and photographed were in London, Leicestershire and Oxfordshire, and the most obvious changes were found in the physical organization of education. The old conventional barriers between subjects 'were dissolving fast'; a great variety of books was in evidence, science was taught by direct experience, 8-year-olds were seen acting an unwritten play in French, a little girl was making and tuning an oboe, and 9-year-olds were playing chess with their teachers at lunchtime. The character of the individual school and the curriculum was very much dependent on the head: at one school 30 per cent of the children played an instrument; some schools were experimenting with French; in others, wide use was made of television, carefully prepared and followed up.

In November of the same year, announced in a cover design by David Hockney showing ranks of children in a school hall, almost the entire issue was devoted to 'A guide to state education'.[62] This issue marked National Education Week, the first ever in Britain (though established on a grand scale in the United States), and referred to the NUT Exhibition at TUC headquarters in Bloomsbury, a Design Centre exhibition of school furniture, and open days in schools across the country, 'so that parents can see what problems faced teachers, and what the latest teaching techniques are'. 'Education has become political dynamite'; the average parent wished to give children the best chance in an increasingly competitive world, but was confused by a welter of conflicting advice.

Brian Jackson, Director of the Advisory Centre for Education and publisher of the quarterly *Where?* sought to resolve some of this confusion in 'Education from A to Z'. Here was advice on how parents should test the strengths and weaknesses of primary schools: they should look at the buildings and the playground ('Are interesting things added?'); they should observe how the children behave at the school gates after school:

> If they are uninterested or oppressed they may burst out like an exploding bomb — sudden, noisy, disrespectful of each other. If the school captures their interest and meets their needs, their exit will be quieter, slower, with, here and there, children lingering to talk to their teacher or to finish some absorbing piece of work.

Prospective parents should also visit the school and look around: the entrance hall would give a sense of values in the school ('Are there prohibitive notices or attractive posters?');

> Are the children noisy or quiet? Ask yourself whether the noise arises from boredom and disorder or whether it is the interested hum of a busy workshop; if the children are quiet try to decide whether it is because they are held in check by strict punishment, or because their energies are devoted to their lessons. Is their courtesy merely a keeping of school rules or does it arise from the beginning of an understanding of other people's needs?

Parents were also encouraged to press the headteacher on the degree of parental participation in the school. Ultimate decisions, however, would depend on your own view of education, and what you wanted for your child.

On 7 July 1968, surrounded by leopardskin fashions as a threat to the species, Her Majesty the Queen on tour, and afloat with the Burtons in their £100,000 refitted yacht, was 'Mrs Pyrah, teacher'.[63] This highly individualistic primary teacher from the West Riding stood before a blackboard overflowing with the rich vocabulary she had cultivated in her young pupils. Without formal training, Muriel Pyrah had developed her own form of integrated day and produced startling results in the 11+ exam. Alec Clegg had spotted her and publicized her work widely.

In the later 1960s, however, the educational interests of the *Sunday Times Colour Magazine* were directed far more towards the sixth form, universities and polytechnics, reflecting no doubt the current expansion in higher education, arrival of the post-war bulge in their late teens, — and the consumer potential of this new generation. There were references to adolescent problems, teenage rebellion, and new independent learning methods adopted in 'the sixth' (which were not without relevance for contemporary developments in primary teaching), but two items relating directly to the primary sector were to be found in 1969, and both significantly reflected distinct aspects of the challenge which was gradually being mounted to what was by now 'traditional progressivism'. Under the title 'What are our primary schools for?' was reported the formation of a Primary School Research and Development Group at the University of Birmingham, launched by Professor Philip Taylor who had 'devised a new approach to research in education'.[65] 'Research and development' was a term fashionable in industry and was linked, as in this project, with the process of consumer research. Hence a questionnaire to *Sunday Times* readers: Dr. P. Ashton, a member of the group, was to investigate the aims of primary education, and a form, returnable via the *Sunday Times* office, sought readers' experience and views, prompted by questions such as:

> Is it a vital stage when skills and attitudes essential to profitable secondary education are laid down?
>
> Does it give six years of experience, learning, interest and enjoyment whose effects last a lifetime?
>
> Is it concerned solely with experiences from 5 to 11 irrespective of what comes later?
>
> Is it really a way of keeping children occupied until the real business of education begins at 11+?

'Goodbye Mr. Chips' was a well-worn journalistic cliché for descriptions of educational innovation, but it was particularly ironic as the headline to an article by Tony Osman which investigated 'the mechanized world that awaits our children'.[66] At the head of the page was a bizarre, surrealistic photograph of eight children using teaching machines ('The talking page') outside on the school field, whilst in the background children danced, a scene which echoed the deliberately fantastic flavour of the text: 'Children of the seventies will be taught in a totally different way from those of the sixties'. Speculating on the future use of computers in school, and offering the 'sci-fi' style of Buckminster Fuller's geoscope as an example, the article concluded that expense would prohibit their widespread educational application. The irony was that the microchip, here unforeseen, was shortly to help realize a part of Osman's vision.

Teaching machines did not belong in the Utopia of most traditional progressivists, but it is noteworthy that Lena Jeger's article of 1963 had included these, for two junior schools in Leicestershire were undertaking pioneer work on 'programmed learning' in consultation with the universities, and overseen by the Ministry of Education. Though doubts were expressed as to the possibility of substituting machines for human beings in the educational process, (and automated teaching should not be used to make up for teacher shortages), it was recognized that machines might fulfil one progressive ideal — that of enabling individual children to work at their own pace. In Osman's account, a number of general points were made underlying the debate on progressivism. Schools had been a proven failure for a large number of people; nearly a fifth of the population was not practically literate, and acquaintance with 'our heritage' was low; the 11+ was now recognized as having failed to predict accurately children's abilities; a period of rapid change might mean four or five changes of job in a lifetime, and children must be educated for flexibility in future. The problem lay, however, in parents understanding what was going on in their children's schools:

> Change in education is not easily accepted. This is just as well. In important fields — medicine is an example — no alteration should be accepted merely because it is a novelty; the risks are too high. There has to be good evidence that change will bring an improvement.
>
> Another conservative element in education is unconscious. The adult of today was subjected to the education of yesterday. Firstly, this tends to obscure the consideration of any other kind of education ... Secondly, there is the feeling that if education could be more pleasant, and at the same time more effective than one's own, then one has in some way been swindled ... People unconsciously think that if it's not difficult, it's not learning.

In noting these common psychological blocks against the acceptance of change in education, the author was anticipating the popular debate about progressivism that was about to break in the nineteen seventies.

Notes

1 Edmonds, E.L. (1962) *The School Inspector* (International Library of Sociology and Social Reconstruction), London, Routledge and Kegan Paul, p. 153. Browne, S. (1979) 'The accountability of Her Majesty's Inspectorate' in Lello, J. (Ed.) *Accountability in Education*, London, Ward Lock Educational.

2 Ministry of Education (1949a) *Story of a School, A Headmaster's Experiences with Children aged Seven to Eleven* (Ministry of Education Pamphlet no. 14), London, HMSO; Ministry of Education (1949b) *Seven to Eleven: Your Children at School* (Ministry of Education Pamphlet no. 15), London, HMSO.

3 NUT Archive, PSAC Minutes, 29 September 1949.

4 Ministry of Education (1949b) *op cit*, p. 33.

5 *ibid*, p. 35.

6 Armfelt, R. (1950) *Our Changing Schools; A Picture for Parents*, Central Office of Information for the Ministry of Education, London, HMSO, p. 103.

7 R.N. Armfelt had been educated at Cranleigh and King's College, Cambridge, and taught at Dulwich College for one year before joining Kent Education Committee in 1925.

8 *Times Educational Supplement*, 4 December 1959, p. 677.

9 *ibid*. The '*Times Ed*' was 'secondary grammar' orientated in this period; it was evidently cautious, if not conservative on the selection issue.

10 *Times Educational Supplement*, 27 November 1959, p. 657. The comments of both David

Eccles and the '*Times Ed*' quoted above offer evidence of an awakening consumer consciousness in education, a phenomenon dealt with later in this chapter and elsewhere.

11 *Village School* (1941), British Film Institute (1980) *National Film Archive Catalogue* vol. 1 no. 3413.
12 *Children's Charter* (1945), *ibid*, no. 3952.
13 WILKINSON, A. (1987) 'Aspects of communication and the Plowden Report', *Oxford Review of Education*, 13, 1, March, pp. 117–8.
14 *Times Educational Supplement*, 13 January 1967.
15 *Times Educational Supplement*, 10 January 1969.
16 Mervyn Benford, speaking at the NAPE Conference 'Plowden Twenty Years On', Oxford, 28 February 1987. Leonard Marsh, speaking on the same occasion, suggested that the Report itself was of less significance than the mass of commentary it provoked.
17 *Times Educational Supplement*, 24 April 1970; 27 August 1976, Bob Doe: 'How dream went wrong'.
18 HALSEY, A. and SYLVA, K. (1987) 'Plowden: History and prospect', *Oxford Review of Education*, 13, 1, March, p. 3.
19 PLOWDEN, B. (1987) '"Plowden" twenty years on', *Oxford Review of Education*, 13, 1, March, p. 119.
20 see chapter 3 above.
21 The Labour government's economic plan was however already in trouble; Plowden assumed 3.75 per cent growth, which was not in the event achieved.
22 *Times Educational Supplement* 13 January 1967.
23 COUNCIL FOR EDUCATIONAL ADVANCE (1969) *Plowden, Two Years On: LEAs Report on the Steps they have Taken to Implement the Plowden Report since its Publication*, (repr. from typescript, May 1969). NUT publicity for Plowden included its evidence submitted in 1964, given full-page treatment in *The Teacher* which also published a regular 'Plowden Forum' feature, whilst the Committee was deliberating. It also published its evidence as a pamphlet, *First Things First*, in 1964. Annual reports of the Union record informal contacts with Lady Plowden and the Committee (1965) and a conference decision to base a Primary Education Campaign around the eventual publication of the Report.
24 *Times Educational Supplement* 28 April 1967, 'Plowden too far from the classroom', a report of Schiller's address to the London Association for the Teaching of English, 22 April 1967.
25 *Times Educational Supplement*, 25 September 1972, Anna Sproule: 'Meeting of the Plowden Club'.
26 *Times Educational Supplement*, 20 August 1976, 'Plowden progressives prepare to hit back at critics'; *Times Educational Supplement*, 8 September 1978, Graham Bond, correspondence.
27 *Times Educational Supplement*, 27 August 1976, 'No way to defind a cause'.
28 NUT (1960) *Fair Play for our Primary Schools*, London, NUT, p. 5.
29 see chapters 1 and 5 above.
30 NUT (1960) *op cit*, p. 7.
31 NUT (1963) *The State of Our Schools*, London, NUT; NUT (1960) *The Education Story*, London NUT; NUT (1964) *First Things First* (Memorandum of evidence to the Plowden Committee) London NUT.
32 *Schoolmaster* 29 January 1960, p. 255; *Radio Times*, 22 January 1960, 25 April 1960, 16 October 1960; *The Listener*, 28 January 1960, p. 190.
33 NUT *Annual Report 1965* p. 76, and *1967* p. 107.
34 NUT *Annual Report 1965* pp. 74–5 and 77.
35 NUT *Annual Report 1967* p. 106.
36 NUT *Annual Report 1965* p. 75. An earlier Council for Educational Advance had been formed 1942–44 as an alliance between the NUT, TUC and WEA, and had made

representations to the President of the Board of Education on the drafting of the 1944 Bill, but had since lain dormant. For the 1963 Campaign for Education, see below in this chapter.

37 12 March 1946 Home Service: *Brains' Trust.*

38 BBC Written Archive R16/499 Lady Simon to Joseph Trenaman 30 September 1952; and Briggs, A. (1979) Sound and Vision: The History of Broadcasting in the United Kingdom, Vol 4, Oxford, Oxford University Press, p. 131.

39 1 December 1960 North, N. Ireland, *Voice of the people*; 16 December 1960 Home Service, *Ten O'Clock.*

40 7 June 1960 Light Programme *Woman's Hour*: 'Margaret McMillan created the nursery school in this country. Mary Davies, principal of Rachel McMillan College at Deptford and recording of nursery school mother on cooperation between school and home'; 27 June 1960 Network 3 *Parents and Children*: 'Margaret McMillan centenary — work of Margaret McMillan and her sister Rachel'; 27 November 1960 Home Service *Margaret McMillan: Portrait of a Pioneer*: 'fought for the health comfort and education of small children, founded the nursery school. Recollections by her friends and fellow workers'.

41 23 November 1960 Light Programme *Woman's Hour*: 'Science and children: 1. Mothering. Scientific research which is being done to help in understanding and education of children'; 30 November 1960 '2. Reading. Very little known about how children learn to read'.

42 6–27 May 1960 Home Service *A Day at School; Radio Times*, 6 May 1960.

43 5 January 1960 Home Service *Teachers and Children*: 'Some characteristic remarks made by teachers (and parents) . . .' repeated 25 April 1960 Network 3 'Certain methods in the junior classroom . . .'; *Radio Times*, 5 January and 25 April 1960.

44 BBC Written Archive Scripts 4 November 1946 Home Service *Teachers in the Witness Box.* Reference was made by the announcer to the possibility that some might be listening as members of a discussion group, and for these a booklist to help further discussion was available from BBC Regional Offices.

45 Dempster, J. B. (1973) *What's Happening in Primary Schools?*, Newton Abbot, David and Charles; Dempster later appeared on TV to comment on the Plowden Report (10 January 1967).

46 BBC Written Archive Scripts 5 January 1960 Home Service *Teachers and Children.*

47 *Oxford English Dictionary, Supplement* vol. 1, (1972).

48 Blishen, E. (Ed.) (1963) *Education Today: The Existing Opportunities*, London, BBC; published, according to the Preface, 'by popular demand'.

49 *ibid*, p. 7.

50 *ibid*, p. 26.

51 *Radio Times*, 12 January 1954.

52 *Radio Times*, 21 October 1954 and 18 January 1955.

53 Maclure, S. (1974) *Educational Development and School Building: Aspects of Public Policy 1945–73*, London, Longman, p. 38.

54 *South Today* 6 February 1967, *Midlands Today* 22 February 1967, *Look North* 8 March 1967 Other examples included: *Look East* (4 April 1967) 'Miss Bowers and her village school at Great Waldringfield', *Midlands Today* (17 April 1967) 'Wigston Primary School "which is open plan and has fitted carpets throughout"'.

55 BBC Written Archive TV index 22 February, 1 March and 20 March 1965.

56 BBC Written Archive Radio Index 5 January–9 February 1953. Light Programme *Parents and children* six-part series (prod. Eileen Molony); BBC Staff Lists; BBC Written Archive file R16/499: letter 9/52 Trenaman to Lady Simon; Briggs, A. (1979) *op cit*, p. 56; Molony, E. (1946) *The Mermaid of Zennor*, Leicester, Edmund Ward.

57 *Radio Times* 12 January 1976: *State of Play — Pre-School Education Now*; BBC written Archive TV Index 20 February 1976; *Peninsula* was SW edition of *Nationwide* — under the heading 'Are our children learning?' on 23 March 1976 was a discussion of the advantages and disadvantages of teaching primary school children in mixed ability

groups. On 30 March 1976 under the same title — different methods of grouping children, the reasons behind them, and professional disagreements were discussed. (BBC Written Archive TV Index).

58 BBC Written Archive TV Index 19 May 1976.

59 *Radio Times* 26 April and 7 June 1976. In the summer of 1976, however, it was the problem of teacher employment that stole the media limelight.

60 GRIFFIN, P. (1986) 'The prize curriculum', *Times Educational Supplement*, 15 August; MACLURE, S. (1984) *op cit* p. 7.

61 *Sunday Times Colour Magazine*, 21 July 1963.

62 *Sunday Times Colour Magazine*, 10 November 1963.

63 *Sunday Times Colour Magazine*, 7 July 1968.

65 *Sunday Times Colour Magazine*, 8 June 1969.

66 *Sunday Times Colour Magazine*, 7 December 1969.

8 *Case Study of a Local Education Authority*

Reference has already been made to the Damascus-style 'conversion' as a theme found in some progressivist texts. A case in point was Vincent Rogers, from the University of Connecticut, who wrote of his visit to Britain:

> My English friends and advisers guided me initially to Oxfordshire, where I visited the Bampton, Brize Norton and Tower Hill primary schools. I have not been quite the same since.[1]

These villages lie within a short distance of one another in West Oxfordshire, near the Gloucestershire border. At Bampton, the head was R.T. Smith, then serving also as a member of the Plowden Committee, and later to join HMI; at Tower Hill, Tom John, who also joined HMI; at Brize Norton, George Baines, who went on to be head of the celebrated Eynsham primary school.

In examining one local education authority, we may see the operation of a progressive ethos, the working of modes of dissemination which served to communicate curricular ideals and practices. In a decentralized system such as the British, there is little typicality in the way LEAs work, but Oxfordshire was one of a handful of authorities which gained a reputation for the progressivism of their primary schools. Leonard Marsh, who had become acquainted with Oxfordshire schools during his time as a teacher trainer in Cheltenham, credited a number of Oxfordshire teachers in his book *Alongside the Child*, the work of whose schools was illustrated there. As a case study Oxfordshire local authority shows how the variety of agencies considered elsewhere in this book were at work in one county.

Certain Oxfordshire schools became showpieces, much visited by students in training, by teachers from other authorities, by visitors from abroad. Some schools were the subject of attention by the press and their activities were filmed and televised. Eileen Molony's television series and Lena Jeger's *Sunday Times* feature, described in the previous chapter, both portrayed particular Oxfordshire schools. Here was a novel feature in the dissemination of curriculum development, facilitated by new media of communication, and one, it might be argued, which focussed attention on *appearances*, however strenuously their protagonists stressed the underlying philosophies, — and which created the impression of *exceptional* schools, however self-effacingly their headteachers rejected this notion, stressing their ordinariness and the potential of progressive methods for universal application.

Certainly such publicity created a 'county image', although some teachers at work within the authority argued that there were only about twenty truly progressive schools. Marsh, whose experience was predominantly based on Oxfordshire, stated in his evidence to the House of Commons Select Committee on Teacher Training that the headteachers were crucial; many absorbed the ethos of a county somewhat unconsciously, taking local conditions for granted until they had the opportunity to compare other counties, but that variations were to be found not only between local authorities, but between individual heads within one county.[2] Some headteachers in Oxfordshire remained impassive or even hostile towards developments urged by the county advisers.

County Ethos

A text which offers the flavour of Oxfordshire progressivism is the opening chapter by Edith Moorhouse in a collection of essays edited by Vincent Rogers. Setting out to describe 'the philosophy of the British primary school', Edith Moorhouse began, as many progressivist writers did, with a contrast between past and present. Children streamed by ability, classified by chronological age, seated in rows and lectured at by a teacher who subjected them to a compartmentalized curriculum, — this was the image of 'teaching in the twenties'. But

> when children *have* been freed from the limits of achievement that teachers in a formal situation imposed, their accomplishments at times have been amazing and surprising.[3]

In place of traditional formalism, some admirable ideals were proposed, and two fundamental principles were expounded: 'appreciation of individual differences', indeed the *uniqueness* of individual children, and 'learning by discovery'. The argument, however, was advanced in a remarkably unproblematic way, and embraced assumptions which were already being questioned in the challenge to progressivism, as the social and professional climate changed. First, the school was to seen to have a compensatory role not only in providing the 'space, material, experiences, freedom and companionship' which were lacking in many home backgrounds, but also in making good the linguistic and emotional deprivation of many homes. As an extension of this, the class was to be considered a 'family', and vertical grouping for continuity of teacher contact was advocated because:

> If one is concerned with the development of the whole personality of the child, and not only with the learning of basic skills, then much of the education is absorbed and cannot be measured or passed on to another teacher.

The possible implications of such ideals for the professional and contractual nature of the teacher's role were not here considered, nor were questions of accountability which were soon to loom large in educational debate.

The second principle, learning by discovery, was predicated on the observation of young babies and toddlers learning. The principle was not opened to question, and alternative models of learning were not explored. The ideal of making discoveries was illustrated by an anecdote in which the teacher took children to study and compare a woollen mill and some abbey ruins, when a snail attracted the attention of one boy, his questions aroused the interest of the group, and snails became the topic which snowballed into intensive study; the idealism of such an account is clear, yet it was increasingly to be questioned whether such an approach could provide a realistic model for curriculum planning. The principles here advocated were:

> the uniqueness of each child and the need for each child to discover himself (sic) and to come to terms with the world around him. We teachers are more concerned with the balance of experiences . . . than with subjects, and more with the wholeness and harmony of growth . . . than with instruction and academic learning.

Other aspects of the account reflected the priorities of Oxfordshire's provision and resourcing of primary education: variety and quality of books, plants inside and outside the school as an object for close observation and substantial study, animals in school for their contribution to young children's emotional development, and for topic work, and above all the physical conditions and environment of the school as a learning medium:

> teachers who believe in discovery transform old buildings, exploit all the advantages of wall space . . .

Especially characteristic of Oxfordshire was the concept of 'celebration'. Thus, for Edith Moorhouse, materials and objects were to be displayed and 'celebrated', and assemblies were when the school was gathered together 'to celebrate something good'. Another text reflecting this 'county ethos' is an essay by George Baines, successively head of two well-publicized schools. A confessional view of education was implied by his quotation of the metaphysical writer Thomas Traherne:

> 'Is it not strange, that an infant should be heir of the world, and see those mysteries which the books of the learned never unfold',

adding:

> This almost divinity of a human child is something for which I have great reverence.[4]

A spiritual aura was recalled by visitors to the county, one of whom referred to the hushed tones which one automatically adopted in certain schools, as if entering a cathedral. And as the medieval cathedrals conveyed their ideals through the richness of their art, so too did these schools. A vision of the teacher's role was thus described by Baines:

> I am ... sure that teaching is an art and teachers are artists. The ideal is still that of Rousseau's *Emile* — one child, on teacher, the interaction of two personalities, the teacher teaching what he (sic) *is* more than what he *knows*, and, as an artist, involved and giving of himself, giving of himself with love.[5]

Some teachers found that such a missionary zeal did not conform to their perception of the teacher's role, others found it too precious for their tastes. Baines' vision is problematic in relation to the role of the teacher within in a state system of universal compulsory schooling, and might conflict with some teachers' perceptions of their professional status; the ideal also made considerable demands on the teachers in his own school

> After the children have left, school is a hive of activity, changing and arranging displays, setting up activities, making records and discussing ways of preparing and using the environment to the best advantage. We ... work to make the building inspiring, stimulating, practical and satisfying ... It is hard work for teachers and standards are high. There is no room for slackers.[6]

One Oxfordshire village school was the subject of a booklet in the Schools Council series already described in chapter 5.[7] Its author was Robert Smith, former head of the school, who subsequently served on the Plowden Committee and later joined HMI. Like other heads, he had been attracted into the county by reports and recommendations of the developments taking place there. His account opened by setting the school in the context of the village and its history. A continuing sense of village identity was evident, owing to its geographical position, and the opening pages dwelt on the traditional buildings as a response to the physical environment and way of life, and on the unbroken tradition of Morris dancing.

> Weston, like so many of the towns and villages of Oxfordshire, is very English.

At the same time, environmental and social change was a factor of which the school must not only take account, but indeed compensate, for example in providing open access to the school playing fields to make up for the loss of traditional playing space of rural children, the agricultural land which modern farming methods had destroyed.

A new school building was opened in September 1960. What parents witnessed as they visited on a normal school day towards the end of that school year is described by one especially articulate and perceptive parent, and another narrative chapter provides a description by a teacher of the work which surrounded the chance discovery of a Romano-British skeleton in the village. Progressive curricular preferences are evident in the emphasis on local history and also on an active discovery approach to science (the latter reflecting a particular interest of the head teacher), careful attention to creativity and aesthetic awareness, and the resourcing of classroom libraries — real books, including adult reference works, growing to a collection of 3000 titles in the school after five years. These descriptive elements, however, are balanced by a highly effective analysis of curriculum planning which is marked by frequent reference to Piagetian ideas: maths, moral education and history are all planned to accord with the developmental ideas of Piaget. Another chapter illustrates how carefully planned support for a probationary teacher led to cooperative teaching in the infant area. Though it was stressed that innovation at Weston was not designed as a controlled experiment, yet the criterion for success was the quality of learning and development achieved by children. An overall general improvement in children's reading compared with earlier years was found, including fewer backward readers and many more in advance of their age. Children were writing earlier, with a richer and more extensive syntax and vocabulary, and social behaviour improved distinctly.

Some of the organizational factors supporting this success, were credited in Smith's closing paragraphs. He referred to help received

> from colleagues who were running schools which were based on a common philosophy and had adopted similar methods.[8]

He acknowledged his fortune in the 'frank advice, honest criticism and practical help' received from HMI. And he credited also LEA support for innovation and development — help from the advisory service, thoughtfulness about the design, furnishing and equipping the school for workshop methods of teaching. Also significant perhaps was the large proportion of staff who left for promotion elsewhere, at least two of his staff becoming heads at other schools in the county.

Advisers and In-Service Training

The growth of advisory services within LEAs provided an effective means of curriculum development and reference has already been made to the West Riding in this respect, where Alec Clegg as CEO was the instigator. Jim Hogan, who worked as a Deputy Education Officer for Alec Clegg, laid emphasis on the quality of advisers, who had a

> significant advantage over all serving teachers ... to see a great deal of the methods adopted by other people and the results which they achieved,

and who had to be able to identify good practice. They did not have to be skilled practitioners themselves but to be able to inspire and to encourage.[9] Winkley (1985), in his recent study of LEA advisers, concluded that the most important single figure in the shaping of the advisory services was the CEO, to whom the advisers are directly accountable.[10] Oxfordshire enjoyed the services of Alan Chorlton as Director of Education, one of the new breed of young CEOs, in the post-war period. After education at Rugby School, he followed a career very similar to that of Clegg. At Cambridge, Chorlton and Clegg were near-contemporaries, both reading modern languages, and subsequently on the postgraduate course at the London Day Training College, 1931/32. Entering educational administration in Buckinghamshire a year later, he worked as Deputy Director in Sussex and subsequently in Hertfordshire under John Newsom before appointment as Director in Oxfordshire at the age of 36. His Deputy, George Ranken, appointed at the same time, was two years younger, also a Cambridge graduate.

With reorganization and the loss of senior classes, rural schools, already small, became even smaller. Oxfordshire in 1945 had 173 primary schools, of which 100 had only one or two teachers (fifty more had three or four teachers). The rural school was a 'problem' of current concern, (although as we have seen, its virtues were central to the progressive ethos). Chorlton therefore decided to appoint an Assistant Education Officer with special responsibility for small rural schools, and to this post in 1946 came Edith Moorhouse, who had latterly taught in Hertfordshire, Chorlton's previous county, at a two-class country school and at Wall Hall Emergency Training College.[11] The role envisaged was an advisory one, attempting to counter the isolation of rural schools.

Chorlton stayed in Oxfordshire for twenty-five years. Edith Moorhouse remained in post for twenty-two years. In the course of that time she built up a team of advisory teachers (their title was only later changed to that of 'adviser'), whose purpose was to work alongside teachers in the classroom, the first appointed in 1947, a second in 1949, reaching a strength of four from 1951. Though some of her early appointments, such as John Gagg whose books and articles have been noted in an earlier chapter, moved on to other posts, other appointees remained for periods of thirty-three years, twenty years and seventeen years, thus establishing a considerable continuity within the county.

That 'remarkable woman',[12] Edith Moorhouse, recognized the problems of intellectual and professional isolation of teachers in small village schools scattered across a rural county, and sought to counter this problem by in-service training. Such a project required the allocation of resources, however, and her personal efforts were directed not only to the schools but to the committees and administration responsible for provision. She was also actively involved at a national level with two of the agencies described in chapter 5, the School Broadcasting Council and the School Library Association. The role of advisory teachers, as Edith Moorhouse saw it, was to participate in the work of the classroom, to promote dialogue about classroom practice with individual teachers and groups of teachers, but not to prescribe particular techniques that might be seen as county policy. Edith Moorhouse preferred the exercise of 'influence' to that of 'authority' (she herself has been described as a 'combination of sometimes bossy toughness and great tact').[13] The aim of the advisory team was not only to create a more thoughtful, responsive teaching force, but also to 'establish a coherent educational philosophy'; former Oxfordshire heads testified to having gained strength personally from the 'unequivocal philosophy of education' promulgated by the advisory team, according to an unpublished study by Bennett, former adviser:

> ... I don't think anyone could work in Oxfordshire for eleven years without absorbing its powerful ethos of child-centred education
>
> ... knowing that there was a clearly defined and regularly expressed philosophy of education which was shared by the advisory team.
>
> We knew and took for granted that advisers share a common view of education.[14]

Successor to Edith Moorhouse in 1968 was John Coe, who remained as Senior Primary Adviser for a further sixteen years, thus considerably extending the continuity already established in Oxfordshire's primary advisory service. Coe had an appropriately progressive pedigree, having been one of Christian Schiller's first students at the London Institute and head of a large new primary school in Essex (a county in which progressivism prospered patchily, more as a result of laissez-faire than of any county policy). He had then worked as an 'inspector' (adviser) in the West Riding from 1964. The year that he was appointed to Oxfordshire, Coe wrote of 'a way ahead'. Making the usual stark contrast between unenlightened formal methods of the past, on the one hand, and on the other, 'the success of our work ... so splendidly confirmed by Plowden', he went on to underline the principles of integrating and expanding the curriculum and of a warm personal relationship between teacher and child, principles which made the modern teaching task more complex and more demanding than before. Moreover,

> The doors of our classrooms are open as they have never been open before. There is a growing informality in school life.[15]

John Coe sought to select members of his team with a unity of view, a fundamental philosophical commitment, and reflecting this is the fact that four Oxfordshire advisers wrote at various times for the *Froebel Journal*.[16] Winkley's study of four authorities describes the Oxfordshire ('Orpheus') model of advisory service as one with a high degree of integration and a high degree of autonomy.[17]

In-service training in Oxfordshire was based on the principles of personal education and personal experience for the teacher, combined with mutual support and exchange amongst teachers from different schools.

> So many teachers were taught and trained in a purely academic way. Now they must try to welcome the new philosophy: that is, only by sharing creative experiences, in painting, drawing, poetry, in making music, in movement or dance can they themselves find fulfilment and confidence and so become sensitized enough to be able to recognize the hidden graces and talents of their children.[18]

Such an approach, including the concentration on the arts in this particular description, was characteristic of the courses organized by local advisers and HMI, and had close similarities with a style of in-service training developed in the West Riding at Woolley Hall. Until the new University Institutes of Education adopted this function, the LEA organized day courses to widen the horizons of teachers on subjects of interest not directly related to teaching (Russia, America, music, were examples), held at grammar schools whilst local primary schools closed for the day. Residential courses for long weekends based at an Oxford college, and later annual week-long courses at Brighton Training College, became a regular feature. By the early 1960s there were two or three residential courses run annually at country house residential centres in Gloucestershire.[19] At these courses HMI with various specialisms, such as Ruth Foster for movement and Len Comber for science, and other outside experts, took the Oxfordshire teachers through a variety of experiences, especially in the visual arts and with a tendency to integrate arts such as poetry, art and movement. Crafts such as bookbinding, spinning and weaving also figured prominently, as did the natural sciences. Poetry readings became an important feature, and several teachers testified to the inspiring and 'uplifting' effect of these courses where the focus was on personal development and self-awareness. Courses on a similar pattern were run nationally at Dartington Hall by Robin Tanner, and he invited select Oxfordshire teachers to these. Teachers from the county also went on occasion to Woolley Hall, whence visits were made to schools in the West Riding, and professional contacts established. On the county courses, informal discussion played an important part in allowing teachers to exchange views and to get to know one another, and this, together with the follow-up work of the advisory teachers, led to 'group meetings' of teachers in particular areas, amongst whom 'a warm feeling of friendship and a sharing of experiences' developed.[20]

To stimulate an interest in creative work and in 'good visual standards', these meetings were elaborated into group exhibitions whereby four or five neighbouring schools would mount an exhibition of children's work in a central hall, accompanied by talks for teachers and managers from the advisory teacher about the work displayed in relation to 'fundamental principles of primary education'. Schools were closed for the day, and teachers, children, parents and school managers were invited to view the work displayed. The Director of Education and the chair of the LEA's Primary Sub-Committee would talk to managers over tea. The good relationships thus built up between neighbouring schools, and between the schools and the authority, were important for the dissemination of innovation amongst small rural schools often geographically remote, and impressed many visitors to the county. Such a mode of in-service training was significantly facilitated by developments in transport: the growth of private car ownership amongst teachers made such meetings easier and more frequent, and the LEA provided a group of schools with a mini-bus to assist in such meetings, as well as for school journeys. In the complex historical process of curriculum development the role of innovators and administrators cannot be judged in isolation from changing social and economic circumstances.

Other forms of in-service nationally included provision made by the institutes of education. Some teachers in Oxfordshire recalled their interests being aroused by various aspects of courses offered by the University of Oxford Institute of Education, long courses of one evening per week, and occasional day conferences. These events featured speakers as disparate as George Macbeth the poet, and Max Beloff the historian, whose contributions were aimed at the personal education of the participants, but other sessions were directly addressed to the concerns of progressive primary education: Dr J.M. Tanner, Professor of Child Health and Growth at the University of London, and a member of the Plowden Committee, spoke on the topical subject of the adolescent spurt and its variability, Sybil Marshall made an impression on one headteacher, and another first learned of Piaget from a course there. Carefully selected teachers were seconded by the LEA for a year to the full-time course run by Christian Schiller 1955–64, and later to Dorothy Gardner's course on child development, both at the London Institute of Education.

An important strategy lay in appointment of heads, both Moorhouse and Coe focussing on the appointment of candidates whose abilities and dispositions they knew. Coe observed that the 'pace-setting' schools in the county (of which he identified about twenty in 1968) became a source of future headteachers able to work elsewhere on similar principles. But applications for headships also came from outside the county from those who knew of Oxfordshire work, felt drawn to it and wanted to work for a supportive authority. The senior primary adviser and local HMI had considerable influence in making appointments, and the pattern of appointments to first teaching posts and to headships, illustrates the links maintained with particular institutions of teacher education and other progressive local authorities, together with the process of 'talent-spotting' through a network of contacts nationwide and through national courses. Edith Moorhouse, who had been born and brought up in the West Riding, trained at Bingley Training College and taken her first teaching job in that LEA (albeit before Clegg's time as CEO), maintained her contacts with Yorkshire. From South Yorkshire two new heads came who were to play a particularly influential role in future developments. One having taken Schiller's course at the London Institute, was attracted to Oxfordshire, to head Long Hanborough school with its new open-plan extension built in 1959. He then encouraged a colleague from Sheffield to apply for the headship of Bampton School, which opened in new buildings in 1962. The first of these heads returned to Yorkshire after three years to become a primary teacher-trainer, subsequently sending two of his most talented students to join the staff at Bampton (and both of these later achieved headships in Oxfordshire). The head of Bampton was subsequently selected as a member of the Plowden Committee, and later joined HMI, one of three of Oxfordshire's noted progressive headteachers of this period to join the Inspectorate. John Coe brought to a headship in Oxfordshire a teacher whose first appointment had been to his school in Essex, and who had subsequently followed his footsteps to the West Riding. Thus networks of teachers succeeded not only in mutual encouragement and reinforcement of their progressive philosophies, but in the promotion and dissemination of progressive practice by recommendations and appointments to key posts.

HMI: Robin Tanner

It has been shown in chapter 1 that arts and crafts occupied a prominent place within the progressive primary school curriculum and Oxfordshire had a particular reputation in this respect. It is more than a mere coincidence that a primary school curriculum dominated by the arts and crafts should have flourished here, when Oxfordshire and the Cotswolds had played an important a part in the 'arts and crafts movement' of the late nineteenth and early twentieth centuries. William Morris and Burne-Jones had discovered their interest in the reform of art through a return to 'pre-Raphaelite' styles and practices whilst students at the University of Oxford in the 1850s. Morris had later made his country home at Kelmscot on the upper reaches of the Thames in West Oxfordshire. Under his influence arose a larger movement for a return to medieval ideals of the decorative arts as a moral force and to craft guilds as the means of production. A Guild of Handicraft had been brought to Chipping Campden by C.R. Ashbee, a disciple of Ruskin and Morris who, in his campaign for social reform through art and handicraft, had turned his back on the East End of London and found in the Cotswolds an unspoilt environment suited to his resurrection of medieval craft guild traditions. So the arts and crafts movement became associated particularly with this area, rather as the poetry of William Wordsworth had made the Lake District a locus for the 'Romantic movement' of the early nineteenth century. The direct link to Oxfordshire's progressive primary practice is embodied in the figure of Robin Tanner and illustrates the potential influence of HMI in the process of curriculum development.

Robin Tanner, artist and educator, etcher and HMI, was born on Easter Sunday 1904; son of a carpenter and joiner, he grew up in Chippenham, a small town in Wiltshire.[21] From being a pupil teacher at Ivy Lane School, Chippenham, he undertook a teacher training course at Goldsmith's College in the early 1920s. Goldsmith's played an important role in the development of primary progressivism, and undoubtedly the close connections maintained between art and education within the college were a contributory factor. In the 1920s a group of Goldsmith's art students were rediscovering Samuel Palmer's romantic landscape etchings. The painter Graham Sutherland was one of these, who described the impact of Palmer:

> It seemed to me wonderful that a strong *emotion*, such as was Palmer's, could change and transform the appearance of things . . . the idea of the way in which emotion can change appearances has never left me.[22]

Having taken a teaching post in Greenwich, Tanner continued his study of life drawing and etching through evening classes at Goldsmith's, and in these years was influenced by an exhibition of Samuel Palmer at the Victoria and Albert Museum. Influential, too, were paintings by pupils of Cizek, the noted Hungarian teacher from Vienna who exhibited his children's work in London at this time. Robin Tanner also discovered in these years the work of the etcher F.L. Griggs whose artistic vision as well as his adopted home gives him a place in the arts and crafts movement; for Griggs, whose perception of the romantic qualities of Gothic architecture led him into active championship of the preservation of old buildings and of the countryside, had set up home in Campden, Gloucestershire where the Guild of Handicrafts continued its activities through the first decades of this century.

Tanner himself soon returned to his boyhood home at first to engage full-time in his art studies and etching, but later to resume working as a teacher at Ivy Lane School, Chippenham. At this time he also read Mackail's Life of William Morris. A published account of his wedding so vividly illustrates the arts and crafts aesthetic that it is worth quoting in full:

> Heather wore a dress of wool and silk dyed with madder, which Robin had designed for her some three years earlier, and which had been woven by her aunt. Robin's elder sister had made his shirt of natural shantung ...
>
> Their small house had been designed a year earlier as a wedding present from Heather's uncle, a pupil of Voysey. Traditional mullioned windows were set in thick walls surrounding a large central chimney stack that rises through a particularly steep and heavy tiled roof ...
>
> Much of the honeymoon was spent scrubbing the woodblock floors and in the long and arduous task of getting them to absorb the polish of wax and turpentine until they mellowed to a warm smooth surface ... Robin's father, a carpenter and joiner and a sound craftsman had made the fitted dresser and from Gordon Russell's workshop in Broadway had come several pieces ... From Michael Cardew's pottery at Winchcombe they acquired cheap slipware pottery ...[23]

Colour, texture, the appreciation and sympathetic handling of natural materials were more than abstract qualities, they were a way of life. This was an ethic, not merely an aesthetic, embodied in his teaching. His pupils decorated their classroom walls with murals depicting the seasons. Teachers visited his school and he gave weekend courses, especially in the craft of making books. Amongst many visitors to the school was the young HMI John Blackie.[24]

On his appointment as HMI in 1935, Robin Tanner moved to Leeds, but returned to his native Gloucestershire two years later. Through the Inspectorate he met and found a sympathy with Christian Schiller, and later made acquaintance with the Elmhirsts at Dartington and the craftspeople whom they patronized, such as the fabric printer Phyllis Baron, and the potters Lucie Rie, Bernard Leach and Hans Coper. In 1956 he was given responsibility as HMI for Oxfordshire.

The ethics and aesthetics of Ruskin and Morris shone through the pages which he wrote on art and craft for the Ministry of Education's book of suggestions first published in 1959. Art and craft teaching reflected the 'gradual recognition that in every one of us there is some native power of imaginative expression'. Only very slowly, out of the old ideas of 'industry' and 'imitative arts' and the entirely separate ideas of 'drawing' and 'handwork', had emerged 'the conception of art and craft considered as one broad aspect of living'.[25]

Though there is no direct reference to John Ruskin (the restoration to respectability of Victorian thought was only beginning in the late 1950s), the following words of Tanner are as Ruskinian as might be:

> The foolish separation between Art and Craft in our present-day life which has led to the making of so much that is ugly to look at and unpleasant to use should be a warning. We know that if an artist is not a craftsman the less artist he, and we also know that a craftsman worthy of the name is always an artist. Indeed, printing is as much a craft as weaving is an art. The education of children should surely aim at fulfilling their creative powers as both artists and craftsmen; and at the same time it should foster their growth as discerning people, able to choose and select, to discriminate between the true and the counterfeit, to reject the shoddy and false and hold fast to that which is good — in short, to form firsthand judgments, to grow in critical awareness and in the capacity to enjoy the arts and crafts of mankind.[26]

A most powerful statement of his beliefs was made by Tanner in an essay on 'creativeness' in education, written for the Froebel Journal at the end of his career as HMI.[27] His premise was that 'every child is at heart an artist', making dances, music, paintings, as an instinctive activity. Children also had a natural curiosity about materials, and through school activities they could acquire the application and discipline which would lead to absorption.[28] Education was to be for self-knowledge and not simply a contrivance for 'getting on in the world'. Tanner's central argument rested on two admirable principles. First, for a full emotional life, intellectual growth was to be fostered not just through book-learning, but through the five senses; IQ was but one criterion of many, the deceptive concreteness of which had misled a great number of people, and many children transcended their 'innate intelligences' daily. Second, art was a necessary transfiguring language, the only true international one. The authorities quoted in the space of a relatively short article are of interest in representing a sort of 'Great Tradition': Isaiah, Leonardo da Vinci, Matthew Arnold, Rilke (poet and biographer of the sculptor Rodin), W.R. Lethaby (one of the leading spirits of the arts and crafts movement) and Virginia Woolf (whose own creativity extended beyond literature to the visual and decorative arts). Finally, the article incorporated a view of the teacher's role which reflected an assumption of consensus on education:

> The role of the teacher is . . . a wonderful invention, deliberately designed to foster the fullest possible growth in children. Through the ages great men and women have lent themselves to this craft. Faith in it is so great that parents are quietly compelled to expose their children to the influence of teachers on five out of every seven days.[29]

The last sentence is open to interpretation as a classic statement of 'social control' in education.

Tanner's way of working within the county is of interest for it followed that of his colleague Schiller in seeking to select what, on the botanical analogy so commonly adopted in progressivist discourse, were described as 'growing points'. That was, a small number of headteachers who corresponded in their practice with his ideas, and whom he aimed to cultivate by visiting them frequently and supporting them in their personal development and in the development of the curriculum and teaching method within their schools. It could be said of both Tanner and Schiller that they interpreted the inspector's role as that of an adviser. Such policy could and did give rise to charges of elitism, and feelings of resentment from outside the chosen groups that resources and attention were unfairly concentrated on a few schools which were ready to adopt the philosophy on offer. It was defended by others as being the only feasible way of making some real impact with limited resources. The schools so supported were found in specific geographical locations where heads could meet locally and offer mutual support, and were located mostly in the north and west of the county, as well as two rapidly growing urban centres of population, Bicester and Kidlington. Thus, Tanner's work strengthened the process already initiated by the advisory team, of encouraging local schools to help one another. Lady Plowden, visiting for her Committee, commented that:

> The thing about Oxfordshire, as compared to the West Riding or Hertfordshire, was the sense of purpose, the groups of excited young heads all working together.[30]

It was more than coincidence that a number of the most noted schools were therefore situated on the fringes of Tanner's beloved Cotswolds, very near to Kelmscot: Langford, Brize Norton, Bampton and Tower Hill, Witney, were frequently visited and became known for the standard of their arts and crafts, and two of the heads went on to join HMI. Another school where a high standard of art prevailed was West Kidlington, whose head, Geoffrey Elsmore, eventually rose to be Chief HMI for Primary Education. The circle of heads would meet Robin Tanner regularly on his visits to the county, when he stayed at 'The Lamb' in Burford.

Other aspects of Tanner's activity included the organization of national courses, such as those at Dartington Hall, to which Oxfordshire teachers would be invited. Through these courses other like-minded teachers would be encountered, and follow-up support would be arranged. He would also encourage the visiting of schools where good practice could be seen in action. Tanner played a key role in spotting talent outside the county and encouraging visits to Oxfordshire schools by teachers who appeared to hold promise for the progressive practices encouraged in the county. Two notable headteachers whom Tanner had met in the course of national duties and attracted into the county by arranging for them to visit Oxfordshire were George Baines from Buckinghamshire and Christopher Jarman from Hampshire.

Tanner's influence on classroom practice was enormous in Oxfordshire's model progressive schools. His belief in the importance of the school environment derived from the values of the arts and crafts movement. As a young teacher at Ivy Lane School, he had asked permission of the head if he might 'civilize' the room. The children scraped varnish from the pitchpine doors and desktops:

> We used glass and it got the varnish off marvellously, then treated the wood with beeswax and turpentine, so that in the end it looked lovely, as though Gordon Russell had made it. The children commented when we'd finished: 'doesn't it look expensive?', and that was quite the word.
>
> The environment of the school is such a force — if you live in a slum you behave appropriately, but if it's shipshape and worth looking at you somehow rise to it.[31]

This attitude towards the school environment harmonized with the policy of Edith Moorhouse and with the experimental work of the Ministry of Education's architects in the Development Group.

Many primary schools were still housed in Victorian buildings and efforts were encouraged to improve the classroom by whatever means available. One device which had singular impact in Oxfordshire schools was his introduction of corrugated card, a commercial display material which could be introduced to mask old and decrepit walls and to provide a fresh, bright background for the display of children's work. Tanner recalled how he found corrugated card at Kettle's in New Oxford Street, a 'wonderful shop' which supplied card and paper for display. Six foot high white card could be used to model space and as a background and could 'make the meanest classroom rather good.' He used it at Dartington and introduced it to Oxfordshire in 1956, putting up displays of children's work. George Baines, who had seen corrugated card in use on a course at Woolley Hall and wrote to express his disappointment at being unable to obtain the material, recalled how Robin Tanner arrived one day at school bearing a roll. He later came to work in West Oxfordshire. Christopher Jarman, headteacher and later adviser in the county, eventually wrote a standard work on display in the primary school.

Aspects of the curriculum in practice which reflected the influence of the arts and crafts movement included the importance accorded to calligraphy and development of italic handwriting as the norm, which became affectionately known outside the county as 'Oxfordshire gothic'. Observational drawing and printing, the favoured media of Tanner's own artistic production, were very much in evidence in Oxfordshire's 'model schools'. The powerful qualities of Tanner's own engravings were often reflected in topic work, — a nostalgia for the past and a romantic view of rural England. Even the formal qualities of his works — their dense structure and horror of empty spaces could be found reflected in a characteristic approach to classroom display.

School Buildings

A particular feature of Oxfordshire as of one or two other progressive authorities, was the interest taken in developing new buildings. As the outward sign of curriculum change, building forms had a particular impact on the professional and public imagination, and thus the buildings themselves may be seen as vehicles of dissemination. It is also significant that open-plan schools were more accommodating of visitors; a group could enter the school and observe, even participate in, a range of activities, without having to penetrate the sanctum of each individual classroom. Teachers having a shared responsibility for the environment and the activities within it were perhaps less threatened by such visits, and children less distracted by the presence of several adults.

Two species of literature considered in earlier chapters also helped to disseminate the architectural achievements of Oxfordshire. In the Ministry of Education's *Building Bulletin* no. 3, in its second edition of 1961 entitled *Village schools*, two of the six new buildings discussed were in Oxfordshire (the others were in Lincolnshire, Cambridgeshire, Berkshire and Texas), and of four remodelled schools two were Oxfordshire projects and two from Northamptonshire. The Schools Council series *British Primary Schools Today* included one volume entitled *Trends in Primary School Design* by Eric Pearson, HMI, attached to the Development Group of the Architects and Building Branch at the Ministry of Education from its earliest days until his retirement. Three of the seven buildings described were in Oxfordshire.

Pearson described Oxfordshire in glowing terms as

> in the van of progress in primary school design, innovation emerging from evolving educational and social philosophies.[32]

Its collaborative model of planning he considered almost unique in public administration:

> Oxfordshire's achievements in primary school building largely rest on the informed opinion of its teachers, which in turn is created by education officers and architects. One spurs the other in a cycle of consultation and collaboration.

Notwithstanding, his detailed description seemed to offer the teachers a relatively minor role, and rather late in the planning process:

> The administrative process for school building in the county is simple and effective. An Assistant Education Officer acts in liaison with the County Architect's Department. He prepares documents and convenes meetings. The County's Education Officers and advisers draw up a framework of requirements for a new school. On this is based the first sketch plan, which is often preceded by discussions between education officers and architects about educational trends. The plan is then studied by the Director of Education and his officers. Revisions are suggested and discussed by the architects, and sensible compromises reached. A revised sketch plan is then sent, with a request for comments, to other interested parties, ie the local school managers and headteacher (if appointed), and any specialists who normally advise the authority. A final sketch plan is then drafted, which is submitted to the Education Committee for its approval.

Christopher Jarman, an Oxfordshire adviser, pointed out that by 1980, Oxfordshire would have been operating open-plan schools for twenty-one years. 'There are in the county teachers who themselves entered open-plan primary schools as 5-year-olds, and who have experienced no other kind. Some of them will soon be headteachers in open-plan designed schools.'[33] Jarman went on to describe the experience of open-plan schools in Oxfordshire as one of 'organic growth over many years' arising from teachers' requests for more convenient spaces in which to provide the best possible facilities for primary age children.[34]

The authority was seeking ways of improving and changing the many Victorian rural schools in the county. One such, described by Eric Pearson, was Brize Norton village school.[35] Here a combination of modest building improvements and ingenuity on the part of the teacher, produced an informal and domestic setting from a lofty schoolroom. The insertion of 'French windows' broke the rigid boundary between outside and inside created by the solid Victorian walls and high windows; the installation of a cooker and sink were practical and domesticating assets; more domesticating still were the rug, sofa and indoor plants provided by the teachers. New tables, chairs and mobile storage units were supplied by the LEA, practical, flexible and more economical of space than traditional school desks. Most significant too in the adaptation of this old school building was the use by the teachers of corrugated card screens, to modify space within the classroom and to provide surfaces for display. This was a device attributable to the influence of HMI Robin Tanner.

The plans of remodelled schools in Oxfordshire, at Clanfield in the west and Sibford Gower in the north-west of the county, were illustrated in the second edition of the Ministry's *Building Bulletin* no. 3 (1961) and showed the process of opening up space in Victorian village schools by demolishing walls and enlarging windows.[36] Terraces and patios broke down the barriers between interior and exterior, extending available teaching space to the immediate school surrounds, each classroom with its own external door. Planting of banks and trees in asymmetrical plan provided interesting spaces. The emphasis in the interior plans was also on asymmetry, not simply for aesthetic reasons, but for functional ones too, in the creation of specialist areas such as workshop, library and home bay (on architectural principles that William Morris had adopted in designing his own home). 'Plain rectangular classrooms', stated the Bulletin, 'cannot easily provide the variety of facilities required', but

> the success of this plan will depend to some extent on effective noise control by the introduction of absorbent surfaces.

In the three-class schools, classrooms were made into independent units insofar as they were given their own cloakroom and lavatories, thus expressing in a practical way the 'family unit' aspect of the class. Warborough C.E. School was a new three-class building by the County Architect, also illustrated and described in this Bulletin.

But the star feature of this *Bulletin* was Finmere School, designed by the Ministry's Development Group in collaboration with Oxfordshire County Council. Most of the photographs were devoted to this building, illustrating its interior, very domestic with rugs of contemporary design, wallpaper in the Home Bay, a divan with valenced counterpane, an Ercol rocking chair, potted plants and fashionable light fittings; large windows flood the interior with light, whilst partition walls create specialist bays and provide support for ample bookshelves and for displays of children's work. Outside, the school's south elevation is shown, with its paved patio, flower beds, plant tubs, bird table, and veranda with woodwork benches. Oxfordshire's special place in the development of primary school architecture was secured at Finmere, opened in 1959 and widely regarded as the launch of a new phase in the planning of primary schools. Finmere was an experimental plan in collaboration with the Development Group at the Ministry of Education, and was a brand new school.

Finmere represented the rare opportunity to build a new *village* school, at a time when the national population growth was mostly urban. The architects, David and Mary Medd, had studied the variety of educational experiences being improvised by teachers in many of the adapted village schools, sitting with children in the classroom throughout their day and following their movements about the school. As a consequence the building was planned as a series of linked working areas, each with a degree of privacy but related to the whole. Each had a character of its own imparted by a variety of wall and floor finishes, lighting, furniture and equipment. The school was for about fifty children ranging from 5 to 11 years old, working individually or in cooperative groups, with two teachers, grouping and regrouping according to ability, age and interests. Pearson's description of this process epitomized the Oxfordshire progressive curriculum with its priorities and emphases:

> Children may carve in wood or stone, model in clay, construct in varied materials, collect, spin, dye and weave their own wool, draw and paint, bake and cook, explore streams and hedgerows, browse among books, write prose and poetry, calculate, estimate and investigate, and any or all or these activities may be followed at one and the same time.[37]

A pre-existing pond and trees were deliberately preserved as part of the school environment, which was also landscaped with earth removed for the footings, for greater interest and educational possibilities. Inside, a sense of domesticity was conferred by the sitting room with its wall fire and rocking chair, and a bedroom alcove for rest, whilst a kitchen area and cooking stove were provided, — not mere toys but rather providing the realism which allows children to work as they would with their parents. Two sliding partitions were provided to define the two 'classroom' spaces from a shared central area if necessary, but these were rarely closed as cooperative teaching was developed which was found to be the happiest arrangement for the social development of the children. On similar lines a larger school was built in 1962 at Tower Hill, Witney, to cater for a growing estate on the edge of the town, the design on this occasion the work of a private architect.

The impetus given to primary school design in Oxfordshire by this earlier work, and by experiments in cooperative teaching arrangements, prompted the local authority to make a further experiment in the planning of large primary schools, carried out at Eynsham, a growing village on the outskirts Oxford. This was to be a 'first school' to cater for 320 5–9-year-olds, and was planned by the County Council's own architects in consultation with LEA advisers.

> It is greatly to the credit of the local authority's advisers and teachers that they did not compromise in this experiment. As an educational and social concept, its demands on the people who use it are more complex than those of the Eveline Lowe school [see chapter 6], assuming as it does that a group of teachers are ready to combine their experience and skill and to surrender their territorial independence, in the education of a large community of children.[38]

Though specialist 'bays' and 'home bays' were provided, the space was open on a much larger scale than at Finmere and Tower Hill; the architects were not asked to retain some form of classroom as a safety net if the experiment should prove unsuccessful. Pearson goes on to note that the teachers were ready to make this advance, and played a major role in the initiation of the scheme.

It was argued in chapter 6 that the school building itself worked as the physical expression of an educational ideal. There was, nevertheless, a tension in the building at Eynsham, between conflicting ideals and between ideals and practical constraints. A variety of texture and space were established and a sense of informality in the arrangement of space had a positive effect on pupils and on their relationships to teachers. But standardization and economy also informed the design; flat roofs and large expanses of glass tend to depersonalize a building by distancing it from hand-made craft traditions. By comparison with the pitched roofs and solid walls, a degree of domesticity was lost. Yet this impersonality was successfully countered by the angles and outside spaces embraced by the form of the building and adorned with ponds, benches, trees, shrubs and flower beds, and interior surfaces included some high quality brick, wood block floors, carpets, quarry-tiles for wet areas, together with tasteful wooden furniture, including Ercol chairs and tables. Certain material problems adversely affected the quality of the environment: flat roofs are continually prone to leaks, resulting in stained ceiling tiles and walls; single glazing, used with more abandon before steep increases in the cost of fuel, meant that the school could be quite cold in winter and insufferably hot on a summer's afternoon; white-painted wooden weatherboarding which does much to soften the effect of glass expanses, required extensive maintenance and is now replaced by plastic (despite its unsympathetic texture, quite smart in appearance). Queen's Dyke Primary School, Witney, built by the county architect just three years later than Eynsham adopted what has since become familiar as the 'post-modern' style; pitched roofs, smaller windows, less open space, and interestingly irregular areas (including triangular teaching bays), and a wealth of wood and brick surfaces, — more immediately expressive of Oxfordshire's progressive values.

At Eynsham, just as in the modified Victorian school buildings, the teachers made the building work an expression of their educational ideals. Most striking as you entered Eynsham was the role of the arts and crafts in the decor. Drapes and fabrics in the designs of William Morris or Sanderson, and plain hessians in 'natural' dyes were much in evidence. Other fabrics had been block printed by children themselves, linocuts on linen and made up into curtains to conceal storage spaces. Pottery also abounded reflecting the artisan productions of local craftsmen, as well as some from further afield, like a West African raku cooking-pot. Functional items such as pencil holders and trays for resources were made of attractive woods, simply turned or carved, and a love of nature was further evident in the teazles, grasses, plants and flowers incorporated in displays. From the children's work, flower and animal drawings, linocuts, fine lettering and penwork were prominently displayed. For the visitor as for the pupil important statements concerning the ethos and curriculum of the school were thus made.

Media and Publicity

In 1958 the County Education Committee agreed to employ the medium of film

> to illustrate the approach of the Authority and its teachers to the educational needs and opportunities of children under 11 living in a rural area.

The Educational Foundation for Visual Aids was enlisted to assist in its production, which was entitled *Village School.*[39] Its explicit purpose was understandable in view of the county's own geographical composition — it included within its boundary 150 very small village schools. Nevertheless, the film is of interest as propaganda for a particular interpretation of progressive primary education, for a pervasive motif throughout the film is the superiority of country to town.

In the film, *Village School*, an introductory sequence showed three geographical areas of the county: remote villages in the north, more closely spaced villages in the Cotswolds, and in the south of the county, the Thames Valley 'more populous, more sophisticated, more affected by outside influences'. To illustrate the last of these is a shot of Henley with cars and antique shops, but this urban environment features no further in the film, for the three schools subsequently depicted were all rural.

The village school 'for all its old-fashioned image and cramped buildings, has something which urban schools have not'. It offered 'an education more balanced and real than might be possible in a town'. In the first place this was ascribed to a sense of integration and awareness of environment.

> In the countryside, home and school are much more closely associated that in any other area and work in school can link up in many ways with children's everyday background.

Turning the local environment to educational use was illustrated first by an example of heavy rural industry, boys studying the workings of a local ironstone quarry, followed up by more formal work in the classroom. Another example showed the children of a Cotswold school engaged in basketwork. This sequence began with the gathering of rushes from a local stream in which the proximity and safety of 'nature' were underlined, as elsewhere in the film, by scenes of children running and skipping from the school gates across open fields. Images such as these (and the unfailingly sunny weather!) subscribed to and reinforced a traditionally idyllic view of the countryside that was contemporaneously transmitted for example through the extensive commercial advertising of Shell petrol and of food products such as Ovaltine.

The activity of basket weaving also reinforced a second theme, that of understanding and valuing the heritage of the past.

> Basketwork is a traditional craft in this area of Oxfordshire and by making it a part of their own craftwork, the children are helping to keep the tradition alive.

This theme was underlined at Wroxton by visits made to the local manor and to the church to study 'their living village heritage, a direct link with Shakespeare's England'. In scenes of children touching the Jacobean panelling and studying the tombs of the Lords of the Manor, an explicit contrast was made in the commentary with museums, which are 'often too impersonal'.

A third implication from this 'making of educational capital out of our local resources' was that of learning through enjoyment.

> Factual knowledge is no less real and solid for having been acquired with pleasure and excitement rather than drudgery and learning by rote.

Thus the children of a school on the River Glyme near Woodstock were seen working in the river, which ran past their school, examining water plants and learning to distinguish between different types. Others were studying maths through measurement of the stream's flow. As the children returned to their classroom the commentary reminded viewers of the skills which the children were learning: 'Here are the biologists and the mathematicians retiring to their desks'. Three of the children were so absorbed that they were left sitting on a bough above the stream, to return later, this detail emphasizing a relaxed approach to timing and to discipline — typical of 'progressivism' and typical by implication of the country life. The integrated curriculum was illustrated, as in all three schools, by the variety of follow-up work: writing, painting, and model-making. Wall displays and table displays proliferated in the informally arranged classroom. The aim of using the local environment was reiterated:

> to give life and meaning to a lot of routine work which can otherwise be dull and meaningless.

The film ended with a restatement of its philosophy, against a low-angle shot of children in the fields silhouetted against the horizon, recalling shots of heroic workers in Eisenstein's classic films:

> Integrating school and life: if the village school can do this for its children then we feel it's doing its job.

The film was shown to teachers in the county for many years after its original production, and thus, embodied in an audio-visual programme extensively used for in-service training, was a theme which provided a significant sub-plot of the progressive ideology. This theme has to be put in the context both of a traditional preoccupation of English culture, and of certain contemporary educational concerns. Raymond Williams has dealt with the literary history of the counterpoint between 'country' and 'city' which has infused English culture ever since Shakespearean retreats to the Forest of Arden and in a variety of responses to the industrial revolution, and similarly in contrasts of 'past' and 'present'.[40] It was emphatically the nostalgia for a pre-industrial past that informed the romantic socialism of the arts and crafts movement which so influenced Robin Tanner. In the post-war period the rural school was widely regarded as an educational 'problem'; the most urbanized nation in the world now had only one in five of its population living on the land, and one of the themes of the Festival of Britain exhibition in 1951 was a division of the nation into townspeople and countrypeople leading quite different ways of life, and that a better mutual understanding of each others' conditions was needed for future progress. W.K. Richmond (1953) argued that educationists had become too predominantly urban-minded. The trend of the age was towards large-scale organizations and mammoth collectives in which the individual and personal choice were suppressed, yet the idea was gaining ground that technological preoccupations and the pressure of impersonal forces were having a deleterious influence. For this reason, the distinctiveness of the rural school should be carefully preserved, a contemporary sociologist observing that:

> with all its handicaps and shortcomings the rural school best represents the social integration of school and community. Teachers know, not only their pupils, but much of the life of the pupils' families. The immediate neighbourhood provides much of the subject matter of the school. The wide range of the age of the children gives a natural setting for the operation of the social processes.[41]

A two-volume work on rural education by Arthur B. Allen (1950)[42] who was headteacher of a rural central school, Great Haseley Endowed School, Oxfordshire, complained of the fact that country schools had been the butt of uninformed comment that their education was thought to be inferior to that of town schools, and that they had been unfairly underresourced. Yet

> The English countryside has grown the food to bring this country through the dark days to victory. The countryside has saved the

> lives and the health of thousands of town children. The nation survives, and will now develop once again because it had the countryside behind it.[43]

Lena Jeger's account of progressive primary education in a *Sunday Times Colour Magazine* of 1963 amply reinforced the idyllic image of the rural school, when she wrote of children 'tiptoeing down an Oxfordshire country lane' after school. The ideal of social unity was woven into her account of two village schools in the county:

> Take Hornton, a remodelled old school where fifty-one children enjoy the most modern ideas. The headmaster, Mr. Backhouse, is a graduate who could earn more elsewhere. But he says that the adventure and reality of education are here, in the village primary schools. At Sibford Gower, where the lintel is dated 1623, picture windows have been cut into old walls, sinks put in each classroom and cloakrooms added. There is a maypole as well as a TV, spinning and weaving as well as radio, and in the hall the cup for choral speaking won at Banbury Arts and Crafts festival. All the village children come to this school. Where else should the doctor's child or the director's twins go? Money could not buy anything better.[44]

Television was considered in chapter 7 as an increasingly significant medium for the dissemination of educational ideas and practices in the 1950s and 1960s. Eileen Molony, the BBC producer who made this her particular specialism, maintained close contacts with Oxfordshire schools. An explicit and powerful statement of progressive ideals, *Eynsham* was one of a series, The Expanding Classroom, made two years after Plowden, and two years after the building of what became one of Oxfordshire's 'show' schools, Eynsham County Primary.[45] Conscious perhaps of the 'Black Paper' debates which were emerging that year, the commentator, David Lucas, referred to doubts which the film purposed to counter with the rhetorical question, against a scene of children utterly absorbed in drawing a stuffed heron:

> Are these children anarchic? Is this what is meant by chaos in the active, integrated classroom?

Three aspects of progressivism featured strongly: attitudes to children, the curriculum, and teacher organisation.

The title sequence incorporated the words: 'The child is the agent of his own learning: Plowden 529', the almost biblical brevity of its citation implying that Plowden's report would by now be extremely familiar to viewers. Inculcating responsibility for their own work was one aspect of the attitude to children reiterated throughout the film. A boy was seen block-printing a cover for the book which he will himself bind and this preparation, it was claimed, ensured that the writing he would do to go in the book would be produced with equal care and pride:

> He is not doing it for reward, but for its own sake, and as his gift to the school community.

Essential to this independence of working was an attitude of trust on the part of the teacher — in a staff discussion, George Baines, headteacher, contrasted this with the more traditional attitude of suspicion towards children. Independence of work was linked with respect for the child's individuality; as David Lucas said of George Baines: 'He knows each child individually and treats each with courtesy'.

The camera lingered frequently on children working alone and enthusiastically amidst a great variety of activity taking place in the open-plan general work areas. Predominantly however, the visual references were to the arts. From the opening sequence of close-ups on exquisitely tasteful displays and on children's paintings and prints, to wide-angle views of the classroom which revealed printed hangings and volumes such as the classic work of calligraphy, Alfred Fairbank's *Book of Scripts* (which appeared frequently behind the interviewer's head!). Flowers, branches, birds and other natural objects were also displayed for their beauty and contributed to the aesthetic quality of the environment. A view of the visual arts, and especially crafts, as the unifying activity of the curriculum was reinforced by a school assembly included in a longer version of this film, at which George Baines took as his theme the principle (from John Ruskin and William Morris) of the honesty of good art. Three bowls, one wicker work, one turned wood and one of moulded glass, were considered for their functional qualities, natural beauty and applied ornament, — the rather extravagant glass object scoring very low on these criteria. Elsewhere, the commentator remarked that 'craftsmanship' was much valued in Oxfordshire schools; it was claimed to have many educational advantages, and the 'morality of art' was clearly implied as one aspect of this. Good presentation, it was claimed, will lead to quality of content.

For all that the text was material design, there were spiritual overtones to the conduct of the assembly. As the commentary observed: the music and the situation imposed their own discipline, and the headteacher's 'delicate control depended on the physical arrangement of the group around him'. Its inspirational tone recalls the suggestion of Edith Moorhouse, mentioned earlier, concerning the 'celebratory' function of a school assembly, and reflected too the style of in-service courses which sought above all to be personally uplifting. Indeed, the commentator remarked that assemblies sometimes attempted a more mystical experience, but that the presence of film cameras prevented this.

Though Oxfordshire progressivism was sometimes characterized by an overemphasis on aesthetics, yet considerable attention was also paid to maths and science in the course of this film. Whilst many of the activities depicted in the general work area were concerned with mathematical skills such as counting, sorting and weighing, there were specialist 'bays' in this modern building where science and maths were the focus of activity. Mechanics was represented by work on a model windmill and crane, physics by experiments with electricity and with lenses, and natural science by the study of bones and feathers. George Baines stressed the importance of observations, acquired through drawing, and the skills of differentiation and classification in studying material objects.

In the maths bay relevant equipment and displays were provided and here the opportunity was taken to stress that although the activities may appear haphazard to an outsider, all was in fact carefully planned.

> Teachers work hard at building into the system concepts which the child can learn.
>
> Time, space, the rhythm of the day, these are the disciplines by which he [the head] works — there is nothing haphazard about it,

David Lucas observed.

A teachers' meeting after school revealed the work involved in team teaching — the necessity for exchange of ideas in planning, and the need to share views on children and their progress; referred to elsewhere were the benefits of younger teachers learning from those more experienced. But at the centre of this team was a headteacher with the force of his convictions, who throughout much of the film interpreted the visual evidence for the viewer: 'I believe, no I don't believe, I *know* each child is an individual'. Thus Molony's film illustrated a feature of progressivism studied in different ways by Cook and Mack (1971), in their publication for the Schools Council, and later by Sharp and Green (1975). The role of the headteacher in a progressive school was crucial in providing a philosophy by which curriculum and teaching methods were to be organized. This crucial role was acknowledged by advisers and HMI in the organization of in-service training in Oxfordshire, and it was reflected implicitly in the architectural design of the schools, for open-plan arrangement such as that at Eynsham denied the possibility of the individual class teacher working independently with her group. For all the educational advantages implied, this structure also had the effect of ensuring greater visibility of individual teachers, and providing for their closer supervision by the head, along the lines of the Panopticon, Jeremy Bentham's model penitentiary!

In the dissemination of ideals and teaching methods, a significant characteristic was the dissemination beyond the county, of Oxfordshire progressivism. Considerable energies were channelled into conveying philosophies and practices from Oxfordshire both to other counties and abroad, particularly the United States. Teachers spoke at conferences far and wide, and Leonard Marsh employed headteachers from the county on his postgraduate course at Goldsmiths; in turn, visitors came in large numbers to observe the better-known schools. A number of Oxfordshire heads and advisers regularly gave lectures and courses in America, and at a time when transatlantic cultural traffic was mostly in the opposite direction, this export of educational philosophy and practice was a striking achievement; the actual impact abroad of such an export drive has yet to be assessed, but it could be argued that at home it served to legitimate establish practices and even to encourage an element of stagnation, inhibiting self-criticism and further development.

Notes

1 Rogers, V. (Ed.) (1970) *Teaching in the British Primary School*, London, Macmillan. p. v.
2 House of Commons Select Committee on Education and Science, *Teacher Training, Minutes of Evidence*, P.P. 1969–70 (135-iv) xi, p. 259.
3 Moorhouse, E. (1970) 'The philosophy of the British primary school' in Rogers, V.R. (Ed.) *Teaching in the British Primary School*, London, Macmillan, p. 11.
4 Baines, G. (1971) 'Learning in a flexible school' in Walton, J. (Ed.) *The Integrated Day in Theory and Practice*, London, Ward Lock Educational, p. 31. Baines' text also shared with the writings of Leonard Marsh an antipathy towards educational research.
5 *ibid*, p. 33.
6 *ibid*, p. 36.
7 Smith, R.T. (1971) *A Rural School: British Primary Schools Today*, London, Macmillan for the Schools Council.
8 *ibid*, p. 75.
9 Hogan, J. (1970) *Beyond the Classroom*, Reading, Educational Explorers Ltd., p. 75ff.
10 Winkley, D. (1985) *Diplomats and Detectives: LEA Advisers at Work*, London, Robert Royce, p. 37.
11 Moorhouse, E. (1985) *A Personal Story of Oxfordshire Primary Schools 1946–1956*, Oxford, privately printed.
12 Jarman, C. (1978) 'The organization of open-plan primary schools, the Oxfordshire experience' in Bell, S. (Ed.) *The Organization of Open Plan Primary Schools*, Gasgow, Jordanhill College of Education, p. 48.
13 Makins, V. (1985) *Times Educational Supplement* 15 November 1985.
14 Bennett, L. (1984) *The Primary Advisory Service in Oxfordshire*, unpublished typescript, p. 20.
15 Coe, J. (1968) 'A way ahead', *The Primary School in Transition. Aspects of Education* no. 8, December.
16 Bennett, Coe, Jarman and Moorhouse all contributed articles to the *Froebel Journal.*
17 Winkley, D. (1985) *op cit*, pp. 70–1.
18 Moorhouse, E. (1970) *op cit*, p. 15.
19 Moorhouse, E. (1965) 'In-service training in Oxfordshire', *Froebel Journal* no. 3, October.
20 *ibid*, p. 26.
21 Biographical details taken from: City of Bristol Museum and Art Gallery (1981) *Robin Tanner RE RWA, paintings, drawings and etchings*, (exhibition catalogue).
22 Quoted in Guichard, K.M. (1977) *British Etchers 1850–1940*, London, R. Garton, p. 13.

23 City of Bristol Museum and Art Gallery (1981) *op cit*, p. 5.
24 Van der Eyken, W. (1969) *Adventures in Education*, London, Allen Lane, pp. 107–13.
25 Ministry of Education (1959) *Primary Education: Suggestions for the Consideration of Teachers and Others Concerned With the work of the Primary Schools*, London, HMSO, pp. 213 and 216.
26 *ibid*, p. 218.
27 Tanner, R. (1966) '"Creativeness" in education', *Froebel Journal* no. 5, June.
28 The absorption attainable by children was a theme of A.L. Stone's pamphlet for the Ministry of Education *Story of a School* (1949). See chapter 7 above.
29 Tanner, R. (1966) *op cit*, p. 5.
30 Makins, V. (1985) *op cit.*
31 Robin Tanner in conversation with the author, June 1986.
32 Pearson, E. (1972) *Trends in School Design: British Primary Schools Today*, London, Macmillan for the Schools Council.
33 Jarman, C. (1978) *op cit.*
34 Jarman, C. (1978) *op cit*, p. 55.
35 Pearson, E. (1972) *op cit.*
36 DES (1961) *Building Bulletin* no. 3 (2nd edn), pp. 58–63.
37 Pearson, E. (1972) *op cit*, p. 34.
38 *ibid*, p. 48.
39 *Village School* (1954), sponsored by Oxfordshire Education Committee, produced by EFVA, directed by Michael Currer-Briggs.
40 Williams, R. (1974) *The Country and the City*, London, Chatto and Windus; Williams, R. (1964) *Culture and Society*, Harmondsworth, Penguin.
41 Richmond, W.K. (1953) *The Rural School: its Problems and Prospects*, London, Alvin Redman, p. 204.
42 Allen, A.B. (n.d) (1950) *Rural Education*, vols. 1, 2, London, Allman and Son.
43 Allen, A.B. (n.d) (1950) *op cit*, vol. 2, p. xiii.
44 *Sunday Times Colour Magazine*, 21 July 1963.
45 First broadcast 1 June 1969, repeat broadcasts November 1969 and August 1970. Two 16mm. film versions are preserved by the LEA, one cut and one longer version. Other Oxfordshire schools were featured in this and in an earlier series entitled *Discovery and Experience* (1967).

9 *Reaction from Progressivism*

The chapters above have illustrated the variety of agencies at work in the dissemination of curriculum change, and the complexity of their interaction. A more widespread progressivism in primary education was not simply a product of professional initiatives, but social and cultural change also governed its progress. The time-lags and contradictions inherent in the gradualism of curriculum change are a product of the social, economic and political contexts, the outside forces which impel or restrain educators in their definition and promotion of the curriculum.[1] For the first two decades after 1945, it could be said that these forces worked in favour of a more progressive approach, but by the end of the 1960s the harmony was beginning to be disturbed.

Progressive primary education was sometimes described as a 'revolution', and was often defined by contrast with a one-dimensional picture of the 'formalism' of the past. The foregoing chapters have demonstrated that such a bipolar view of developments is as inadequate in explanation of curriculum development as it would be in accounting for social change, and the 'conservative' and 'innovatory' cannot be neatly distinguished in this way. Continuity accompanied change, and the development of curriculum and teaching method represented a continuing flux along the whole spectrum from the conservative through the liberal to the radical revolutionary.

In the Introduction, Tom Paxton's lyrics of 1962 were quoted. Illustrating the radical cultural shift that subsequently occurred, Pink Floyd had a hit in 1980 with the single *Another Brick in the Wall* from their album and film *The Wall*. The heavy rhythm of its lyrics:

> We don't need no education,
> We don't need no thought control,
> Hey, teacher, leave those kids alone,
> All in all you're just another brick in the wall,

was accompanied in Gerald Scarfe's animated film by a sequence of scurrying school children pursued by hammers. A deeper cynicism, violently expressed, now made Tom Paxton's protest folksong look ingenuous and naive, but the success of both songs in their time suggests that they spoke to a strain of contemporary popular feeling. Silver (1983) identified opinion as a vital component in any social history of policy:

> An opinion-related history is one in which significant moments of change are explored, counter pressures for innovation and established practice are probed, the subtleties of social interaction and their public articulation investigated. The basis of such explorations lies not in theoretical models or quantifiable data but in historical interpretation of issues, of how they emerge, of their disappearance.[2]

Given the picture of opinion represented by the shift from Paxton to Pink Floyd, the smooth oratory of Schiller or Blackie would be unlikely to continue to serve effectively as the lynchpin, let alone the cutting edge, of curriculum change. Following the student revolts of 1968, open schooling had become deschooling in many quarters, where anti-school was the orthodoxy, bolstered by trends in sociological research. The *Little Red Schoolbook* enjoyed a succès de scandale giving advice to children on sex and drugs, and encouraging them to demand more democracy in the running of their schools.[3] At the practical level, lay-people were demanding a greater say, no longer willing to accept unquestioningly professional expertise. Government took up a new stance from 1976 and the teaching profession was henceforth increasingly called upon to respond to political directives concerning the curriculum. Christian Schiller's later lectures lamented such developments; in 1971, in a lecture at an Oxfordshire in-service course, he used the claim of teachers to professionalism in order to reject pressures for accountability.[4] Schiller died in February 1976. 1976 was a year of great setbacks for progressive primary education. Parental discontent at William Tyndale School had erupted in the previous year, and was revived in news headlines with the completion of an enquiry in June 1976; the school had been one of the model progressive schools in ILEA, and its discontents made excellent news copy. Neville Bennett's *Teaching Styles and Pupil Progress* was published and widely publicized by the national press and media in April 1976. In the new circumstances in which primary school teachers now had to work, and in which the younger teachers were trained, the authority of 'gurus' was open to question. It was also thus to a predisposed national audience that the Prime Minister, Jim Callaghan made his speech on 18 October, carefully orchestrated beforehand by his policy advisers in collaboration with senior DES officials and duly leaked to the press in advance.[5]

Social Reaction

Examining the social context of progressivism in the 1950s and early 1960s, chapter 2 considered as indicative phenomena the standard of living, cultural trends and the mass media, and the status of children and the family. The political mood and cultural climate of the 1960s and 1970s must now be reviewed with particular reference to such phenomena. From 1973 the birth rate had begun to drop visibly, so that in 1975 for the first time since the Second World War, the total population began to fall. By 1978 the NUT Education Committee was reporting to the annual conference that the problem of falling school rolls had become acute.[6] That year unemployment also exceeded one million for the first time in the same period. A national mood of tension had grown throughout 1974 after the long miners' strike of the winter, which had forced a change of government; in June an anti-National Front demonstrator was killed, and the acceleration of terrorism continued with an IRA bombing campaign on the mainland, which by November had claimed twenty-nine lives. A Prevention of Terrorism Act was passed. On the economic front, a trebling of oil prices in 1973 was a psychological blow to a society which had become so dependent on this fuel and on its by-products.[7]

It is tempting to see in educational policy a simple conservative backlash in the 1970s against radical change of the previous decade, or in the social context a reaction in the 1970s and 1980s period of 'cuts and confrontation' against the affluence and consensus of the 1950s and 1960s. However, as both Marwick (1982) and Ryder and Silver (1985) have noted, there is a good deal of continuity as well between these periods. An earlier turning point might be 1963; the rapid loss of African colonies such as Nigeria, Kenya and others in the years 1960–63 and the unnerving drama of the Cuban missile crisis in October 1962, had preceded the assassination of the American President, and at home, the end of the 'Macmillan era'. De Gaulle's veto in January 1963 of Britain's application to join the European 'Common Market' was perhaps another blow to national pride. From 1963 it is tempting to look back to an earlier date, 1956, which saw the debacle of Suez, another injury to national pride after victory in the Second World War, and an indication of the limits of the Western alliance; culturally 1956 could also be said to have been a shock year with the production at the Royal Court Theatre of John Osborne's *Look Back in Anger*, and the arrival of Elvis Presley's *Heartbreak Hotel* and Bill Haley's *Rock Around the Clock*, which seemed to reinforce popular cultural dependence on America. Rather than compare the rival claims of 'watershed' years, the purpose here is to suggest a continuity of events in cultural change.

Continuities and contrasts may also be identified with respect to the growth of affluence. It was suggested in chapter 2 that a rising standard of living assisted the progressive curriculum to develop, but it is also arguable that the progressive curriculum increasingly ignored the social and cultural implications as changes were wrought in the lifestyle of children, and in attitudes to authority. Affluence continued to alter the circumstances of parents as educational consumers through the 1970s; a strengthening of the consumer voice, which markedly altered the context in which the curriculum was delivered, was accompanied by a growth of inequality, revealing the failure of education to deliver what it seemed to have offered at the moment of reconstruction in 1944 or in the more optimistic and expansionist 1960s.

Growing opulence in the 1970s may be symbolized by the credit card. In the 1950s, credit in the form of 'hire purchase' had facilitated increased acquisition of durable goods, and throughout the 1970s purchases on credit eased the way to ownership of ever more sophisticated appliances such as colour television, stereo hi-fi equipment, and freezers. Advertising, Sunday colour supplements and the rise of market research all reflected this.[8] By the late 1970s 88 per cent of households now had a fridge and 71 per cent a washing machine; between 1970 and 1978 those households with a deep-freezer rose from 4 per cent to 41 per cent. By 1977 more than 50 per cent of houses had central heating. Car ownership also expanded; in 1950 there had been 2.3 million on the road; by 1970 11.8 million and by 1980 15.4 million, by which date 11 per cent of households were recorded as having two cars. Wider choices in consumption may be exemplified by a proliferation of foreign restaurants, as British culture became more cosmopolitan; this enrichment of choice derived partly from the impact of immigrant communities, and a taste for foreign foods was also encouraged by holidays abroad, which rose from two million in 1951 to four million in 1961 and nine million in 1978.[9] In terms of material comfort and cultural experience, therefore, many primary school children of the 1970s enjoyed different circumstances from those of the 1950s.

It is significant though, that a substantial proportion of children did not share in these benefits. Affluence went alongside inequality. Criticism of the welfare state had been made by Richard Titmuss as early as the late 1950s, showing how unequal distribution of benefits and increased tax and fringe benefits helped the middle class and the rich; in 1960 less than 10 per cent of all the population owned 83 per cent of all private wealth, and by 1975–76 the top 10 per cent of income earners still gained over 25 per cent of all earned income and 53 per cent of investment income. Townsend's research in 1964 showed that 14 per cent of the population were in total poverty, and in 1982 seven million people were being supported by Supplementary Benefit. In its philosophy of positive discrimination and its proposals for Educational Priority Areas, the Plowden Report acknowledged these facts, but educational policies in the event did little to ameliorate the situation. Moreover the widening gap between rich and poor in the 1970s and 1980s revealed inequalities between north and south and a high proportion of Black people amongst the disadvantaged, factors which contributed to heightening social tension in more recent years.[10]

Increased choice and buying power for many in the market for goods, led to a growth of consumer consciousness and contributed to a more critical approach amongst education's clients, realized in pressing claims for parental participation. We have already seen that a Gallup Poll of 1959 showed 59 per cent of parents claiming a say in their children's education, and some of the 'challenges to progressivism' came from parents as at William Tyndale. These developments are well illustrated in the work of Michael Young as a promoter of consumers' rights, linked to the growth of sociological research which will be further explored below. Himself a product of the progressive independent school, Dartington Hall (and biographer of its founders, the Elmhirsts), with war-time experience in political and economic planning (forerunner of the Policy Studies Institute) and post-war work as secretary of the Labour Party's Research Department from 1945–51, he went on to found and direct the Institute of Community Studies from 1953; he was also founding chair of the Consumers' Association in 1956, publishers of *Which?*, testing and comparing manufactured goods for the benefit of customers. In 1959 he became chair of the Advisory Centre for Education which aimed to offer a similar service for parents in choosing schools for their children, and published the journal *Where?* Brian Jackson, teacher and educational sociologist, was closely associated with this work. Employed by the Institute of Community Studies from 1958, he produced with Dennis Marsden an influential study of education and the working class, became Director of the Advisory Centre for Education, and campaigned against streaming in junior schools.[11]

The protection of the consumer and of the environment was the goal of the many pressure groups which became a particular hallmark of the 1970s. Nationwide consumer movements such as Friends of the Earth and the Campaign for Real Ale were seen to have an impact on industry, and on public policy with the passing of such legislation as the Control of Pollution Act (1974), Community Land Act (1975) and Consumer Safety Act (1978). In education, the consumer's voice might be seen as a challenge to the professional educationists' prerogatives in curriculum planning. The publications of ACE and of the Home and School Council represented an attempt above all to break down the mystique of education for parents, but more radical expressions of consumer consciousness in education included the 'free school' movement, which sought an alternative to state schooling through local cooperative enterprise. A greater interest in the child as consumer was reflected in Blishen's compilation of children's ideals solicited by *The Observer* in 1976, and in Roger White's and Michael Brockington's (1983) study, *Tales Out of School*.[12]

Participatory democracy in its broadest sense is a phenomenon that cannot be dealt with here at great length, but as it is of relevance to questions of professional autonomy later in this chapter, a little more needs to be said here. In 1967 a parliamentary Ombudsman (after the Swedish prototype) was appointed to assist the public in redress against bureaucratic unfairness. A government committee on public participation in planning (the Skeffington Committee) reported in 1969 and legislation on involvement of the community in local planning was passed in 1971. The Education Acts of 1980 and 1986 eventually gave legislative form to the trend towards greater parental participation in the running of schools.

The broadcasting media played a significant part in this general process. It has been argued that local radio, as well as education, enhanced the spirit of local community participation and involvement; the first group of BBC local stations was launched in 1969, followed by the Sound Broadcasting Act of 1972 and Independent Local Radio with nineteen stations in operation by the end of the decade.[13] Examples given in chapter 7 of broadcasters' interest in education during the 1960s may be aptly contrasted with the more searching 'investigatory' style of TV programmes in the 1970s. A BBC *Horizon* programme on the day of publication of Bennett's *Teaching Styles and Pupil Progress* was entitled 'A lesson for teacher'. It was, by contrast with much other press coverage, an extensive and balanced exploration of the significance of Bennett's research but nevertheless set the scene in terms of 'a fierce debate between progressives and traditionalists', illustrated by film of two schools at quite opposite extremes, identifying a range of virtues and vices in each; in particular it interviewed parents, who were unanimously supportive in each case of their own school! Some of the conclusions were sensationally presented, such as the deduction that the child in a progressive school could be held back in some subjects by more than a year over the course of its primary education. Yet its overall message was clearly that the Plowden Report had made claims for progressivism without any research evidence; Bennett's scepticism concerning progressivist assertions that their aims, and hence their performance, were not capable of evaluation, came over with force, and the culminating argument of the programme was that the teacher's ability to sequence and structure the curriculum was of more significance than the context and the environment.[14] More sensational was the *Panorama* coverage of 'The school that came apart', which portrayed the confrontational nature of the educational debate through a dramatic reconstruction of the Public Inquiry conducted by Robin Auld QC for the ILEA. The characters portrayed and the sharp cross-questioning of witnesses conveyed all the tension of a courtroom drama.[15]

Participatory democracy and the consumer movement may be regarded as aspects of a more general questioning of established authority, in the context of which the charismatic and inspirational mode of disseminating progressivism exemplified by Schiller and Blackie was less likely to succeed. 'The Establishment', a term coined in the mid-1950s and highlighted by Hugh Thomas in his book of that title in 1959, was

> The English constitution, and the group of institutions and outlying agencies built around it to assist in its protection ...
>
> The word 'Establishment' simply indicates the assumption of the attributes of a state church by certain powerful institutions and people; in general these may be supposed to be effectively beyond democratic control.

Thomas took up the cudgels:

> To those who desire to see the resources and talents of Britain fully developed and extended, there is no doubt that the fusty Establishment, with its Victorian views and standards of judgment, must be destroyed.[16]

It has been shown that the promoters and facilitators of the progressive primary school curriculum, for all their reforming and liberal tendencies, associated with the drive for social reconstruction in the post-war period, did not stand unequivocally outside, let along against, the Establishment. The adoption of received canons of high culture, the promotion of the craft aesthetic, the rural and the antiquarian, though originally conceived in a democratic spirit, had also an air of conservatism and dogmatism about them. Increasing affluence had not shifted the centres of power by bringing about a 'managerial revolution' or a process of 'embourgeoisement', as some had predicted. Anthony Sampson's *Anatomy of Britain* of 1962, a timely journalistic work which could be included in the category of 'popular sociology' described in chapter 2, demonstrated the resistance to change of established institutions, and that power still lay firmly in the hands of an established elite; twenty years and four editions later, in *The Changing Anatomy of Britain*, his treatment of education was still largely concerned with the grammar schools, the public schools, and 'the private resurgence'.[17]

On the other hand, a prevailing mood of liberalism in the early 1960s reinforced the growth of progressivism and a more liberal approach to education. Christopher Booker's classic study of the decade was entitled *The Neophiliacs* — a society embracing anything that was new, including the 'new morality'.[18] Marwick has subsequently dubbed the 1960s as the 'End of Victorianism'. The growth of progressivism in the 1960s cannot be separated from increasingly 'tolerant' social attitudes reflected in legislation such as the abolition of capital punishment (1965) and of theatre censorship (1968), or the legalization of homosexuality (1967) and abortion (1968), yet much of the 'new morality' was leading towards the destruction of traditional ideals which progressivism espoused. Such 'permissive' legislation came about from the resolution of two forces, the increasingly liberal attitudes of authority, but also the new challenges to authority. Penguin Books' calculated decision to publish a paperback edition of *Lady Chatterly's Lover* in 1959, for example, gave rise to a highly publicized trial for obscenity with 'experts' giving evidence for both the traditional and the new moral order. The farcical character of the trial provided the kind of material which was ripe for anti-establishment satire in the early 1960s, typified by the magazine *Private Eye* and the BBC television programme *That Was The Week That Was.* Just as the BBC with its Director General Lord Reith, in the pre-war years had been regarded as the guardian of the nation's morality, so the institution and its new Director General, Hugh Carlton Green, became a scapegoat for those who attacked declining moral and cultural standards.

By the early seventies, the challenge to authority seemed to prove an even stronger force than the liberalising stance of traditional institutions, however. Thus Germaine Greer's *The Female Eunuch* which appeared in paperback in 1971, stood as a telling counterpart to Hoggart's *Uses of Literacy*, described in chapter 2 as a cult text of the late 1950s. A fashionable and successful book, *The Female Eunuch* challenged many traditional assumptions about sex roles and family life in society, and reflected changing patterns of sexual and social behaviour. Politically, the model of protest movements and extra-parliamentary politics by bodies such as the Campaign for Nuclear Disarmament which characterized the later 1950s, developed in the late 1960s into youth rebellion and campus unrest partly inspired by more extreme movements such as Black Power in the USA. In such developments the objects of attack were traditionally liberal authorities such as the universities and the schools, which now came to be seen by some as instruments of repression, — the 'mind police'.

In such a climate the cosy consensus of primary progressivism was bound to come under strain. In the 1960s innovation and attack on 'Victorian' traditions may have provided an acceptable environment for progressivism but by the 1970s and 1980s it was to suffer both from a questioning of the traditional liberalism handed down by authority, but also from the backlash of those who felt that 'liberation' had gone too far. The new 'toleration' bred a reaction which further heightened the sense of confrontation. Mary Whitehouse launched her counter attack against 'moral laxity' and the Festival of Light movement paved the way for other reactions such as the *Black Papers* on education. This had a political dimension, so that by 1975 it was possible for a political journalist to write of 'Mrs Thatcher's middle-class uprising'. The 1979 General Election further proved that:

> middle-class persons who formerly prided themselves on their

progressive sympathies were now swinging away from Labour and back to a more obvious 'class' support of the Conservatives.[19]

Where increased affluence had a particular impact on culture was the new economic power of youth; as wages, and especially the wages of the unskilled and semi-skilled, rose faster than prices from the 1950s, so young people entering employment benefited. As consumers of pop music and fashions they began to exercise a considerable economic choice freed from traditional dependence on their parents. Analysis of teenage expenditure in 1959 showed that 20 per cent of teenage incomes went on clothing and footwear, whilst their purchases of records and gramophone equipment represented 42.5 per cent of all consumer spending under this heading.[20] Symbols of the 'Swinging Sixties' included the mini-skirt and the Beatles; Philip Larkin's 'Annus Mirabilis' recalled:[21]

> So life was never better than
> In nineteen sixty-three
> (Though just too late for me) —
> Between the end of the *Chatterly* ban
> and the Beatles' first LP.

The Beatles' award of the MBE in 1965 was as much for services to the British economy, the export of records *and* the revival of the flagging corduroy industry, as for their contribution to music. It must be acknowledged that such phenomena did not immediately affect the primary school child, but indirect effects were many; the independent 'teenage culture' demonstrated that the challenge to traditional authority was not simply an intellectal phenomenon, but was a more far reaching and continuous growth across the period from the 1950s, though harsher and more strident perhaps in the 1970s and 1980s.

At a time when progressive educationists were promoting the ideal of the primary teacher's class as a family unit, the family as a social institution appeared to be undergoing considerable change with an increasing divorce rate, but was also under attack in principle. Prominent figures in the 'counter-culture' of the later 1960s, such as R.D. Laing and Robin Blackburn questioned the relevance and benevolence of the family unit.[22] But more established figures too, echoed this growing disillusionment, such as the anthropologist Edmund Leach in his 1967 Reith lectures, describing the family as 'the source of all our discontents'; this phrase caught the attention of the media and educational worlds in a way which was scathingly described by Ronald Fletcher in the third edition of his standard work on the family and marriage in Britain:

> The journalistic country is agog! Editors use a provocative sentence or two to head their colour supplement leaders on 'Why marriage?'. Television producers hang all the bright clothes of

> their educational programmes on this peg of controversy. Colleges of education quote the sentences [of Leach] in their examination questions and ask the students to 'discuss'.[23]

Fletcher's first edition in 1962 had been to counter the right wing criticism that social tendencies and especially the welfare state and education had undermined the traditional family. By 1973 the third edition was countering attacks on the family from critics on the left.

Professional Reaction

Whilst some broader cultural trends were beginning to mitigate against well established progressive practice from the mid-1970s, certain trends in professional discourse and in educational politics were also tending to undermine progressivism. These trends included adverse reactions to Plowden, centralizing tendencies of educational policy, new directions in educational research and their implication for the status of the teaching profession, and the continuing role of the NUT and of the Schools Council both of which took a less committed stance towards the precepts of progressivism.

Bernstein and Davies (1969) observed that the 'horticultural view of child nature and development' and the view of teacher, school and curriculum which this entailed, came 'very close to being the semi-official ideology of primary education in this country',[24] yet there was also professional dissent to counter the euphoric mood of 'Plowdenitis' from soon after the publication of Plowden. Despite the fact that Plowden's Committee had included Oxford University's Wykeham Professor of Logic, the Report was particularly vulnerable to attack on the grounds of its dubious definition of a 'recognizable philosophy of education'. Philosophers were prominent in their searching questions about the premises on which the Committee had set to work. Peters (1969) for example, whilst acknowledging the value of its recommendations and the advance over more authoritarian thinking represented by the Report, found it 'theoretically not satisfactory' and 'far from appropriate to the practical needs of our time'. Concepts such as 'development' and 'children's needs' were 'too often a way of dressing up our value-judgments in semi-scientific clothes'. The exclusive stress on intrinsic motivation embodied in certain psychological theories, especially those of Piaget, was open to question; practical experiments appearing to support them, such as those of Susan Isaacs, had too often been conducted in the context of small classes of intelligent children in experimental progressive schools. Concern about the potential influence of such insecurely based theorizing stemmed from the widespread evidence that the Report was already being treated as an authoritative textbook on the theory of primary education, especially in colleges of education.[25] From a sociological viewpoint, Bernstein and Davies found that Plowden's biological model of the child emphasized too exclusively individual differences, 'stages of development' being considered to the exclusion of sub-cultural differences. Another observation was that compensatory policies of education could not be developed without a better understanding of how school actually perpetuated social and educational handicaps.[26] Further educational discourse in the 1970s, by scholars such as Sharp and Green or the Centre for Contemporary Cultural Studies in Birmingham, led to questioning from a Marxist perspective the 'unproblematic' values on which the Plowden Report had been based, as representing various means of social control. From another political perspective, and in the public domain, the Black Papers on education (originally conceived by Professors Cox and Dyson as a means of boosting the circulation of their conservative *Critical Quarterly*)[27], which had initially railed against Marxism and anarchy in the universities and egalitarianism and comprehensivization in the secondary schools, also turned their attention to primary school progressivism with G.H. Bantock's attack on 'discovery methods'.[28]

At the same time, in the early 1970s, a shift in official policy within the Department of Education and Science initiated a transition from the view represented by Plowden's key statement: 'At the heart of education lies the child' to the enunciation in 1981 that 'The curriculum lies at the heart of education . . .'[29]

Callaghan's 'Ruskin speech' in October 1976, a virtually unprecedented focus on education in a key Prime Ministerial statement, put the issue of school performance in the political limelight, and the Secretary of State, Shirley Williams, associated herself very closely with the 'Great Debate' on education which was launched in 1977. But the work of DES administrators and of HMI had been tending in this direction well before the eruption of this public debate. An adverse report on reading standards in 1972, during Margaret Thatcher's period of office at the Department, had led to the setting up of the Bullock Committee on language; and the survey of primary schools which was eventually published in 1978, pointing up criticisms of curriculum and school performance, had been carried out in the years 1975–77. In chapter 3 above, it was noted that a more 'advisory' role for HMI, characteristic of the work done by Schiller, Blackie and Tanner, had been identified by the House of Commons Select Committee in 1967/68, which had predicted a decline in size of the inspectorate, but from the mid-1970s its function turned increasingly towards 'accountability' in conducting national surveys and as an arm of central control in drafting curricular guidelines. From early in 1975 an HMI Publication Group had worked on curriculum guidelines, resulting in the publication of *Curriculum 11–16* in December 1977, which underlined the need for a 'properly thought out' curriculum to ensure 'pupils' common curricular rights and society's needs', and various subsequent publications, including *A View of the Curriculum* (1980) which sought 'greater coherence and continuity in school education as a whole'.[30] At the same time, the Secretary of State adumbrated a reinterpretation of the division of responsibility for the curriculum as traditionally understood within the terms of the 1944 Education Act, by its Circular 14/77 (November 1977) which sought LEA responses on a number of curriculum issues including local arrangements for coordination and development, curricular balance and breadth, selected subject areas, and 'preparation for working life'. Two years later the DES report on this review concluded that the Secretary of State should take the lead in producing a desirable framework for the curriculum, a matter which had previously been considered the responsibility of local authorities.[31] The government Green Paper *Education in Schools* (1977) noted the transformation in primary schools of a much wider curriculum and of the 'child-centred' approach. Its widespread influence was deemed to have provided a trap for less experienced and able teachers, and the 'challenge' was now 'to restore the rigour without damaging the real benefits of the child-centred developments'; teachers should be able to identify with precision the levels of achievement represented by a pupil's work, and should plan for progression, a measure of uniformity from one part of the country to another should reasonably be expected, and skills such as literacy and numeracy, 'for which the primary schools have a central, and indeed an overriding responsibility', should form a 'protected area of the curriculum'.[32]

Centralization was, of course, a longer term trend from which progressivism had earlier benefited. The setting up of an Architects and Building Branch which, though it worked in partnership with the LEAs, had used the medium of national architectural guidelines to promote open-planning of primary schools, and the dissemination of 'good practice' through the publication of pamphlets, had helped to promote progressive ideals. Implementation of progressive practices in primary schools, had been substantially assisted by the imposition on LEAs of Circular 10/65 and later legislation which pushed forward the abolition of selection at 11+ in reluctant localities. But centralization in curricular matters was eventually to work against the initiatives of LEAs and against the independence of headteachers in their primary schools, through which progressivism had been promoted.

Curriculum had been placed high on the agenda of national politics in 1976/77 when Shirley Williams was Secretary of State, but a high degree of continuity in this centralizing trend was observable following the change of government in 1979. It became something of a personal mission during the ministry of Sir Keith Joseph, and the promise of legislation for a national curriculum made by his successor, Kenneth

Baker, became an urgent reality following the re-election of Mrs Thatcher's government in June 1987.

A further blow to progressivism was the simple but fundamental one of resources. A rising child population in the 1960s had been accompanied by growth in government expenditure, and rising school rolls had encouraged investment in new building. But financial crises and falling rolls from 1973 changed the tack. As school architecture was a proud emblem of progressive primary schooling, the situation of primary school building by the later 1970s may be taken as symptomatic. Despite the much publicized model primary schools which had been the subject of Building Bulletins in the 1950s and 1960s, the overall state of the national primary school building stock in 1977 gave a less rosy picture of progress made since the war. The facts were publicized in a DES report following two sample surveys made in 1975 and 1976.[33] At this time there were 23,000 primary schools and 5000 secondary schools in England and Wales. For historical reasons, a higher proportion of the primary schools were older: 36 per cent having some accommodation dating from before 1903, compared with only 12 per cent of the secondary schools. As many of the older schools were smaller, it needs to be added that the 36 per cent of primary school buildings represented 20 per cent of primary school places built at the turn of the century or earlier. As against this, 45 per cent of buildings (representing 51 per cent of places) had been built since 1945. The quality of the primary school buildings was illustrated by a variety of statistics. Almost half of the classrooms or teaching spaces in pre-1945 buildings were less than 500 square feet, giving accommodation for no more than twenty children by current standards (whereas the average primary class size in 1976 was 29.2). Twenty-two per cent of primary schools were accommodated on more than one storey, a feature by now considered undesirable for this age group, and 30 per cent still had some outdoor lavatories. Falling school rolls removed the pressure for new school building, and a survey made by HMI in 1983, noted as one of its main findings that

> Problems with accommodation and the maintenance and repair of buildings remain and the long term consequences of the deterioration in the capital stock of buildings are particularly worrying.

Planned programmes of maintenance were judged to be less than satisfactory in fifty-nine out of the ninety-seven local education authorities.[34] By 1984 it was revealed that emergency repairs were taking up to 50–55 per cent of the maintenance budget, compared with the normal 35 per cent.[35]

Architectural literature produced by the DES Architects and Building Branch after 1980, reflected growing financial stringency in less voluminous publication and less lavish presentation. The *Architects and Building Branch Broadsheets* now produced, were more modest productions than the *Building Bulletins* referred to earlier in chapter 6. Broadsheet no. 3 (1980) concerned the remodelling of a school at Burslem, Stoke-on-Trent. Significant in curricular terms was the emphasis on flexibility, giving greater autonomy to the teachers in organizing their own teaching space, but also recognizing the likelihood of continuing change in both educational methods and pupil numbers.[36] Broadsheet no. 9 in 1982 offered advice by referring to good examples already in existence such as Chaucer Infant and Nursery School (Ilkeston, Derbyshire — 1974) with it covered work areas linking teaching spaces to grassed and planted banks, and its adjacent adventure playground, and Guillemont Junior School (Farnborough, Hampshire — 1976) with its covered work areas for outdoor craft, enclosed landscape courtyards and work patios, grass mounds, nature ponds, and paved areas for formal and informal games.[37] And reflecting the changing and difficult relationship between school and community, a Broadsheet of 1983 dealt with the question of vandalism in schools. Containing mostly practical advice concerning consultation at local authority and school levels, it also promulgated the principle that involvement of the community, through community use of facilities, would be an effective preventive measure. Heavy policing and fortress-like protection were thus ill-advised; 'Over-prevention will produce a result far removed from the pleasant appearance and civilizing influence which an educational building can bring to a neigbourhood'.[38] The fortieth anniversary of the 1944 Education Act saw many 'progressive' principles such as outdoor education and community use now taken for granted, but the main concern was now not with pioneering new building forms, but with economy and with making the best use of inherited facilities.

Progressivism may be seen in the chapters above as having had equivocal implications for professional status. On the one hand much was left to the wisdom of the individual teacher identifying the needs of each child in her care, with little reference to a curriculum negotiated with other parties in the educational process; in this respect she might be seen as having particular expertise in her understanding of child development. On the other hand were frequent implications embodied in the progressives' of 'confessional' and 'craft' views of the teachers' role. She was to practice the child-centre beliefs and ideals, handed down as enlightenment and backed by scientific (Piagetian) explanation, but hardly open to question or debate; in progressive LEAs the advisory team had considerable influence over classroom practice, and in the model progressive school the headteacher was the guardian of these principles. As craftsperson, the emphasis was on classroom procedure to be acquired by observation of and apprenticeship to good practice. Peters touched an important truth, in observing that the professional role of the teacher was down-graded by the Plowden image; its suggestion was that there is just one ideal method of teaching (usually contrasted with 'formal teaching' and 'rote learning'), reflected in the prevailing pattern of teacher education

> which supplemented a basic training in subjects and the handing on of skills by an attempt to bring about commitment to some sort of ideology.[39]

In 1974, the NUT argued that the imposition by local education authorities on primary teachers, of open-plan schools had implications for the principle of professional autonomy. These included the need to consider the training, experience and knowledge of teachers required to work in open plan schools, and ultimately, a respect for their convictions. More appropriate initial training had to be developed, more in-service opportunities were required to facilitate transfer to new methods and new situations. In particular, team teaching, though not synonymous with open-plan schooling, was frequently a feature and required adaptation of professional skills. The problems for young teachers with relative inexperience, had to be recognized, as also the difficulties for older teachers who had received training and extensive experience in other methods. Many of the latter had given valuable service, and ultimately their own convictions had to be respected. There is a wealth of nuance in two central paragraphs of the report:

> . . . like other professional people, they fully appreciate that change is an essential ingredient in the working life-time of them all.
>
> The fact still remains, however, that there are many teachers, . . . who have given careful thought to the question of open planning and still remain unconvinced about its educational and professional advantages. They are entitled to expect that their views, based upon experience as well as educational theory, will be given equal weight with those of equally experienced colleagues who come to a different conclusion . . .
>
> A change to a new method will be all the more effective, and permanent, it if is brought about only after full consultation with teachers and with their consent, and if proper care is taken at all points to respect their own experience and safeguard their professional position.[40]

The trend of educational research from the 1960s to the 1980s may be seen as adversely affecting the fortunes of progressive education. The antipathy towards contemporary developments expressed by Christian Schiller (1971), the Oxfordshire headteacher George Baines (1971), and later by Blenkin and Kelly (1983) was a vain cry against an ineluctable trend.[41]

In chapter 4 it was suggested that a growing body of educational science enhanced the professional status of primary teachers. The rise of sociology as an academic discipline, and its application to educational research, was discussed in chapter 2 for as its influence in the Crowther (1959) and (1963) Newsom reports. Concepts of deprivation and compensation, embodied in Plowden, implied an important social role for the teacher, and sociology of education in its early structural functionalist phase gave scientific authority to this view. The expansion of higher education after 1963 was marked by a growth in the number of social science courses in the new universities and polytechnics. It has been suggested that social studies were popular because of their accessibility; as Ryder and Silver put it,

> unlike the pure sciences, they appeared to use ordinary language in ordinary ways and to argue on the basis of commonsense knowledge.[42]

But sociology proved a double-edged weapon, for as the focus shifted from 'sociology of education' to 'sociology of knowledge', so harder questions began to be asked concerning the traditionally beneficent role of the teacher.[43]

Linked with Bourdieu's concept of 'cultural capital' and Bernstein's intepretation of the 'classification and framing of knowledge', Young (1971) argued that pupils were socialized within an institutional structure into accepting the traditional high status of the academic curriculum. Insofar as this suggested a rejection of traditional subjects which had 'denied the validity of the child's existing knowledge', this interpretation was welcomed by Blenkin and Kelly (1983). But it may be argued that features identified by Young, such as individualism rather than cooperation, the unrelatedness of curriculum to daily life, and preference of written over oral skills, were still to be found embedded in much progressive practice. Sharp and Green (1975) considered that despite the expression of liberal intentions, the progressive primary school generally contributed to the promotion of a static social order.[44] Research findings, especially in sociology, thus created a climate of uncertainty about the teacher's role. By the mid 1970s, teachers reading contemporary educational research may have concluded that either they had little impact on the child's life-chances, or that their role was one of repression. Classroom-based research came to the rescue with the conclusion that schools did have a considerable impact, but this was of little comfort to the progressives.[45]

Journal publication of educational research flourished in the 1960s and 1970s reflecting increased specialization and new priorities. Periodical literature of education diversified considerably by contrast with earlier journals such as *British Journal of Education Studies*, begun in 1952, which had embraced the whole field of educational research. Two examples were the NFER *New Research in Education* which began in 1969 and the *Journal of Curriculum Studies* (published by Taylor & Francis) which was launched in the same year (including an article by Hirst which offered a challenge to progressivism).[46] Specializing in the primary field, two significant additions to the list were *Primary Education Review*, published by the NUT, and *Education 3-13*.

Founded in 1973, *Education 3-13* grew out of the Primary-School Research and Development Group headed by Professor P.H. Taylor at the University of Birmingham. Its contributors included noted progressivists, such as Sybil Marshall, already discussed in foregoing chapters; Mervyn Benford, an Oxfordshire progressive headteacher wrote in an early issue about his methods and his school at Lewknor, quoting from Christian Schiller as his cynosure. Stalwart Froebelians Molly Brearley and Elizabeth Hitchfield were also published, but the journal was more questioning and open to ideological debate than had been the *Froebel Journal*. Thorny questions of accountability, authority and evaluation were discussed in its pages, and the aims of primary education were a matter for debate — both progressives and Black Paper writers being given their say; aims were even recognized as a legitimate subject for empirical research, and the work of Pat Ashton's project, funded by the Schools Council and located at the University of Birmingham, which had identified no less than seventy-two aims of primary education, was also reported.

The first appearance of the journal *Primary Education Review* was another of the educational events of that cataclysmic year, 1976. This was published by the NUT and deserves some consideration both as an extension of the Union's continuing contribution to curriculum development, and as one example of a new species of professional literature; more sophisticated in its approach to theoretical issues than had been *Teacher's World*, it did not assume a particular ideological viewpoint concerning curriculum and teaching method, as had the *Froebel Journal*. It contained serious discussions and some reporting of contemporary research but in a more readable style than most academic journals.

For the profession there had been public challenges from government and from the media that had to be met by a reinforcement of professional identity. As an early editorial put it:

> Society places upon teachers the responsibility of offering a worthwhile education to children of all abilities, personalities and backgrounds. Teachers, conscious of the demands this makes, are constantly looking for ways to extend their competence and professionalism.

In recognition of the professional interest and concern of primary teachers, the Union had established *Primary Education Review* as

> a forum for open debate on important educational matters, to inform and to provoke.[47]

An editorial response in the spring of 1980 to the new Conservative government's White Paper *A Framework for the School Curriculum* made clear its professional stance, cleverly adapting one of the most famous Plowden tenets, as a defence against centralization:

> At the heart of the educational process is the *relationship between teacher and child* [my emphasis], and particularly at the primary stage ...
>
> Children need partnership between parents, teachers and administrators cooperating in their interests, and they need teachers with professional autonomy and confidence, whose judgment is respected, to decide on the details of curriculum provision to meet individual needs at different stages of learning.[48]

The editorial agreed that the curriculum must be related to national needs, but asked who would define these, and in what terms — manpower planning, social, cultural?

Individual contributors commented on the many ministerial and inspectorial publications which followed the Ruskin speech of 1976. In *Primary Education Review* no. 4, Peter Kennedy discussed the Green Paper *Education in Schools.* Headteacher of Great Wakering County Primary School in Essex, and one-time President of the Union, Kennedy had chaired the Schools Council Working Party on Language Development and had contributed substantially to the Union's thinking on the Bullock Report. Described after his death in 1981 as 'a distinguished and articulate educationalist', he was noted also for his blend of understatement and cutting irony.

> Let us be thankful for the sound judgment of thousands of teachers who ensured that, in spite of the great volume of advice to which they were subjected, not *all* primary English teaching was about creative writing; the teachers who decided that not all the children would get pocket calculators for Christmas and so had better make sure they had learned their multiplication tables; the teachers who, when phonics were unfashionable, still insisted on teaching them and thus helped many children along the road to reading, and the teachers who have lived through all the fashionable developments in the teaching of mathematics, but understood that it meant rather more than allowing children to career round the playground with trundle wheels.
>
> Surely these are the people who brought about the situation described in the Green Paper paragraph 2.1: 'Visitors have come from all over the world to see, and to admire, the English and Welsh primary school revolution'.

He welcomed the Green paper's acknowledgement that primary schools had adopted methods and approaches which better reflected children's growth and development, and that there had not been a general decline in educational standards, but also that whilst the majority of primary teachers recognized the importance of performance in basic skills, some had failed to achieve satisfactory results in them. His main argument was that the promises contained in the Green Paper of better resourcing for staffing and for INSET (paras. 10.26 and 10.32) must be honoured.[49]

Another leading member who promoted the importance of primary education within the Union, and who worked with Peter Kennedy to bring the *Review* into being, was Gwyn Jones. A skilled orator and writer, he was a headteacher and had chaired the Schools Council in Wales. To the HMI Primary Survey published in 1978, he wrote 'A Qualified Amen'. The Inspectorate, he observed, were not accountable, yet wielded an enormous influence on policy-making through the publication of their reports. In an amusing comparison with the three young barristers who in 1846 reported for the Royal Commission on the state of education in Wales, he noted the necessity of relying on subjective judgment, despite the dressing up of the Primary Survey with a panoply of 'scientific' educational assessment. This particularly affected the crucial question of matching children's levels of work to their potential, an essential principle of 'child-centredness' as well as a key professional skill to which the teacher lays claim.

> Children, like all of us, learn in terms of what they already know and every day, every teacher in every class, for every child throughout the kingdom has to assess (a) what the child knows; (b) what he could know; (c) what he's ready to know ... I must confess to some dubiety about the perception of any Inspector, however acute, who, after an hour or two in a classroom, can make judgements about matching on every child, knowing little, if anything, about the child's school history; little, if anything, about the child's temperament and attitudes; and probably nothing of the home background.

Whilst not invalidating the seriousness of the major point about matching, he argued that evaluation, to be convincing and conclusive, would have to adopt instruments reliable enough to inspire the confidence of the evaluated. He was also disappointed about the Report's ambivalence concerning any additional resources for its admirable recommendations on the staffing of schools.[50]

In general the *Review* was balanced in views expressed about the gains and failures of previous decades in development of the primary curriculum and teacher training. Nowhere was this more apparent than in the several articles in the journal from Norman Thomas. After a long career as a primary school teacher in London and Hertfordshire, he had joined HMI in 1962, rising to Staff Inspector of Primary Schools in 1969 and HM Chief Inspector of Schools (for primary and middle years) from 1973 until his retirement in 1981. Whilst still in post, he commented for the *Review* on reactions to the 1978 HMI Survey. Generally pleased by the press response, it had been noticed that the assertions of children in primary schools working aimlessly or lacking control were rarely justified, and there had been widespread recognition of the abundant evidence for primary teachers' concern for their pupils' acquisition of basic skills. As for responses from the profession, he claimed that teachers with whom he had discussed the report did not share the researchers' scepticism concerning inspectors' judgements on 'matching', finding a subjective assessment more reliable.[51] Following his retirement, he addressed the first of a new series of national professional courses for primary school teachers to be held by the NUT at Stoke Rochford Hall on the topic of 'Testing and Assessing'. Here, he put the children's interests first:

> the purpose of assessment should be to improve the education service for children. While, for the most part, the process should have a direct influence on what is done with the children, some indirect effects flow from informing parents, LEAs, the government and the public at large about what children can do.[52]

Commenting in a later issue of the journal about his own report, *Improving Primary Schools*, which he had prepared for ILEA, much of the general philosophy of progressivism was acknowledged approvingly. The Report, based on visits to one in ten of London's primary schools, had recognized the solid success and enterprise, hard work and care for the children; parents as well as teachers had expressed their wish for a broad curriculum with imaginative and creative elements, a happy atmosphere, and conversation as a means of developing children's powers of observation and reasoning, 'though the handful who argued otherwise was a vociferous minority'. But his appeal was to abandoning entrenched positions:

> Isn't it time to have done with the dichotomies that bedevil educational discussion? Mustn't teaching be formal sometimes and informal at others? Isn't it insufficient to say 'I teach a subject', or to say 'I teach children'; don't we have to teach children something?[53]

The role of the Schools Council was discussed in chapter 5 with regard to curriculum innovation in the 1960s. Research by Taylor and others, published by the Schools Council in 1974, entitled *Purpose, Power and Constraint in the Primary School Curriculum*, would hardly hearten progressivists, finding that teachers were generally neutral towards change and unable to visualized a range of alternative possibilities, and confirming school and classroom as being separate zones of influence.[54] Before its demise, the Council made a further contribution to primary curriculum debate in two working papers. *The Practical Curriculum* in 1981 took, for progressive ideology, an unpromising point of departure in Callaghan's Ruskin speech of 1976 and the ensuing 'Great Debate'. Perhaps reflecting its institutional need to take account of the times and bend to the political wind, it adopted the words of the 1977 Green Paper, describing the core curriculum as 'an irreducible minimum to which every pupil should have a right of access'. Nevertheless

> There is a close link between . . . different kinds of experience of the world and many familiar school subjects. Unfortunately teachers of older children have often tended to emphasize the content of their subjects instead of their importance as ways of experiencing the world.[55]

Primary Practice: A Sequel to 'The Practical Curriculum' (1983) introduced a new element into curricular discussion by trying 'to make our children's education future-proof'. Though some references to the need for flexibility, and the likely changes to be found during the modern child's future career, 'the future' had not been weighed as a determining factor of the curriculum — it was hard enough to defend the child against the demands of the adult world here and now. Yet this working paper began on a millenarian note: 'Today's schoolchildren will be young adults in 2000 A.D. Many of them will live into the second half of the twenty-first century', and it took as its point of departure not the 1976 speech, but Neil Armstrong's moon walk of 1969. Underlying its premises was an acceptance of the need for a nationally planned curriculum.[56]

Latterly, more specific professional organizations than those considered in chapter 5, have been founded to defend what are seen as the gains of progressivism against reactionary trends. The National Association for Primary Education was founded long after the demise of the National Froebel Foundation (which might be considered in some respects its precursor), and celebrated the twentieth anniversary of the Plowden Report with a national conference to consider how far and why the realization of its recommendations had failed.[57] The Undergraduate Primary Teacher Education Conference was founded in 1984 in response to specific government measures which sought to restore a more subject-centred curriculum to the primary school.

It may be salutary to recall Reid's (1984) observation that curriculum is largely defined by the 'external publics' such as parents, employers, politicians and others who are consumers and paymasters of education. Teachers have not the power to initiate new topical categories, but merely to represent the topics taught as belonging to existing categories. They are thus not 'manipulators of realities', but 'purveyors of rhetorics'.

> Even where proponents of pedagogical reform can convince professional colleagues of the value of their ideas, they still face

the more essential and highly difficult task of converting outside publics.[58]

Notes

1 GOODSON, I. and BALL, S. (1984) *Defining the Curriculum: Histories and Ethnographies*, Lewes, Falmer Press, p. 3.
2 SILVER, H. (1983) *Education as History*, London, Methuen, p. 11.
3 HANSEN, S. and JESPER, J. (1971) *The Little Red Schoolbook*, London, Stage One (translated from original Danish edition); POSTMAN, N. and WEINGARTNER, C., (1971) *Teaching as a Subversive Activity*, Harmondsworth, Penguin, however, offered teachers some appropriate strategies in the new circumstances.
4 SCHILLER, C. (1979) *Christian Schiller In His Own Words*, ed. C. Griffin-Beale, published by private subscription through A. and C. Black reprinted by NAPE (1983) p. 93.
5 SECRETARY OF STATE FOR EDUCATION AND SCIENCE (1976) *School Education in England and Wales: Problems and Initiatives* (the notorious 'Yellow Book'); The *Guardian*, 13 October 1976; *Times Educational Supplement*, 15 October 1976. Lord Donoughue has recently published a first-hand account of this Prime Ministerial initiative, and of the popular reception which it received despite the resistance of professional vested interests both at the DES and amongst the teachers' unions: DONOUGHUE, B. (1987) *Prime Minister*, London, Jonathan Cape.
6 NUT (1978) *Annual Report*, London, NUT, p. 79.
7 CALVOCORESSI, P. (1978) *The British Experience, 1945–75*, Harmondsworth, Penguin, p. 110. It was only a contributory and secondary source of the escalating inflation however, as imports only accounted for 1 per cent of GNP.
8 RYDER, J. and SILVER, H. (1985) *Modern English Society* (3rd edn), London, Methuen, pp 257–61.
9 MARWICK, A. (1982) *British Society Since 1965*, Harmondsworth, Penguin p. 242; *Social Trends 1980*, p. 29.
10 RYDER, J. and SILVER, H. (1985) *op cit*, p. 217.
11 JACKSON, B. and MARSDEN, D. (1962) *Education and the Working Class*, London, Routledge and Kegan Paul; JACKSON, B. (1964) *Streaming: An Education System in Miniature*, London, Routledge and Kegan Paul.
12 BLISHEN, E. (1969) *The School That I'd Like*, Harmondsworth, Penguin; WHITE, R. and BROCKINGTON, D. (1983) *Tales Out of School: Consumers' views of British Education*, London, Routledge and Kegan Paul.
13 MARWICK, A. (1982) *op cit* p. 247; RYDER, J. and SILVER, H. (1985) *op cit*, p. 237.
14 *Radio Times*, 26 April 1976; *The Listener*, 29 April 1976, p. 254.
15 *Radio Times*, 7 June 1976. The Tyndale enquiry was notable as a cause celebre which became the focus for a wider debate, and for the books produced in its wake: as well as the official report running to some 400 pages, were *The Teachers' Story* published by Writers' and Readers' Cooperative, *The Lessons of Tyndale* published by the Conservative Political Centre, and the less partisan but equally portentous sounding *William Tyndale: Collapse of a School — Or a System?* by two journalists from the '*Times Ed*'.
16 THOMAS, H. (1959) *The Establishment*, London, Anthony Blond.
17 SAMPSON, A. (1982) *The Changing Anatomy of Britain*, London, Hodder and Stoughton.
18 BOOKER, C. (1969) *The Neophiliacs*, London, Collins.
19 MARWICK, A. (1982) *op cit*, p. 211.
20 ABRAMS, M. (1961) *Teenage Consumer Spending in 1959*, quoted in RYDER J. and SILVER H. (1985) *op cit*, p. 226.
21 LARKIN, P. (1974) *High Windows*, London, Faber, p. 34.

22 Laing, R.D. (1972) *The Politics of the Family and other essays*, London, Tavistock; Blackburn, R. (1969) 'A brief guide to bourgeois ideology', *Student Power*.
23 Fletcher, R. (1973) *The Family and Marriage in Britain*, (3rd edn) Harmondsworth, Penguin. The 2nd edition had been reprinted annually from 1966 to 1971; its commercial success reflects the liveliness of contemporary debate, as well as the exponential growth of teacher training, social workers and student sociologists.
24 Bernstein, B. and Davies, B. (1969) 'Some sociological comments on Plowden' in Peters, R.S. (Ed.) *Perspectives on Plowden*, London, Routledge and Kegan Paul, p. 58.
25 Peters, R. S. (Ed.) *Perspectives on Plowden*, London, Routledge and Kegan Paul, pp. ix–x, p. 8.
26 Bernstein, B. and Davies, B. (1969) *op cit*.
27 Cox, C.B. in an interview with Stuart Maclure, in *Promises and Piecrust*, broadcast by Channel 4, April 1987.
28 Bantock, G.H. (n.d.) (1969) 'Discovery methods' in Cox, C.B. and Dyson, A.E. (Eds) *Black Paper Two*, London, Critical Quarterly Society.
29 This contrast is noted by Alexander, R. (1984) *Primary Teaching*, London, Holt, Rinehart and Winston, p. 5.
30 DES (1977a) *Curriculum 11 to 16*, London, HMSO; DES (1980) *A View of the Curriculum*, London, HMSO.
31 DES (1977b) *Circular 14/77*, London, HMSO; DES (1979) *Local Authority Arrangements for the School Curriculum*, London, HMSO.
32 DES (1977c) *Education in Schools; A Consultative Document*, London, HMSO paras. 2.1–2.3.
33 DES and Welsh Office (1977) *A Study of School Building: Report by an Interdepartmental Group*, London, HMSO. Selected statistics were made available in DES (1978) *Statistics of Education SS5: School Building Surveys 1975 and 1976*, London, HMSO.
34 DES (1983) *Report by HMI on the Effects of Local Expenditure Policies on Education Provision in England*, London, DES.
35 DES (1984) *Maintenance and Renewal in Educational Buildings*, A & B Papers no. 7, London, DES.
36 DES (1980) *Remodelling of Jackfield School: An Exercise in Primary Renewal in an Urban Context*, Architects and Building Branch Broadsheet no. 3, London, DES.
37 DES (1982) *School Sites: Recreation, Play and Outdoor Education*, Architects and Building Branch Broadsheet no. 9., London, DES. The first of these two schools had been the subject of Architects and Building Branch *Design Note 11* (1973). The latter had been described in *Building Bulletin* no. 53 (1976).
38 DES (1983) *Vandalism in Schools and Colleges*. Architects and Building Branch Broadsheet no. 12, London, DES.
39 Peters, R.S. (1969) *op cit*, pp. 16–19.
40 NUT (1974) paras. 34 and 35.
41 Schiller, C. (1979) *op cit*; Baines, G. (1971) *op cit*; Blenkin, G. and Kelly, A. (Eds) (1983) *The Primary Curriculum*, London, Harper and Row.
42 Ryder, J. and Silver, H. (1985) *op cit*, p. 265.
43 Young, M.F.D. (Ed.) (1971) *Knowledge and Control: New Directions for the Sociology of Education*, London, Collier-Macmillan; an account of the changing attitude of sociologists towards teachers is found in Hargreaves, A. (1984) 'Educational policy and the culture of teaching', paper presented at the annual meeting of the American Educational Research Association, New Orleans; April, Cole, M. (1982) A theoretical and empirical analysis of teacher consciousness, unpublished MA Thesis, University of Keele.
44 Sharp. R. and Green, A. (1975) *Education and Social Control: A study in Progressive Primary Education*, London, Routledge and Kegan Paul.

45 Bennett, N. (1976) *Teaching Styles and Pupil Progress*; Rutter, M. *et al* (1979) *Fifteen Thousand Hours*, London, Open Books; Galton, M., Simon, B. and Croll, P. (1980) *Inside the Primary Classroom*, London, Routledge and Kegan Paul.
46 *Journal of Curriculum Studies*, 1, (1969).
47 *Primary Education Review*, 4, spring 1978, p. 4. The opinions expressed in the *Review* are those of the authors and not necessarily those of the NUT.
48 *Primary Education Review*, 8, spring 1980, p. 3.
49 *Primary Education Review*, 4, spring 1978, pp. 7–8, and obituary note Primary 12, Education Review, autumn 1981, p. 1.
50 *Primary Education Review*, 6, spring 1979, pp. 7–8, and obituary note *Primary Education Review* 12, autumn 1981, p. 1.
51 *Primary Education Review*, 6, spring 1979, pp. 4–6.
52 *Primary Education Review*, 13, spring 1982, p. 2.
53 *Primary Education Review*, 22, spring 1985, pp. 2–3.
54 Taylor, P.H. *et al* (1974) *Purpose, Power and Constraint: The Primary School Curriculum*, London, Macmillan for the Schools Council.
55 Schools Council (1981) *The Practical Curriculum (Working Paper no. 70)*, London, Methuen, p. 19.
56 Schools Council (1983) *Primary Practice; A Sequel to 'The practical curriculum' (Working Paper no. 75)* London, Methuen.
57 Associated with this conference was the special issue of *Oxford Review of Education* 13, 1, 1987, 'Plowden twenty years on'.
58 Reid, W. (1984) 'Curriculum change and the evolution of educational constituencies' in Goodson, I (Ed.) *Social Histories of the Secondary School Curriculum: Subjects for Study*, Lowes, Falmer Press, p. 72.

Bibliography

ADDISON, P. (1975) *The Road to 1945*, London, Cape.

ALEXANDER, R. (1984) *Primary Teaching*, London, Holt Rinehart & Winston.

ALEXANDER, R., CRAFT, M. and LYNCH, J. (Eds) (1984) *Change in Teacher Education*, London, Holt, Rinehart & Winston.

ALEXANDER, R. and ELLIS, J. W. (Eds) (1981) *Advanced Study for Teachers*, Guildford, SRHE.

ALLEN, A.B. (1950) *Rural Education*, vols. 1 and 2, London, Allman and Son.

ALLEN, G. and others (1958) *Scientific Interests in the Primary School*, 4th ed. 1965, London, NFF.

ARMFELT, R. (1950) *Our Changing Schools: A Picture for Parents*, Central Office of Information for the Ministry of Education, London, HMSO.

ARMSTRONG, M. (1980) *Closely Observed Children: The Diary of a Primary Classroom*, London, Writers and Readers.

BAINES G. (1971) 'Learning in a flexible school' in WALTON, J. (Ed.) *The Integrated Day in Theory and Practice*, London, Ward Lock Educational.

BANTOCK , G.H. (n.d.) (1969) 'Discovery methods' in COX, C.B. and DYSON, A.E. (Eds) *Black Paper Two*, London, Critical Quarterly Society.

BBC Written Archive R16/files on education and school broadcasting 1926–55.

BEARD, R. (1969) *An Outline of Piaget's Developmental Psychology for Students and Teachers* (Students Library of Education), London, Routledge and Kegan Paul.

BENNETT, N. (1976) *Teaching Styles and Pupil Progress*, London, Open Books.

BENNETT, N. and others (1980) *Open Plan Schools, Teaching, Curriculum, Design*, Slough, NFER for the Schools Council.

BERNSTEIN, B. and DAVIES, B. (1969) 'Some sociological comments on Plowden' in PETERS, R.S. (Ed.) *Perspectives on Plowden*, London, Routledge and Kegan Paul.

BLACKIE, J. (1963) *Good Enough for the Children?*, London, Faber.

BLACKIE, J. (1967) *Inside the Primary School*, London, HMSO.

BLENKIN, G. and KELLY, A.V. (1981) *The Primary Curriculum*, London, Harper and Row.

BLISHEN, E. (Ed.) (1963) *Education Today: The Existing Opportunities*, London, BBC.

BLISHEN, E. (1969) *The School That I'd Like*, Harmondsworth, Penguin.

BLISHEN, E. (1980) *A Nest of Teachers*, London, Hamish Hamilton.

BLYTH, W.A.L. (1984) *Development, Experience and Curriculum in Primary Education*, London, Croom Helm.

BLYTH, W.A.L. (1965) *English Primary Education*, vol. 2, London, Routledge and Kegan Paul.

BOARD OF EDUCATION (1931) *Report of the Consultative Committee on the Primary School*, London, HMSO.

BOARD OF EDUCATION (1944) *Teachers and Youth Leaders*, London, HMSO.

Booker, C. (1969) *The Neophiliacs*, London, Collins.

Bowlby, J. (1965) *Child Care and the Growth of Love*, Harmondsworth, Penguin.

Brearley, M., Goddard, N., Browse, B., and Kallet, T. (1972) *Educating Teachers (British Primary Schools Today)*, London, Macmillan for the Schools Council.

Brearley, M. and Hitchfield, R. (1966) *A Teacher's Guide to Reading Piaget*, London, Routledge and Kegan Paul.

Brearley, M. and others (1969) *Fundamentals in the First School*, Oxford, Basil Blackwell.

Briggs, A. (1979) *Sound and Vision: The History of Broadcasting in the United Kingdom*, vol. 4, Oxford, University Press.

Browne, S. (1979) 'The accountability of Her Majesty's Inspectorate' in Lello, J. (Ed.) *Accountability in Education*, London, Ward Lock Educational.

Burstall, C. (1974) *Primary French in the Balance*, Slough, NFER.

Carline, R. (1968) *Draw They Must*, London, Edward Arnold.

Catty, N. (Ed.) (1921a) *Training in Appreciation: Art, Literature, Music*, London, Sidgwick and Jackson.

Catty, N. (1921b) *A Study of Modern Educational Theory and its Applications*, London, Sidgwick and Jackson.

Calvocoressi, P. (1978) *The British Experience, 1945–75*, Harmondsworth, Penguin.

CCPR (1960) *Sport and the Community, Report of the Wolfenden Committee on Sport*, London, CCPR.

Central Statistical Office (1979) *Social Trends no. 10, 1980 Edition*, London, HMSO.

Central Statistical Office (1980) *Annual Abstract of Statistics, 1980 Edition*, London, HMSO.

Centre for Contemporary Cultural Studies (CCCS) (1981) *Unpopular Education: Schooling and Social Democracy in England since 1944*, London, Hutchinson.

Clegg, A. (1974a) 'A subtler and more telling power', *Times Educational Supplement*, 27 September.

Clegg, A. (1974a) 'The shadow and substance of education' in University of London, Goldsmith's College, *The Changing School: A Challenge to the Teacher* (Report of Conference 1974).

Coe, J. (1968) 'A way ahead', *The Primary School in Transition: Aspects of Education* no. 8, December.

Cons, G.J. and Fletcher, C. (1938) *Actuality in Schools*, London, Methuen.

Cook, A. and Mack, H. (1971a) *The Teacher's Role: British Primary Schools Today*, London, Macmillan for the Schools Council.

Cook, A. and Mack, H. (1971b) *The Headteacher's Role: British Primary Schools Today*, London, Macmillan for the Schools Council.

Cooper, B. (1985) *Renegotiating Secondary School Mathematics*, Lewes, Falmer Press.

Cunningham, P. (1987) 'Open Plan Schooling: Last stand of the progressives?' in Lowe, R. (Ed) *The Changing Primary School*, Lewes, Falmer Press.

Daniel, M.V. (1947) *Activity in the Primary School*, Oxford, Blackwell.

Daniel, M.V. (1951) 'The library in relation to education in the primary school', *School Librarian*, 5, 6, December.

Davis, D. (1948) 'The school library in the infants' and Primary School', *School Librarian*, 4, 2, July.

Dean, D.W. (1986) 'Planning for a post-war generation: Ellen Wilkinson and George Tomlinson at the Ministry of Education 1945–51', *History of Education*, 15, 2, June.

Dent, H.C. (1977) *The Training of Teachers in England and Wales 1800–1975*, London, Hodder and Stoughton.

DES *Architects and Building Branch Broadsheets*, London, DES.

Department of Education *Building Bulletins*, London, HMSO.

DES *Design Notes*, London, DES.

DES *Reports on Education*, London, DES.

DES (1967) *Children and Their Primary Schools*, (The Plowden Report) London, HMSO.

DES (1972) *Teacher Education and Training*, (The James Report) London, HMSO.

DES (1974) *Statistics of Education vol. 4 (Teachers)*, London, HMSO.

DES (1977a) *Curriculum 11 to 16*, London, HMSO.

DES (1977b) *Circular 14/77*, London, DES.

DES (1977c) *Education in Schools: A Consultative Document*, London, HMSO.

DES and Welsh Office (1977) *A Study of School Building: Report by an Inter-departmental Group*, London, HMSO.

DES (1978) *Statistics of Education SS5: School Building Surveys 1975 and 1976*, London, HMSO.

DES (1980) *A View of the Curriculum* London, HMSO.

DES (1983) *Report by HMI on the Effects of Local Expenditure Policies on Education Provision in England*, London, DES.

DES (1985) *Education 8 to 12 in Combined and Middle Schools*, London, HMSO.

DONALDSON, M. (1978) *Children's Minds*, London, Fontana.

DYMOND, D. (Ed.) (1955) *The Forge: The History of Goldsmiths' College 1905–1955*, London, Methuen.

EAGLETON, T. (1983) *Literary Theory, an introduction*, Oxford, Blackwell.

EDMONDS, E.L. (1962) *The School Inspector*, (International Library of Sociology and Social Reconstruction), London, Routledge and Kegan Paul.

Education

EVANS, K. (1979) 'The physical form of the school', *British Journal of Educational Studies*, 27, 1.

EYKEN, W. VAN DER (1969) *Adventures in Education*, London, Allen Lane.

FEATHERSTONE, J. (1971) *An Introduction: British Primary Schools Today*, London, Macmillan for the Schools Council.

FLETCHER, R. (1973) *The Family and Marriage in Britain*, (3rd edn) Harmondsworth, Penguin.

FROEBEL FOUNDATION (1972) *Designing Primary Schools*, London, Froebel Foundation

Froebel Journal

GOLBY, M. (1982) 'Microcomputers and the primary curriculum' in GARLAND, R. (Ed.) *Microcomputers and Children in the Primary School*, Lewes, Falmer Press.

GOODSON, I. (Ed.) (1985) *Social Histories of the Secondary School Curriculum: Subjects for Study*, Lewes, Falmer Press.

GOODSON, I. and BALL, S. (1984) *Defining the Curriculum: Histories and Ethnographies*, Lewes, Falmer Press.

GOSDEN P.H.J.H. and SHARP P. (1978) *The Development of an Education Service, the West Riding 1889–1974*, Oxford, Martin Robertson.

GOULD, R. (1954) 'The teacher in the twentieth century', *Advancement of Science*, 11, 4, June.

HALSEY, A. and SYLVA, K. (1987) 'Plowden: History and Prospect', *Oxford Journal of Education*, 13, 1.

HAMILTON, D. (1980) 'Adam Smith and the moral economy of the classroom system', *Journal of Curriculum Studies*, 12, 4.

HANSEN, S. and JESPER, J. (1971) *The Little Red Schoolbook*, London, Stage One.

HOGAN, J. (1970) *Beyond the Classroom*, Reading, Educational Explorers Ltd.

HOLMES. E.G.A. (1920) *In Quest of an Ideal*, London, Richard Cobden-Sanderson.

HOUSE OF COMMONS SELECT COMMITTEE ON EDUCATION and SCIENCE, *Her Majesty's Inspectorate*, (England and Wales) PP 1967–68 (400–1).

HOUSE OF COMMONS SELECT COMMITTEE ON EDUCATION AND SCIENCE, *Teacher Training, Minutes of Evidence*, PP 1969–70 (135–iv) xi.

HUMPHRIES, S. (1981) *Hooligans or Rebels?*, Oxford, Blackwell.

HUTCHINSON, M.M. (1960) *A Simple Gardening Project with Young children: From Seed to Seed* (rev. edn), London, NFF.

HUTCHINSON, M.M. (1961) *Practical Nature Study in Town Schools*, London, National Froebel Foundation.

Hyndman, M. (1980) 'Utopia reconsidered: Edmond Holmes, Harriet Johnson and the school at Sompting', *Sussex Archaeological Collections*, 118.

Isaacs, N. (n.d) (1965) *Piaget: Some answers to Teachers' Questions*, London, National Froebel Foundation.

Isaacs, N. (1955) *Some Aspects of Piaget's Work*, London, National Froebel Foundation.

Isaacs, N. (1961) *The Growth of Understanding in the Young Child: A Brief Introduction to Piaget's work*, London, Educational Supply Association.

Jackson, B. (1964) *Streaming: An Education System in Miniature*, London, Routledge and Kegan Paul.

Jackson, B. and Marsden, D. (1962) *Education and the Working Class*, London, Routledge and Kegan Paul.

Jarman, C. (1972) *Display and Presentation in School*, London, A. and C. Black.

Jarman, C. (1978) 'The organization of open-plan primary schools, the Oxfordshire experience', in Bell, S. (Ed.) *The Organization of Open-plan Primary Schools*, Glasgow, Jordanhill College of Education.

Jones, K. (1983) *Beyond Progressive Education*, London, Macmillan.

Kogan, M. (1971) *The Government of Education: British Primary Schools Today*, London, Macmillan for the Schools Council.

Lawrence, E. (1952) *Friedrich Froebel and English Education*, London, Routledge and Kegan Paul.

Lawton, D. (1981) 'The curriculum and curriculum change' in Simon, B. and Taylor, W. (Eds) *Education in the Eighties: The Central Issues*, London, Batsford.

Lines, K. (comp.) (1950) *Four to Fourteen: A Library of Books for Children*, London, National Book League.

McGill, H.M. (comp.) (1952) *Books for Young People: Group 1, under eleven*, London, Library Association.

McKenzie, M. and Kernig, W. (1975) *The Challenge of Informal Education*, London, Darton Longman Todd.

Maclure, J. S. (1968) *Curriculum Innovation in Practice*, London, Schools Council/HMSO.

Maclure, S. (1984) *Educational Development and School Building: Aspects of Public Policy 1945–73*, Harlow, Longman.

Mann, B.F. (1962) *Learning Through Creative Work (the under-8s in school)*, London, NFF.

Manning, P. (Ed.) (1967) *The Primary School: An Environment for Education*, Liverpool, University of Liverpool Department of Building Science.

Marsh, D.C. (1965) *The Changing Social Structure of England and Wales, 1871–1961*, London, Routledge and Kegan Paul.

Marsh, L. (1970) *Alongside the Child in the Primary School*, London, A. and C. Black.

Marshall, S. (1963) *An Experiment in Education*, Cambridge, Cambridge University Press.

Marwick, A. (1982) *British Society Since 1965*, Harmondworth, Penguin.

Medd, D. and Medd, M. (1972) 'Designing primary schools' in National Froebel Foundation *Designing Primary Schools*, London, National Froebel Foundation.

Ministry of Education (1946) *School and Life*, [First] Report of the Central Advisory Council for Education (England), London, HMSO.

Ministry of Education (1948) *Out of school*, Second Report of the Central Advisory Council for Education (England), London, HMSO.

Ministry of Education (1949a) *Story of a School: A Headmaster's Experiences with Children aged Seven to Eleven* (Ministry of Education Pamphlet no. 14), London, HMSO.

Ministry of Education (1949b) *Seven to Eleven: Your Children at School* (Ministry of Education Pamphlet no. 15), London, HMSO.

Ministry of Education (1950) *Challenge and Response* (Ministry of Education Pamphlet no. 17), London, HMSO.

MINISTRY OF EDUCATION (1952) *School Broadcasts* (Ministry of Education Pamphlet no. 20), London, HMSO.

MINISTRY OF EDUCATION (1954) *Early Leaving: A Report of the CACE (England)*, (Chair: Sir Samuel Gurney-Dixon), London, HMSO.

MINISTRY OF EDUCATION (1957) *The Story of Post-war School Building*, (Ministry of Education Pamphlet no. 33), London, HMSO.

MINISTRY OF EDUCATION (1959a) *15 to 18: A Report of the CACE (England)*, (Chair: Sir Geoffrey Crowther), London, HMSO.

MINISTRY OF EDUCATION (1959b) *Primary Education: Suggestions for the Considerations of Teachers and Others Concerned with the Work of the Primary Schools*, London, HMSO.

MINISTRY OF EDUCATION (1963) *Half Our Future: A report of the CACE (England)*, London, HMSO.

MITCHELL, F.W. (1967) *Sir Fred Clarke, Master-teacher, 1880–1952*, London, Longmans.

MOON, B. (1986) *The 'New Maths' Curriculum Controversy: An International Story*, Lewes, Falmer Press.

MOORHOUSE, E. (1970) 'The philosophy of the British primary school' in ROGERS, V.R. (Ed) *Teaching in the British Primary School*, London, Macmillan.

MOORHOUSE, E. (1985) *A Personal Story of Oxfordshire Primary Schools 1946–1956*, Oxford, privately printed.

MULHERN, F. (1979) *The Moment of Scrutiny*, London, New Left Books.

NFF Education Committee Minutes 1949–1963.

NFF Bulletin

NIAS, J. (1981) '"Commitment" and motivation in primary school teachers', *Educational Review*, 33, 3.

NIAS, J. (1985) 'Reference groups in primary teaching: Talking, listening and identity', in BALL, S. AND GOODSON, I. (Eds) *Teachers' Lives and Careers*, Lewes, Falmer Press.

NUT *Annual Reports*

NUT Archive, Primary Schools Advisory Committee (PSAC) Minutes 1949–1959.

NUT (n.d) (1959) *The Curriculum of the Junior School, Report of a Consultative Committee*, London, Schoolmaster Publishing Co. Ltd.

NUT (1944) *Educational Developments of the National Union of Teachers: Statement by the Executive for Presentation to the Easter Conference 1944*, London.

NUT (1949a) *Transfer from Primary to Secondary Schools: Report of a Consultative Committee*, London, Evans/NUT.

NUT (1949b) *Nursery-Infant Education: Report of a Consultative Committee Appointed by the Executive of the National Union of Teachers*, London, Evans/NUT.

NUT (1949c) *The teachers' part in the post-war world, an address delivered by the P.M. the Right Hon. Clement Attlee CH MP to the Annual Conference of the National Union of Teachers*, London, NUT.

NUT (1960) *Fair Play For Our Primary Schools*, London, NUT.

NUT (1963) *The State of Our Schools*, London, NUT.

NUT (1959) *The Education Story*, London, NUT.

NUT (1964) *First Things First*, London, NUT.

NUT (1974) *Open Plan schools*, London, NUT.

Oxford Review of Education, 13, 1 (1987) special issue: 'Plowden Twenty Years On'.

PEARSON, E. (1972) *Trends in School Design: British Primary Schools Today*, London, Macmillan for the Schools Council.

PETERS, R.S. (Ed.) (1969) *Perspectives on Plowden*, London, Routledge and Kegan Paul.

PILE, SIR W. (1979) *The Department of Education and Science*, London, George Allen and Unwin.

PLOWDEN, B. (1987) '"Plowden" twenty years on', *Oxford Review of Education*, 13, 1, March.

PLUCKROSE, H. (1977) 'Open plan schools — an environment for learning' in NATIONAL FROEBEL FOUNDATION *Designing Primary Schools*, London, National Froebel Foundation.

Postman, N. and Weingartner, C. (1971) *Teaching as a Subversive Activity*, Harmondsworth, Penguin.

Primary Education Review

Probert, H. and Jarman, C. (1971) *A Junior School: British Primary Schools Today*, London, Macmillan for the Schools Council.

Pullan, J.M. (1971) *Towards Informality: British Primary Schools Today*, London, Macmillan for the Schools Council.

Razzell, A. (1968) *Juniors, A Postscript to Plowden*, Harmondsworth, Penguin.

Reid, W.A. (1986) 'Curriculum theory and curriculum change: What can we learn from history?', *Journal of Curriculum Studies*, 18, 2.

Richards, C. and others (comps.) (1984) *The study of Primary Education: A Source Book*, vol.1, Lewes, Falmer Press.

Richards, C. (Ed.) (1978) *Education 3–13*, Driffield, Nafferton Books.

Richmond, W.K. (1953) *The Rural School, Its Problems and Prospects*, London, Alvin Redman.

Robinson, P. (1971) Ideology in teacher education', unpublished MSc (Econ) thesis, University of London, Institute of Education.

Rogers, V.R. (Ed.) (1970) *Teaching in the British Primary School*, London, Macmillan.

Rowland, S. (1984) *The Enquiring Classroom: An Approach to Understanding Children's Learning*, Lewes, Falmer Press.

Rowland, S. (1986) 'Where is primary education going?' *Journal of Curriculum Studies*, 19, 1.

Royal Institute of British Architects (n.d) (1948) *New Schools: The Book of the Exhibition by the Royal Institute of British Architects*, London, RIBA.

Ryder, J. and Silver, H. (1985) *Modern English Society*, (3rd edn) London, Methuen.

Salford Diocesan Schools Commission and Manchester Education Committee (n.d) (1969) *St. Thomas of Canterbury R.C. Primary School: An Educational Brief*, Manchester.

Schiller, L.C. (1969) 'The progressive ideas in state schools' in Ash, M. (Ed.) *Who Are the Progressives Now?*, London, Routledge and Kegan Paul.

Schiller, C. (1972) 'Introduction' in National Froebel Foundation *Designing Primary Schools*, London National Froebel Foundation.

Schiller, C. (1979) *Christian Schiller In His Own Words* ed. C. Griffin-Beale, published by private subscription through A and C. Black, reprinted by NAPE (1983).

Schoolmaster and Woman Teacher's Chronicle (later *The Teacher*).

Schools Council (1967) *Curriculum Development, Teachers' Groups and Centres (Working Paper no. 10)*, London, Schools Council.

Schools Council (1968) *The first three years 1964/67*, London, Schools Council.

Schools Council (1969) *The Middle Years of Schooling 8–13 (Working Paper no. 22)*, London, Schools Council.

Schools Council (1981) *The Practical Curriculum (Working Paper no. 70)*, London, Methuen.

Schools Council (1983) *Primary Practice: A Sequel to 'The practical curriculum' (Working Paper no. 75)*, London, Methuen.

Scottish Education Department (1946) *Primary Education: A Report of the Advisory Council on Education in Scotland* (Cmd 6973), London, HMSO.

Selleck R. (1972) *English Primary Education and the Progressives, 1914 to 1939*, London, Routledge and Kegan Paul.

Sharp, R. and Green, A. (1975) *Education and Social Control: A Study in Progressive Primary Education*, London, Routledge and Kegan Paul.

Silver, H. (1983) *Education as History*, London, Methuen.

Simon, B. (1986) 'The 1944 Education Act: A Conservative measure?', *History of Education*, 15, 1, March.

SLA (1953) *Suggestions for Primary School Libraries*, London, SLA.

SLA (1958) *The Library in the Primary School: Report of the Primary Schools Sub-Committee*, London, SLA.
SMITH, R.T. (1971) *A Rural School: British Primary Schools Today*, London, Macmillan for the Schools Council.
Social Trends, 1980.
STEWART, W.A.C. (1986) *The Educational Innovators, vol. 2, Progressive Schools 1881–1967*, London, Macmillan.
Sunday Times Colour Magazine.
TANNER, R. (1966) '"Creativeness" in education', *Froebel Journal* no. 5 June.
TATTERSALL, E. (1976) 'The West Riding Philosophy' in OPEN UNIVERSITY *The West Riding: Changes in Primary Education*, E203 Case Study 2.
TAYLOR, P.H. *et al.* (1974) *Purpose, Power and Constraint in the Primary School Curriculum*, London, Macmillan for the Schools Council.
Teacher's World.
THEAKSTON, T.R., ISAACS, N and others (1955) *Some Aspects of Piaget's Work*, London, NFF.
THOMAS, H. (1959) *The Establishment*, London, Anthony Blond.
THORNBURY, R.E. (Ed.) (1973) *Teacher's Centres*, London, Darton Longman Todd.
Times Educational Supplement.
UNIVERSITY OF LONDON, GOLDSMITHS' COLLEGE (n.d) (1974) *The Changing School: A Challenge to the Teacher: Report of a One-day Conference*, London, Goldsmiths' College.
UNIVERSITY OF LONDON, GOLDSMITHS' COLLEGE (1974) *Prospectus for 1975–76*, London, Goldsmiths' College.
UNIVERSITY OF LONDON, GOLDSMITHS' COLLEGE (1979) *Postgraduate Prospectus 1980–81*, London, Goldsmiths' College.
VAN DER EYKEN, W. (1969) *Adventures in Education*, London, Allen Lane.
WALKERDINE, V. (1984) 'Developmental psychology and the child-centred pedagogy: The insertion of Piaget into early education' in HENRIQUES, J. and others (Eds) *Changing the Subject: Psychology, Social Regulation and Subjectivity*, London, Methuen.
WALLACE, R.G. (1981) 'the origins and authorship of the 1944 Education Act', *History of Education*, 10, 4, December.
WALTERS, E.H. (1951a) *Activity and Experience in the Infant School*, London, NFF.
WALTERS, E.H. (1951b) *Activity and Experience in the Junior School*, London, NFF.
WALTON, J. (1971) *The Integrated Day in Theory and Practice*, London, Ward Lock Educational.
WARD, C. (1976) *British School Buildings, Designs and Appraisals, 1969–1974*, London, Architectural Press.
West Riding Education Committee Papers, Brotherton Library, University of Leeds MS 731.
WHITE, E.W. (1975) *The Arts Council of Great Britain*, London, Davis-Poynter.
WHITE, L (1972) 'Designing schools for young children' in NATIONAL FROEBEL FOUNDATION, *Designing Primary Schools*, London, National Froebel Foundation.
WHITE, R. and BROCKINGTON, D. (1983) *Tales Out of School: Consumers' Views of British Education*, London, Routledge and Kegan Paul.
WILKINSON, A. (1987) 'Aspects of communication and the Plowden Report', *Oxford Review of Education*, 13, 1.
WILLIAMS, R. (1961) *The Long Revolution*, Harmondsworth, Penguin.
WILLIAMS, R. (1973) *The Country and the City*, London, Chatto and Windus.
WINKLEY, D. (1985) *Diplomats and Detectives: LEA Advisers at Work*, London, Robert Royce.
WRAGG, E. (1985) 'Flowers from a secret garden', *Times Educational Supplement 1910–1985*, (Supplement to *TES*, September).

Index

Index